WITHDRAWN

Recalling
the Good Fight

The Internationals—united with the Spaniards we fight the invader

Recalling
the Good Fight

*An Autobiography
of the Spanish Civil War*

John Tisa

Bergin & Garvey Publishers, Inc.
Massachusetts

First published in 1985 by
Bergin & Garvey Publishers, Inc.
670 Amherst Road
South Hadley, Massachusetts 01075

56789   98765432

Printed in the United States of America

LIBRARY OF CONGRESS CATALOGING IN PUBLICATION DATA

Tisa, John.
    Recalling the good fight.

    Includes index.
    1. Tisa, John. 2. Spain—History—Civil War,
1936–1939—Personal narratives, American. 3. Spain.
Ejército. Brigada Internacional, XV—Biography.
4. Soldiers—Spain—Biography. I. Title.
DP269.9.T56 1985   946.081′092′4   85-8111
ISBN 0-89789-078-7
ISBN 0-89789-079-5 (pbk.)

Spanish Civil War posters photographed by William T. Tisa.

*Photographs are courtesy of the author and the Spanish Civil War Collection of the
Brandeis University Library.*

To those fifteen hundred or more brave young volunteers of the Abraham Lincoln Brigade for whom the bells tolled in the Spanish Civil War of 1936–1939, this book is dedicated. And to an equal number who returned to their homes in the Americas, most of whom were able to carry on the good fight against world fascism in World War II and thereafter.

CONTENTS

PART THREE · *Madrid: May—November 1937*

PART FOUR · *Aragon and Catalonia: December 1937—September 1938*

PART FIVE · *Withdrawal of the International Brigades: September 1938—April 1939 and Beyond*

Illustration insert begins on page 81.

Foreword

The thing to remember about the men and women who volunteered for service on the side of the Spanish republic is that they offered their lives unconditionally. They were not given any financial incentives. Money was never mentioned by recruiters, neither was their insurance to cover wounds and illnesses sustained, nor honors or pensions. All they were promised was an opportunity to serve in a fight variously termed The Good Fight, The Pure War, and The Wound in the Heart, but which for them was simply the war against fascism. The men and women who came to Spain from all over the world, 3,200 from the United States, to form the International Brigades were committed to the proposition that Nazi/ Fascist aggression would eventually embroil both east and west in a world war of devastating proportions, if it was not stopped in Spain. The measure of their commitment to this purpose can be found in the soil of Spain where half their number lie in unmarked graves. As "No Pasarán" was the war cry of the Spaniards at whose side they fought and died, "Make Madrid the Tomb of Fascism," were the watchwords inscribed on the banners they carried into battle. The failure was not theirs, but that of the fainthearted appeasers of the western world who abandoned Spain to the ravaging hordes of what became the Axis powers. The holocaust that ensued was the price paid for the lack of nerve and the illusions harbored by men in high places in the western democracies.

Johnny Tisa was one soldado who, against all odds, left home and hearth to do what had to be done. No two men experience or see an action in exactly the same way; but the convictions and principles which moved him to place himself in peril was common to us all. The spirit of anti-Fascism which pervaded the "war" as he "saw it," in the end became the stiffened spine of the allied armies, the underground resistance, and the heroic partisans who together brought victory in the Great War Against Fascism: recompense and honor enough.

Milton Wolff
Last military commander of the Abraham Lincoln Brigade

Prologue

Revolt in Spain

by Frank Ryan

Military revolts in Spain had been too frequent in that land overstocked with monarchist generals to be more than one-day's news to the outside world. so, it was with casual interest that most people outside Spain read in their newspapers, in mid-July 1936, that Franco and other generals were attempting another *putsch*. Nor were feelings quickened to anything save amusement when Franco's first proclamations described him as the "Saviour of Christianity," the bulwark of the Catholic Church against a reign of "Godless Communism." For, was it not a Franco, who a few years previously, had described that same Catholic Church in Spain as "a church which converts Jesus Christ into a trinket to gain its reactionary and imperialistic desires!"

And, to the few who knew of the black revolt that had been threatening for months, first despatches from the Popular Front Government of Spain were reassuring. The revolt was confined to the army; the airforce—what there was of it—and the navy remained loyal. In Madrid, Valencia, Albacete, Bilbao, Barcelona, and hundreds of smaller towns the workers of Spain, armed often with only sticks and stones, had—by sheer force of numbers—overpowered the revolting garrisons. There was not a single case where the civil population took over power in the name of the insurgents. There were hundreds of cases to the contrary—in themselves eloquent testimony that the 28,000,000 Spanish people did not want Franco's rule. After the first few days' fighting, the insurgents had been driven out of all towns in Spain save Cadiz, Seville, Burgos, Salamanca, and a few places of lesser military importance. Only in Morocco had they succeeded in establishing themselves in power. Insofar as it was a civil war, Franco was definitely losing by early August.

Suddenly flagging world interest quickened. There were stories out of Spain that made this Generals' revolt different from all that had preceded it. For these Generals had German aeroplanes and Italian tanks at their disposal. Franco's rôle, hitherto largely comic-opera, took new significance. It was now recalled that Sanjurjo, killed in an aeroplane crash while on his way to take command of the revolt, had paid two visits to Hitler. This revolt had not originated in Spain. Else, how explain the liberal supply of German and Italian war machines and munitions? Franco was now revealed as the agent of the International Assassins who had climbed to power over the corpses of the workers and intellectuals of Italy and Germany. So a similar fate was planned for those who opposed Franco!

At this stage, the governments of Britain and France, in what then appeared a well-intentioned effort to end German and Italian interference, formulated the Non-Intervention Pact. All signatories to the Pact—including Germany and Italy—pledged themselves to refrain from aiding either side in Spain. The immediate result of the Pact was that the Spanish government could not receive even those arms that it had ordered and paid for before the outbreak of the revolt. Nevertheless (it was argued, and hoped) the rebel Generals deprived of foreign aid could not now hold out for long against the overwhelming masses of the Spanish people.

Throughout the month of September, German and Italian representatives sat in on non-intervention conferences, in pledge of the neutrality of their respective governments, and solemnly discussed ways and means of localizing the war. And throughout that month, their pledged word was broken daily. German and Italian air squadrons in Spain were augmented; German and Italian artillery and tanks were imported in increasing numbers. As a result, just when victory for the people seemed certain, German and Italian aid enabled Franco to take the offensive.

Morocco was Franco's base. Here, the relatively small Spanish population was quickly dealt with in the now traditional Fascist manner. There remained in the Moroccan population a hatred of Spain which was dominant and bitter. The savagery with which the Spanish had crushed Abd el Krim's war of independence was still a vivid and bitter memory. Hence, it was not difficult to delude many Moroccans into the belief that—since Franco was in revolt against the Spanish government—he was opposing the tyranny that had so long oppressed them. They did not realise that the government against which Franco was in revolt was the very antithesis of the Primo de Rivera Dictatorship that had subjugated them. They did not realise that Franco aimed at an even more ruthless rule than that of Primo de Rivera. All they realised was that now it was their turn, that they were now the invaders. So, they came into Spain—in German and Italian aeroplanes, obligingly provided for them, nursing age-old wrongs, neither giving nor seeking quarter.

With the Moors came the Foreign Legion, the outcasts of humanity, not ten percent of whom were Spanish. Together the Moors and Legionnaires were concentrated in Cadiz and Seville. With sufficient troops and war materials now at hand, Franco undertook the offensive.

Driven from the outskirts of Cadiz by the Moors, forced back from Seville by the Foreign Legion, the untrained Republican militia had neither rest nor respite. At Badajoz, they turned at bay. The Fascists were around them; behind them was the Portuguese border. Escape that way was impossible; Fascist Portugal handed over all Republican refugees to Franco. So, the militiamen fought to the death. The wounded, the noncombatant sympathizers, the people—without distinction by age or sex—whom the victorious Fascists considered suspect were herded together into the bullring. When Fascist machine-gunners had finished their work two thousand corpses cluttered the ring in bloody piles. The reek of human blood that rose that summer afternoon from the bullring of Badajoz was to seep out of Spain and stir a worldwide wave of sympathy for the people—sympathy that neither official "explanation" nor ecclesiastical apologia could abate.

At Geneva, German and Italian representatives still continued to pledge themselves to nonintervention. And in Spain, Franco's armies were driving up from Seville to meet Mola whose armies were pushing south from Salamanca. German Junkers and Italian Capronis bombed the roads ahead for them. German artillery and Italian tanks found it easy, though not as easy as they had expected, to counter the rifles, the blunderbusses, and the pistols of the militiamen.

These raw militiamen were fighting stubbornly. The shadow of feudal slavery from which they had so recently escaped was again hanging over them. If Franco won, the reign of terror would be worse than it had ever been. "Better die on our feet than live on our knees," they cried, as they flung themselves again in the path of the invading armies.

Thanks to one-sided nonintervention, the self-constituted saviour generals of Spain were able to join forces and turn their united armies eastwards towards their final objective: Madrid. The modern version of a Christian Crusade, the army that was fighting (as its leaders blasphemously proclaimed) "for God and Spain" was, stangely enough, composed of Mahommedan Moors ("the infidel Moors" of Spanish history) and the Godless scum of the Foreign Legion! Ahead of them were the people, cluttering the roads into Madrid, in flight from their saviours! But, not all were able to flee. So, there are other stories out of Spain besides that of Badajoz. Of villages captured or surrendered without struggle, peasants shot down unarmed and untried, others more slowly put to death by revolting tortures, castrations, crucifixions, women turned over to the Moors ("one woman to every twenty Moors").

On the whole, it was a triumphant march, this advance through the provinces of Badajoz and Caceres. The Moors and the Foreign Legion had carte blanche since these were the very provinces in which a few months previously the peasants had seized the estates. (What matter if they had done it legally, and offered the absentee landlord rent!) Yet, these peasants were now stubborn. They erected barricades around their mud-hovel *pueblos*, and with their shotguns disputed the entry of the Saviour Army. They caused delays before they could be roasted, dead and wounded together, in the flaming ruins of their hovels.

So triumphantly—although at times timorously—Franco advanced towards Madrid. Thanks to German planes and Italian tanks, Toledo was approached. The besieged cadets in the Alcazar were relieved. Their "heroism" was front page news. (The girls they had seized and held as hostages during the siege did not live to tell of their rape.) Toledo fell, and Moor and Legionnaire had another field day, grenading the wounded in the hospital wards.

And at Geneva, German and Italian representatives still sat at nonintervention conferences, pledging the neutrality of their governments.

A Franco victory seemed certain. And what that victory would mean Franco proclamations made clear. In decrees published and interviews given, the traitor general envisaged the Fascist future of Spain. The republic was to be abolished, the government was to be totalitarian. Agrarian reform, even of the limited nature conceded by the government, was to be revoked, and the estates of the grandees restored. The 20,000 landowners would again dominate 28,000,000 people. Trade unionism would be outlawed; strikers would share the fate of the miners of Barrio-Real who died before Franco's firing-squads in July. Finally, state rights would be abrogated; Catalonia and Euzkadi would lose their newly-won independence.

These Fascists aims were necessarily part of Franco's alliance with Mussolini and Hitler. The world would come to know them. What the world was not to be told was that the Balearics had been handed over to Mussolini, and Morocco to Hitler, and that the mines of Spain were to supply both these dictators with the minerals they needed for war purposes.

Franco's one claim to sympathy abroad was that he was the champion of the Catholic Church in Spain. But when Franco raised the religious issue, backed though he was by a formidable array of Catholic prelates in Spain and abroad, it had an unforeseen and disconcerting result. It proved clearly the cleavage between those prelates and their Catholic flocks. Despite the support of the prelates, there was no rush of Catholic volunteers for Franco's crusade. From Ireland alone a miniature Franco brought a few hundred men to "fight for the faith." A few months later they were home again, disgusted with the minor—and the major—Franco, disillusioned with the "Christian" crusade of Mahommedans and Legionnaires.

The Catholic church in Spain was notoriously reactionary. It had allied itself with monarchism, and fought tooth and nail against the republic. Its concern with wordly affairs, its dominance in big business clouded its claim to be the church of Jesus Christ. Where—as in the Basque provinces—it was a church of the people, it sided now with the people. The Catholic clergy of Euzkadi were against Fascism, and against Franco. For that, many of them paid before Franco's firing squads with their lives. So, even if Franco believed that the clerical oligarchy of Spain were his allies, and he was their champion, the Basque clergy and many of the poor priests of Spain regarded him as their enemy, and his rule as the very antithesis of all that Christ had taught.

As the issues of the war became more generally understood the democratic citizens of the world rallied in greater numbers to aid the people of Spain. From many countries came ships laden with food and clothes and medical supplies—for "nonintervention" prohibited any other aid from democracies. The workers of the Soviet Union set the example which was quickly adopted. In France, Belgium, Sweden, and Norway a great movement of solidarity with the Spanish people was organized. In America, workers and intellectuals combined their efforts. The American ambulance, now a familiar sight on Spanish highways, is only one of the proofs of that solidarity. Canada was early in the field with its invaluable Blood Transfusion Unit. The workers of Great Britain sent food ships and medical units. From Denmark to Ireland, from Cuba to Chile and the Argentine aid was organized. There was scarcely a country in which democrats did not in one way or another contribute support to the Spanish people.

Mexico, never a signatory to the Non-Intervention Pact, exercised from the beginning of the war its right to send arms and munitions to the Spanish republican government. The effects of this aid were at last being felt. Helped by the increasing equalization of arms, the government forces were now able to slow up Franco's advance on Madrid. So Franco, depending on speed for success, had to seek more troops. He found the rank and file cannon fodder from Italy; Mussolini sent whole divisions, equipped and officered before they embarked. Hitler supplied the pilots, the tank crews and technicians for Franco's various army departments.

This open invasion had inevitable repercussions. It needed only such brazen intervention to clarify the issues at stake in Spain. It was now a question as to whether a people who had overwhelmingly rejected Fascism at the polls were to be allowed to solve their own destinies, or whether they were to be annihilated in an unofficial but overwhelming invasion, and their country made another base for international Fascist designs. The issue was at last crystal clear: Fascism versus Democracy.

The challenge insolently thrown down by Mussolini and Hitler was quickly answered. Throughout the world democrats—workers and intellectuals alike—stirred. If their governments would not act then they would. The untrained, ill-armed militia of the Spanish Republican Army would not have to fight unaided any longer. International Fascism was throwing its forces into Spain; international democracy would do likewise.

So a momentous decision was spontaneously taken, and acted upon throughout the world. From the far corners of the earth came the Volunteers of Liberty, men of different—and differing—parties; workers, intellectuals of practically every nation under the sun, all with one common aim—to smash Fascism.

Sympathy for justice brought some volunteers, hatred of injustice brought others. Some like Hans Beimler came exultantly to fight for a just cause. Others, like Ludwig Renn, hating all war, came realizing that the Fascist menace had to be crushed now lest it overwhelm the world. Communist, socialist, Labour Party, republican, liberal, and nonpolitical men found in the fight against Fascism a common rallying ground. Intellectuals like Ralph Fox interrupted their work and studies in the revolutionary struggle and came to give their aid on the battlefield. Revolutionary poets like Charles Donnelly came to fight the themes they had sung. Doctors and nurses came not from any abstract motives of relieving suffering but in order to help human progress by aiding those who were fighting the battle of all humanity.

From twenty-five nations they came: some with military experience, some claiming it, but all with fighters who valued their principles above everything else, who were ready to sacrifice home and family, livelihood, and even life itself for the cause they believed in. They stowed away in boats, they hitchhiked across continents. Governments raised barriers against them. The French border was closed to them, but they came. In Spain, in September, they were numbered only a few. As the menace of a Fascist victory loomed larger, they arrived in greater numbers. In October, they were counted in hundreds. They could now be organized in their own units. André Marty, veteran French revolutionary, undertook the task.

Outnumbered and outclassed in arms, the militiamen retreated from Toledo. Getafe and Carabanchel fell. The Moors were in University City. German and

Italian planes were bombing, and even machine-gunning Madrid. The nonintervention committee was to blockade land and sea frontiers. The pirate ships of Hitler and Mussolini menaced the Mediterranean. The French border patrols were guarding the mountain passes of the Pyrenees. Nevertheless, the hundreds of volunteers became thousands. Their first brigade, organized in forty-eight hours, hurriedly equipped—four different types of rifles, three different types of machine-guns—rushed into action in the suburbs of Madrid. That was November 1936. The Defense of Madrid is already history.

So began the greatest crusade in history. So, for the first time, the forces of international democracy assembled as allies on the battlefield. So, for the first time, they fought side by side, for their own cause.

So began the International Brigades.

FRANK RYAN

Frank Ryan wrote "Revolt in Spain" as an Introduction to the *Book of the XV International Brigade* in Madrid in 1937 while that city was under siege and suffering repeated bombardment and punishment from the air. He was an Irishman, member of the Irish Writers' Union, as well as a prominent writer, lecturer, and leader of the Irish Republican Army, indeed one of its founders. A student and admirer of the Irish revolutionary martyr James Connolly, Ryan had fought for Irish independence since his youth. He likened the Spanish struggle with that of his own country, and organized a column of volunteers that named themselves the Connolly Column in honor of their distinguished hero. He served in Spain as a Major and was promoted to Executive Officer of the 15th International Brigade, but was captured by Italian Fascists in 1938. Ryan was a prisoner in Spanish Fascist prisons for two years before he was turned over to the Gestapo. On June 10, 1944, Frank Ryan died as a Nazi prisoner in Dresden, Germany. He was forty-two years old. By publishing his "Revolt in Spain" as a Prologue to this book, it becomes a fitting tribute to this brave and unusual man.

—J.T.

Homage to the International Brigades

Part One

JOINING THE INTERNATIONAL BRIGADES

January—February 1937

ONE

The Call of Conscience

When on a cold 5 January 1937 I walked up the gangway of the SS *Champlain*, a French passenger liner, with passport number 359 499, issued a few days earlier, little did I suspect how completely my life was to change. Rubber-stamped in bold purple letters on one of the back pages of the passport I was clutching with my frozen bare hands was the officially stern warning: NOT VALID FOR TRAVEL IN SPAIN.

At twenty-two years of age, I was facing the high seas for the first time—except for occasional deep-sea fishing trips off the coast of my native South Jersey. But the Atlantic was also the first leg of my journey toward meeting other volunteers then assembling in Paris from remote parts of the world to join the Spanish people in defense of their young Republic. All shared enthusiastically the expectation of dealing a quick, mortal blow to the rapaciousness of German and Italian fascism. Peoples of the world, especially the socially and politically conscious, seemed well aware that a group of Spain's right-wing career army officers—the regulars—under traitorous generals, were leading an organized, armed, and premeditated insurrection against their own government, to which they had previously pledged loyalty, in what was widely recognized as a conspiracy with Hitler and Mussolini to bring about another fascist dictatorship on the European continent.

More than two years later, about mid-April 1939, I was to step down that same gangway in New York City harbor, this time descending from the SS *Washington* and into the hands of waiting FBI agents, who promptly, though not discourteously, seized my passport, which by then had expired anyway. This time I didn't step so briskly, and I was lean and somewhat dejected. I was returning from the crucible of Spain, where Spanish Republican armed forces had finally yielded to the power of Hitler's tanks, artillery, and air superiority. Franco's ground troops, aided by well-equipped and mechanized Italian infantry, had stalked and ultimately overrun government positions.

Because the International Brigade Headquarters unit that I was part of remained in Barcelona till the day it fell, I witnessed the collapse of Republican fronts as Franco's triumphant forces pressed us with brutal ferocity to the French frontier. I was the last American volunteer of the Abraham Lincoln Brigade to leave Spain in that massive retreat from Barcelona to France during January and February 1939, except for U.S. prisoners of war still lingering in Franco's jails with an uncertain future; their release came at a much later date. By the time our headquarters unit tripped across the Pyrenees into France, the other American volunteers of the Lincoln Brigade who had survived, the well and the wounded, had already been repatriated and were safely in the United States. I voyaged back alone.

From Le Havre until our ocean liner sailed past the Statute of Liberty, I spent hours each day staring aimlessly into the stormy sea reviewing the turbulent events of the last three years. I was oblivious of the people around me and resisted all their attempts to involve me in the games they were playing.

Instead, I repeatedly asked myself: What went wrong? Why did we lose to the fascist juggernaut? How was it possible for evil to have triumphed over what I was idealistically certain had been a lofty and rightful cause? Answers did not come easily. There was no one on board I could talk to.

I knew that in my two years in Spain—an experience I was never to forget nor to regret—I had already lived a lifetime. Since then I have lived additional lifetimes: in the U.S. Army Air Corps and in the Infantry during World War II; in the trade union movement of the 1940s and 1950s (I had also worked for it in the 1930s), both in the American Federation of Labor and in the CIO; and in and out of several critical medical surgeries at the hands of skilled specialists and occasionally under the scalpel of the unskilled. However, for me, no experience before or after measures up to that of the Spanish Civil War in uniqueness, scope, dedication of purpose, and intensity—so much compacted into so short a period of time.

Though unfamiliar with weapons and with war and its terrors when I arrived in Spain in January 1937, I became a seasoned combat soldier by the spring of that year. Almost overnight I learned about killing, dying, and survival. I also learned about the military intricacies and political complexities of the raging civil war. Before long, my initial views of the war and my restless urge to quickly man the barricades of trade union solidarity struck me as being simplistic, and if I was romantic, I soon found the enemy firepower and the savage fighting to be sobering. As my political understanding broadened, I saw that the Spanish people were not only defending their trade unions and their newly elected Republic but were also engaged in a life-and-death war against the organized and combined forces of world fascism.

It didn't take me long, therefore, to become totally committed, with others—especially the Cubans, with whom I seemed to be more in tune temperamentally and culturally—to the goal of ending global fascism, whether of the Hitler or the Mussolini brand, or of any other brand in Europe, Asia, or America. I knew which side I was on. The friendships and associations at the front and behind the lines speeded up my political maturity; they sharpened my awareness of many world problems of the day and helped me grasp clearly the events of that decade. Each of my 746 days in Spain was a day for action, and also a day for learning.

Among the conclusions I came to, one was unequivocal: a firm conviction that Franco's armed insurrection, despite Hitler's and Mussolini's massive military and financial intervention, could and would have been promptly and decisively crushed had not the Republic been so shamefully betrayed by European and world democracies, especially the United States. As we shall see, American foreign policy and its Embargo Act, directed against Spain and passed by the U.S. Congress in January 1937, played an important and exceptional role in that betrayal.

Almost from the day I returned from Spain and through all the years that followed, I was repeatedly asked: "Why did you go to Spain to join *their* civil war?" My motives were simple and to me entirely clear. I never doubted that the road I had chosen was absolutely correct.

During the strikes and struggles of the South Jersey trade union movement, I had picked up the slogan "Workers of the world unite, you have nothing to lose but your chains"—a slogan I had no difficulty in embracing. The Spanish brothers and sisters and their trade unions, I reasoned, were under fire by insurgent generals: union workers' centers, offices, and headquarters were being raided, closed down, and in some cases reduced to rubble, while their leaders and supporters were being rounded up by the thousands and murdered, sometimes en masse in the community bullring. If I believed workers of the world must unite for justice, peace, and freedom from capitalist exploitation and profiteering, for that is how I interpreted the slogan, then how could I hesitate to join the Spanish workers, in their blue or gray monos (overalls), in defense of their Republic? I hesitated only long enough to get a passport.

Of course, there were additional contributing reasons, instinctive, less refined, and not always arithmetically figured out, but no less fundamental. For instance, in our Italian neighborhood, there were those who loudly supported Mussolini, the Duce, the black-shirted dictator of Italy. "He put Italy back on its feet, didn't he?" they would say. "The trains are now running on time, aren't they?"

On the other hand, refugees from Italy and the black-shirt fascist movement spoke calmly, with only occasional emotionalism, about personal experiences in their native country. They told us, the young men—young women were not to be burdened with these tragic stories—how democracy was crushed, how the strong Italian socialist movement that had flourished after the First World War was drowned in blood, how the people became victims of an increasingly exploitive, militaristic, and violent form of government, and how the freedom Italians loved so much were buried in terror. They mentioned the names of comrades and others held as political prisoners, still without a trial. They seemed to know what was going on in Italy day after day, as if these events were happening just around the corner. They spoke with shame of Mussolini's invasion of Abyssinia and of his senseless bombing and strafing of the civilian population, as if this brutality were a personal reflection on them. Strangely, I too remember feeling this shame and relating to their feeling of guilt. The many stories from recently arrived, sensitive Italians who spoke in their native tongue appealed to my young, impressionable mind. I chose sides.

Then there was Hitler, the dominant partner of the Berlin-Rome-Tokyo axis, who blatantly advocated war on his neighbors and the world, who publicly promoted the burning of books and the extermination of Jews, who was violently liquidating political parties and the trade union movement and sending nonconforming German citizens to prisons, torture chambers, and death camps in order to carry out his "final solution" for Jews and "Communists." Again, it was not hard for me to choose sides.

Eventually, people came to refer to the volunteers in Spain as "premature antifascists," a recognition that these volunteers were fighting fascism long before the world was ready to do so, that they were not soldiers but simply antifascists, and that they understood the high stakes and were prepared to make the supreme commitment.

In coalition with the ruling establishments, the powerful Catholic church of Spain was actively supporting the politically conservative military, who were plotting to overthrow the Republican government. It also favored the extreme right-wing elements, admirers of Hitler and Mussolini and their ideologies. Since the church was the nation's largest landholder and owned the most fertile farmland, its attitude was not surprising; it feared the Republic's planned agrarian reforms and vigorously opposed them. As a result, it strengthened the "hate-the-government" factions. In the meantime, Franco and his army officers were developing conspiratorial relationships with Berlin and Rome as they plotted a coup against the Republic. A civil war against the legitimately and recently elected government thus became inevitable.

*   *   *   *

As well as being a soldier, I was an editor of our frontline newspaper, the *Volunteer for Liberty*; coauthor of *The Book of the XV Brigade*, printed in Madrid in 1938; a Fifteenth Brigade historian; and headquarters staff member of the Political Commissariat of the International Brigades.

In the Barcelona headquarters, I was assigned to the historical section of the International Brigades, where important documents relating to the detailed participation of the Americans were at my disposal. This assignment spanned the fall months of 1938, after volunteers of the International Brigades were withdrawn from combat duties and sent to bases in northern Catalonia, near the French border, to await repatriation.

Luigi Gallo, inspector general of the Political Commissariat of the International Brigades, asked me if I wanted to be repatriated along with other Americans, as I was entitled to, or stay with him and the headquarters group and take on the monumental task of assembling detailed and complete documentation on the military and political role of American volunteers in Spain. He added that John Gates, Lincoln Brigade political commissar, had urged him to name me for this assignment. When without hesitation I accepted it, he cut me short with warnings of the risks of encirclement, defeat, and capture, since International Brigade headquarters personnel would most likely be among the last to evacuate Spain, should that become necessary. He emphasized clearly that our group would be guardians of all documents, which would precede us in leaving. However, every effort would be made for us to get out in time. Knowing Gallo to be a responsible and intelligent leader who would stick to his ship to the bitter end, yet a man who would want to get out alive as sincerely as anyone else, I didn't think for a moment that I was taking too much of a risk of enemy entrapment by staying. At headquarters we shared faith in his skill, courage, and integrity.

Gallo's real name was Luigi Longo. Though my association with him lasted about a year and a half and was very close during the last months and weeks of the civil war, I did not learn his real name until after the end of the Second World War, when it was safe for Italian Communists, underground antifascists, and partisan fighters to reveal their true identity.

Gallo (Longo) distinguished himself not only in Spain, where his role is now legend, but particularly in the Italian antifascist partisan movement. He was perhaps more than anyone else responsible for the effectiveness of the resistance and for its close working relationship with Allied forces. For this Gallo, by now Longo, was lauded as a war hero by the U.S. government and awarded the Bronze Star, a medal pinned on him in a public ceremony by American General Mark Clark, under the express and written orders of President Harry S. Truman.

It is widely known and acclaimed in Italy that it was Longo's *partigiani* who captured Mussolini as he tried to escape to Switzerland. In August 1964, after the death of his longtime friend and comrade Palmiro Togliatti, Longo became secretary-general of the Italian Communist party.

Because my diary, papers, letters, documents, pamphlets, and books refer to Longo by his nom de guerre, Gallo, I shall not change it, but I do ask the reader to bear in mind this one and the same identification.

In my new assignment, I accumulated enormous amounts of material from official orders, battle plans, field dispatches, government directives, and reports written by military officers and political commissars. I had at my disposal diaries of division and brigade commanders and officers. Gallo emphasized that no holds should be barred and that whatever the facts revealed should be stated; if some whose toes got stepped on should complain, so be it. Battles, whether won or lost, were to be described forthrightly and in detail, with map illustrations where applicable. Conclusions, lessons learned, and military or political evaluations were to be based on facts and treated objectively. This kind of history was being prepared by each language group.

Alonzo Markham Elliott, an Englishman with whom I worked closely, handled sections dealing with the British and the Irish. Since the English-speaking volunteers—British, Irish, Canadian, Cuban, and American—were grouped largely in the Fifteenth International Brigade, it was natural for Alonzo and me to collaborate as we had when we put together *The Book of the XV Brigade*. (We did so under the careful guidance and dominant personality of a great Irishman, Frank Ryan, who later was captured by the enemy and doomed to die at the hands of the Nazis.)

Elliott, known to his friends as "Lon," was born in 1912 in Ipswich, Suffolk, England. Awarded a degree in modern languages at Cambridge University and trained as a teacher, he didn't like teaching very much and was not very good at it, he told me. Before going to Spain in 1937, he worked for a progressive bookshop in Cambridge for a short time. I first met him while on leave in Madrid in the summer of that year; we struck up a warm and compatible relationship that has lasted to this day. His command of Spanish and several other languages was almost flawless; his French came in especially handy when we had to travel clandestinely from southern France to Paris after the retreat from Catalonia. In World War II, while he was serving in the British army as a motorcyclist, he and his cycle collided with a truck. The accident landed him in a hospital for almost a year and ended his military service.

We were unable to complete our special documentation assignment in Spain, for the war came to an abrupt and tragic end before we could do so. Driven by the fast-moving fascist forces to the French frontier in February 1939, we eventually slipped into France in the dead of night. Whispering to each other, we consoled and assured ourselves that this was only a "shortening of the lines." Madrid fights on! We admitted that it was a major battle lost and a long world war in the making, but as sure as day follows night we would be back. Prescience? Not at all. No one I knew and none with whom I spoke would claim such mystical powers. Yet the sense of an impending cataclysm was chilling our bones. It was, we felt, the logical consequence of historical events, and Great Britain, France, and the United States would pay dearly for their betrayal in permitting the rape of Spain. Unfortunately, these countries were to drag down with them peoples and nations undeserving of the holocaust that befell them.

* * * *

Like others, I tried keeping a diary; obviously, care had to be taken, for a detailed and indiscreet diary could be of value to the enemy should it fall into their hands. Often there were other difficulties: lack of paper, pencils, and places where one could write, as well as the cold, the rain and wind, and most of all, the enemy, who gave us little comfort or rest. From time to time, despite these obstacles, I managed to put down on paper some of the actions and impressions of the day, sometimes writing in a state of physical exhaustion. It became easier to keep a diary once I joined the staff of the political commissariat headquarters, in Madrid and in Barcelona. Later, I was able to recover only a part of my diary, notes, and letters, and of the biographies, unpublished stories, and anecdotes written by other volunteers. Hundreds of pictures taken by brigade photographers, professional and amateur, mysteriously disappeared, just as illustrations and art work produced by volunteers, especially the delightful cartoons and art work of the extraordinarily prolific and talented American Deyo Jacobs, were lost. Inevitably, during war, with sudden and rapid shifting movement of troops and headquarters, documents and valuables get lost, misplaced, ignored, burned, and even unintentionally left behind. Hence the frequent gaps in dates and events in the pages that follow.

I realize, too, that diary writing, originally intended for the diarist alone, has its shortcomings. It is often cryptic and a form of shorthand that is hard for others to read, unless they happen to be intimate with the diarist himself or know a great deal about him. In my diary, I find that occasionally people pop in and out and we never see them again, and too often they are not identified in the first place in their relationship to me, the International Brigades, or to others. I have tried to correct these faults and to help reduce frustrations for the reader by providing additional information and clarification where possible. In a few cases I have been able to give an up-to-date biography of individuals referred to in the diary, but where I was not able to do so, for lack of information, I had to leave the abbreviated name or initial, with the hope that the reader will not be too annoyed.

This book does not pretend to be a history of the Spanish Civil War, or of the International Brigades, or even of the Abraham Lincoln Brigade. Moreover, I shall not spend time trying to convince the reader of the justice of the Spanish people's impatient crusade aimed at wiping out their medieval past and of their giant efforts to propel their country into the twentieth century. History has already done so. Competent professional scholars and historians have produced scores of books detailing this subject. By chronicling some of my personal experiences, perhaps I can shed additional light on the period. Experiences of each volunteer, of course, varied, but if the reader gets some feel at least of what it was like for this American volunteer to be in Spain while history was being made, then my hope for this book will be fulfilled.

The events of our first crucial months—February, March, and April 1937, a period characterized by daily high-noon confrontations with the enemy in the struggle for control of the vital Jarama mountains, their passes and roads, to prevent Madrid from being entirely encircled at that early stage of the war—were partially told in *The Story of the Abraham Lincoln Battalion*, which I wrote in between battles and completed in Madrid during May 1937. Five hundred specially bound and numbered copies of this document were published in New York that year by the Friends of the Abraham Lincoln Brigade and distributed in the United States to raise money for the Spanish Republican cause. Later, the same group published *The Story* in pamphlet form for general circulation, though the authorship of this document was not revealed at the time. It can be found in most libraries that specialize in historical materials on the Spanish Civil War. In recent books written about that war, sections of my material have been liberally quoted and generously referred to, but understandably the accounts were often attributed to "Anonymous."

Much of *The Story of the Abraham Lincoln Battalion* later became part of a larger book I mentioned earlier, *The Book of the XV Brigade*, of which I was one of the authors. Thousands of these books fell into fascist hands by the end of the war, before we could get them out of Spain, but many volunteers were able to get at least one copy to bring back home. This book can be found in libraries that stock special collections on Spain.

Because my *Story of the Abraham Lincoln Battalion* was written while the action was taking place, I, too, shall dip into it occasionally. So if at times sentences, paragraphs, and certain vignettes sound familiar to readers of works on the Spanish Civil War, I hope they will understand why. Unlike other authors, however, who of necessity simply quoted from my material, I am in the unique position of presenting additional information, expanding the original in some areas, weaving diary entries into appropriate sequences, quoting from personal letters and other items, and inserting hitherto unpublished facts in my possession.

Still, the reader should remember that the ensuing chapters are largely recollections of events that took place almost fifty years ago, from 1936 to 1939, and that I have organized these recollections into their present form only recently. During a few of the fifty years, I found it difficult, often impossible, to talk freely about the Spain I got to know during her civil war. The hurt of defeat and disaster frequently overwhelmed me into bitter silence. I found myself at times evading questions, postponing discussions about the war, turning down speaking engagements, and sidetracking queries about my views on the course of significant current events in that country. I realize now, even self-critically, that I hid and indulged that hurt too long. Perhaps the reason was a sense of guilt at having left Spain on the very day of her defeat in the certain knowledge that thousands who remained and the many more thousands trapped by Franco's revengeful troops would go to their graves or suffer long years of imprisonment, in many cases brutalities and hardships worse than death. Maybe it was the endless heartbreaking letters from former acquaintances asking for help: a friend, a comrade, a refugee hiding somewhere, a letter from a French internment camp, from Central and South America receiving Spanish war refugees. All needed assistance. They asked for the kind of aid I found myself helpless, in most cases, to give.

When on occasion I was able to mail a ten-dollar bill, always in cash because in those days I never had quite enough money to start a checking account, to a friend in the Dominican Republic, Ecuador, Mexico, or some other Central or South American country, I was startled to find how many more new friends I suddenly heard from. It was as if my United States home address was hooked into some international chain letter, or, in today's lingo, into some world computer.

Many of the materials and documents I had sent home from Spain remained for too many years in boxes in our leaky garage, and a goodly number of them were destroyed by the dampness and mice. However, in recent years I made a greater effort to salvage anything that may have historical value. Time has erased many of my early nightmares. I became more objective, less personal, more detached from the happenings of those Spanish war years, as if I no longer belonged—just an interested spectator, perhaps. Yet not really. It was terribly difficult for me to get to work on this book. As soon as I had convinced myself that I was ready to start sorting out material and writing, I found excuses for delay, for getting busy instead with organizational activities—trade union, political, peace movement, and veterans' activities, as well as other work, including earning a living for my family. The present always seemed to be more important than the past.

In preparing this book, I relied on my sketchy diaries, letters, personal documents, scraps of papers with orders from field commanders, rosters, notes, printed flyers to enemy troops and to our own, posters, and many items that served to recapture more accurately the events of that period. My brother Dominic and his wife, Antoinette, kept neat scrapbooks of the letters, pictures, postcards, and documents I had sent them, which did not appear to be important at the time but proved to be helpful in placing events in a more sensible order. I thank both of them for saving this material. My recent book, *The Palette and the Flame: Posters of the Spanish Civil War*, was made possible because of the care they had taken in preserving the posters I had sent them.

What spurred me to publish both that book and my present recollections was the profound and sincere empathy for the Spanish people and the Republican cause that I found in all strata of our society once I began talking about my experiences. It is one of America's healthier attributes, inherited from our own revolutionary past, I'm convinced, that prompts our ready support of peoples battling to break from aristocracy, plutocracy, and tyranny.

Particularly among our youth today, there is a robust interest in the Spanish Civil War. Many in our young generation of Americans demand facts about this disquieting chapter of world history. They are scrutinizing this history and want to lay bare what really happened in Spain during the late 1930s. "Why," they ask, "was the Spanish Republic defeated after almost three years of valiant resistance to the legions of fascism?" Then they raise the key issue: "What was the role of European democracies and that of our own United States of America?" I have spent pleasurable days with writers, authors, and historians, answering hundreds of questions on tape recorders, but the most satisfying time I spent was with graduate and undergraduate college students who were writing their theses or papers on some phase of the war. Their perceptive and searching questions seemed to be motivated by a realization of the growing dangers of our own militarism and of our government's apparently irresistible compulsion to intervene in the internal affairs of other nations in support of reactionary, counterrevolutionary, militarist, or fascist elements and repressive regimes.

TWO

The Crucible of Spain

When the Franco rebellion against the new Spanish Republic began in July 1936, I was too absorbed in labor union activities to pay much attention to what appeared to be minor shooting skirmishes in a far-off land. The fact that I had had three years of Spanish in high school made me slightly curious as I read the daily newspaper reports of the conflict in Spain—but only slightly curious. Besides union activities, I was wrapped up in the antiwar student movement, the League Against War and Fascism, the Unemployed Union, and the young socialist and young communist movements of those depression years. During the summer months, while still in high school, I had worked at the Campbell Soup Company in Camden, New Jersey, and had taken part in the abortive strike of 1934 there. Our home was just four blocks from the plant, which at the time was the largest cannery in the country, if not the world. The giant Radio Corporation of America—to us local people it was the Victor Talking Machine, the Victrola with a dog's cocked ear listening to "His Master's Voice"— had its plants sprawled next to Campbell's. Camden also boasted one of the largest shipyards in the country: the New York Shipbuilding Company.

Unemployment was high. Families were still being evicted from their homes, and, in spite of President Roosevelt's pump-priming works projects, it was still the depression, with the homeless and the hungry roaming the streets. But workers in our city, as throughout the nation, were stirring. Sit-down strikes in the factories were just beginning. Industrial unionism was taking hold, and John L. Lewis was becoming the hero of the American oppressed worker. It was also the year of the Committee for Industrial Organization, which was threatened with expulsion from the conservative American Federation of Labor.

Though we had lost our strike at Campbell's in 1934, a small group—not more than a dozen or so—kept the spark and hope of unionism alive while the defeated majority went underground for fear of reprisals. The dozen diehards became chartered by the American Federation of Labor as Federal Local No. 20224, unaffiliated with any national union, since there was none covering our jurisdiction.

Early in 1936, out of work, I took a job with the WPA (Works Progress Administration) writer's project, but I continued my trade union activities at Campbell's. In November 1936, when the American Federation of Labor held its national convention in Tampa, Florida, I went as a delegate from our federal cannery local, under the assumed name of Roy Hawthorne. I did so on the advice of my sympathetic WPA director, who said he could not justify my absence from the job and still qualify me to draw pay while I attended a union convention. In those depression days, a paycheck was indispensable.

It was an incident at this AFL convention that aroused my interest in Spain. A Spanish woman, a consul representing the legally elected government, requested permission from the AFL officialdom to address the delegates on behalf of her people, to tell about the military uprising and the intervention of Italian and German armed forces. When her request was denied, many delegates were furious; so we listened to her outside the convention hall as she told about the military rebellion, whose aim was to set up a fascist state patterned after Italy and Nazi Germany and to destroy legitimate trade unionism and the infant Republic, which, she emphasized, had been democratically elected. She made clear that the defeat of the Spanish Republic would be the beginning of a new world war. She called for support for the workers of Spain from the trade unions of the United States. We were ashamed that this great convention of trade unionists would not even listen to her, let alone support the Spanish Republic and our fellow workers in Spain. On my way back from Tampa, I could think of nothing else but how to get to Spain.

Once back home, I contacted Pat Toohey, district organizer for the Communist party, whom I knew I could trust with this crazy idea. He was not surprised at my inquiries, and I learned from him that the Central Committee of the U.S. Communist party had already adopted a resolution calling on its leaders, members, and friends to organize an American column to join the then forming International Brigades in Spain and that Communist parties throughout the world were doing likewise. As a matter of fact, Pat added, the Communist party of Eastern Pennsylvania had by then put together a committee to help in organizing such a column, and this committee was already raising funds for its work, publicizing the cause of the Spanish Republic, recruiting volunteers, and arranging for passports, equipment, transportation, and many other details. He also told me the Young Communist League was playing a leading and vigorous role in the work of the committee.

When I appeared before the committee, I learned that its function was also to check a volunteer's political awareness, stability, integrity, usefulness, and reliability. I must have passed the test because, along with others, I was led to Dr. Leof, well-known in Philadelphia and highly respected as a dedicated activist in socialist causes. Stripped to the waist, we lined up for his friendly medical inspection, but his eyes were bad, and if anyone had anything wrong with him, I doubt that he would have caught it. He did not look below the belt, for if he had, he might *not* have okayed Joe Bianca as a volunteer. Joe was a Philadelphia longshoreman, who later in Spain had a leg blown off—his wooden one.*

My first difficulty, however, was in getting a passport speedily. In Philadelphia, where I was born, there was no record to be found that I existed. I discovered that when I had been enrolled in grammar school, my mother, who did not speak English and could neither read nor write, gave the school my name but could not spell it. The teacher, I'm sure, did the best she could and spelled it the way she thought it sounded. Therefore, throughout grammar and high school I spelled my name "Tisso," and my Camden High purple-and-gold graduation book bears this surname. This is the way my brothers spelled it, and so did my mother when she had to learn to endorse her Campbell Soup paychecks. Finally, through records of the South Philadelphia Catholic church where I was christened, I was able to unravel the name confusion for myself and my family. My mother had to relearn to endorse her name. When years later, in October 1952, I was subpoenaed to appear before the House Committee on Un-American Activities, I was asked, among other things, if I had ever used the alias of "Tisso." The committee, I discovered, knew the answer, but its purpose in asking was intentionally devious. My refusal to affirm or deny my old name, since I was exercising my constitutional rights under the Fifth Amendment to refuse to answer questions, seemed to imply that I had hidden behind a secret alias—exactly the impression the committee wanted to create. The local press reported this but did not make as much of it as, I'm sure, the Un-American Committee had hoped.

By the time I got my passport, it was almost the end of 1936, and the first group of Americans—ninety-six, as we later learned—was already on the high seas, having left on the SS *Normandie* the day after Christmas.

At exactly midnight, my father ushered in the New Year 1937 in his traditional ceremonial way. While my three brothers and I looked on with awe, he emptied his revolver into the cold night air, as we listened to more shots fired by neighbors. Then came the fastidious cleaning of the weapon and its careful storage, till the next year, in a little brownish cloth bag with a pull string, probably one of the old tobacco pouches used in those days.

A few hours later I was on my way to New York City and to the Sloane YMCA on 34th Street, which turned out to be a rendezvous for many others scheduled for Spain. The only ones in my family in whom I had confided were my two younger brothers, Dominic and Charles. I pledged them to secrecy. My parents were good and simple peasants from the old country who had come to New Jersey from the small town of Delia, Sicily, in 1911, and they would not have approved, nor would they have understood why I felt I had to go. To them my antiwar activities, my participation in labor strikes and secret training with a cane for defense against police attacks, and my association with the Unemployed Councils and with the radicals of the city were just youthful aberrations that their son would sooner or later outgrow. Their ambition for me was that I should pursue the trade of a barber, which they so carefully had me learn; at the very least, they wanted me to hold down a good job in

---

*I got Joe's story from a letter he had sent Pat Toohey, to which I was privy. But those who knew him well were certain Joe did *not* have a wooden leg. This claim more likely was his roguish way of twitching his Irish friend's nose. Joe Bianca was killed in August 1938 near the town of Gandesa, in the Arc of the Ebro. Bill Bailey, who later acted in the documentary, *The Good Fight*, said he dug Joe's grave on Hill 666 and placed a marker at the grave site.

one of the factories, preferably Campbell Soup, get married, have children, and become a quiet and conforming member of our closely knit Italian community in South Camden. My father had also tried to convince me to marry the daughter of one of his *paesani*, with whom, my mother proudly confided, he had a private arrangement for a handsome dowry and $1,500 in cash. I'm sure I was a great disappointment to him and to my would-be father-in-law.

From Sloane House, I was directed uptown to the headquarters of the Julio Mella Club, a left-wing organization comprising mainly Cubans, many of whom were refugees from the Batista dictatorship. At this club I met others like myself, with passports, listening to briefings and impatiently eager to leave for Spain. It was here that I met and became close friends with many Cubans with whom I was to travel and serve in Spain.

Our group leader was Rodolfo de Armas, about five feet eight inches tall, broad-shouldered, and muscular. His wide, chestnut-brown face had a high, shiny, prominent forehead with deep-set, sparkling brown eyes, the left one crossed. When he spoke, one felt that one was in the presence of a powerful tractor in motion. He wasted no words, and one moved fast under his command. Always serious and in a hurry, he seemed intolerant and angry, until one got to know him; then one understood his vigor, his short temper, and his anxiety that everything be done quickly and perfectly. To his friends he was no mystery; he was considered to be one of the gentlest of human beings, as well as the most advanced Marxist of all the Cubans. Forced to flee the Batista terror, Rodolfo had left his family, friends, and roots behind to work in the United States with other Cuban exiles and to wait with them for a triumphant return home. Some were never to make it. He and his fellow Cubans loved to sing anti-Batista and revolutionary songs and did so at the club in Harlem, on the ocean in time with with the gentle sway of the ship, and in Spain at the training bases. I learned these songs and sang with them. Each Cuban had his own blood-curdling story of life in Cuba under the fierce dictatorship, and each was going to Spain on a personal mission to fight fascism, for to them the defeat of Hitler, Mussolini, and Franco would be their vengeance on their own dictator, Batista. To them the defeat of European fascism would inevitably lead to the defeat of American fascism—Central, South or North—and they were resigned to the realization that their path back home had to be by way of Spain. Though many of them were young communists or had Marxist sympathies, there were some who were just against Batista for his cruelties and let it go at that. Rodolfo, however, by the magnetism of his personality and the soundness of his reasoning, was able to pull together in common bond the various political shades among these antifascist Cubans.

From the club, a group of about fifteen of us was sent down to a lower Manhattan Army-Navy store. It was obvious we were expected because when we arrived—it was during the early hours of the morning, before the store's regular opening time—the managers lined us up single file, U.S. Army fashion, and shoved World War I GI issue into our arms as we quickly paraded through the upper and lower levels of the store. They asked for no money; we had none to offer. The doughboy khaki uniform was complete: overseas cap, pants with leggings, shirt, jacket, boots, gas mask, hatchet, and other tools, enough to fit tightly into one suitcase. The old-fashioned army pants and leggings I got were too large, so back at the Y I traded them with someone whose pair was too small. That's the way it went. In Spain I could never properly wrap these World War I style leggings. They kept unraveling or dropping down to my ankles. Even with the use of many safety pins, I had trouble, and as soon as I was able to, I discarded them for less embarrassing trousers. I could not imagine myself on the battlefield, advancing with rifle in one hand and holding up my leggings with the other.

As we steamed out of New York Harbor on 5 January 1937 and watched the Statue of Liberty disappear into the horizon, I could not believe that I was not to see her again for more than two years. I had told my brothers that I would be back in six months at the latest. This was what many in our group understood. We signed no contract or agreement to that effect, however. As a matter of fact, some were impatient to get to Spain, for fear Franco would be defeated and the war over before they got their licks in. I prayed for that miracle to happen because, mid-ocean, I was already homesick. There were some fifty of us on board, with a squad leader for about every ten men.

Throughout our one-week trip, the sea was calm and the sun shone every day. I did not get seasick as I had expected; instead, I listened, enraptured, to the stories about the anti-Batista conflicts told by the Cubans, and then thrilled at their antifascist songs and love songs strummed on the guitar. They spoke of their revolutionary hero, José Martí. They were a happy bunch, not caring who knew where they were going. They roamed the ship and invaded the upper, first-class decks and often were ordered back to our third-class hole. I gate-crashed with them because I too wanted to see how the rich lived. The non-Cubans in our ranks were more reserved, playing cards, shuffleboard, and other deck games to pass the time and appear as inconspicuous as possible. They followed strictly the briefing instructions on behavior we had received in New York. Despite such caution, I doubt that many passengers in third class were deceived as to our mission. Often, after dramatic reports on the progress of the war, which we got from the ship's wireless, heated discussions about the Loyalist government raged between passengers and the secret volunteers. Squad leaders had to intervene to remind us of our decorum.

Every morning, while the sun was still bright, I would briefly sit on a deck chair next to a young woman who wore black sunglasses. She intrigued me. She was wrapped warmly in several blankets, and she protected her long blond hair from the wind with a head kerchief. Though she was an easy conversationalist and friendly enough, I could never get her to look toward me as we talked. I was curious about the color of her eyes, but she just stared through her dark glasses into the clear blue space above us. I thought her a snob. At Le Havre, as the ship docked, I saw her at the railing watching the ship's maneuvers through her ever-present sunglasses. We again exchanged pleasantries, but again she looked straight ahead, and I could not get her to turn toward me. As the gates opened for passengers to disembark, her traveling companion took her gently by the arm, turned her around, and led her slowly off the ship. It was then, for the first time, that I realized she was blind.

We had no difficulty clearing customs. The French government, at that point in history reflecting the overwhelming support of its people for the Spanish cause, placed no obstacles in our way. Indeed, when the customs official opened my suitcase and saw khaki, he quickly closed it, smiled, and winked in solid approval. As he returned the case, he whispered audibly, "Viva la Republica." I felt good. My companions experienced the same welcome treatment. Had I been challenged, I was prepared to say I was on my way to Switzerland to climb mountains.

After an overnight pause in Paris, we boarded the train to southern France and

Perpignan. I don't remember too much about Paris except that we were perpetually accosted by street women. In spite of stateside warnings agains the dangers of venereal disease, some of my companions insisted on a last fling. Sure enough, a few weeks later severeal had to be sent back to France from Spain with serious doses of that incapacitating infirmity.

Together with my Cuban comrades, we roamed Paris like any other fast-moving tourists and marveled at its antiquity. At a glass-enclosed sidewalk cafe, we ordered by pointing to the menu, since none of us knew French. When we got the strangest foods, we traded with one another, family style. One of our guys wanted a toothpick. To the waiter he said, "I want . . . " and demonstrated by sticking his thumb nail between his teeth and simulating spitting. The waiter, in perfect English, said, "Oh, you want a toothpick."

The Paris railroad station was jammed with thousands of volunteers on their way to Spain. Dozens of cars were filled to capacity with young men and a few women from all over the world. Seats were hard to come by. Standing room only was almost literally the case. Some of us sat on the floor, others stood in the aisles or with heads out of the train windows. No one complained at being jostled, stepped over, or even accidentally stepped on. The man next to you, though he didn't know you or speak your language, was friendly, comradely, and helpful. We shared each other's food. We broke three-foot-long French bread with each other amid wine toasts, followed by cheese, salami, sausage, and fruits. Some with sleeping bags shared them with others who needed to rest after a tedious journey from this country or that. But the excitement of our togetherness, the eagerness to talk and to listen to stories of the hardships some volunteers had in getting there, made rest a weary dream. One German, who had escaped his native land, had swum across the Rhine with two others. Midstream, he said, the Nazi police had fired on them; his two comrades were hit, and drowned with fascist bullets in their bodies.

The trains moved southward slowly and deliberately through the bright French countryside, while the crewmen threaded past the tangle of people greeting us as hospitably as if we were guests in their own homes. That was the first and last time I was ever on a train where the conductor didn't ask for a ticket. As we slowly passed the neatly tilled fields, farm workers, peasants, and their families dropped their work, raised their clenched fists, and kept them in the air until we were out of sight. Each time the train stopped, which seemed like every few minutes, men, women, and children gathered to hand us flowers, fruit, wine, and candies. As the train moved again, these French people stretched out their hands and grabbed ours, running with the train, throwing kisses, wishing us luck and victory. They waved vigorously till we lost them in the distance. These receptions were repeated dozens of times all the way to the Spanish border. We believed it to be the longest, sweetest greeting that any group of Americans had ever received in a foreign land. Never were there so many men and women together, from all parts of the world, speaking the common language of antifascism yet actually able to communicate with each other only through inner understanding—or an occasional translator.

Once we crossed the French frontier into Spain, we were quartered in a tremendous ancient fortress, occupying many acres of the highest ground in Figueras, the Catalonian frontier town.

We climbed out of the train with stiff, jerky movements, and stood together in small groups. A single lamp cast a thin light on the ground and faintly illuminated sections of the immense fortifications. Finally, we got our suitcases and filed off behind a uniformed soldier, who led us under an arch into a tremendous passageway, thirty feet high and wide enough for two cars to travel alongside each other. The passageway turned to the left and descended sharply, deep into the belly of the fortress. In the central aisle, men stood talking under dimly lit bulbs, which hung at intervals from the vaulted ceilings. Some of the volunteers were stretched out on the ground, and others were sitting on beds. There were hundreds of men and some women, from many nations, chattering gaily in numerous languages. They quickly crowded around the arriving groups. Where were they from? Americans who had arrived just a few days earlier asked about friends they had left behind. Were more Americans coming? Was there anyone from Toronto? Detroit? Chicago?

In this underground medieval castle, more than a thousand men and a smattering of women had gathered, with room for thousands more. A German with dark, tragic eyes had escaped from a concentration camp and hitchhiked to get here—mostly, he had walked. Several German Jews and an Arab had trekked hundreds of miles zigzagging their way to this fortress. In the shadow of one of the pillars stood a group of pink-cheeked Austrians in ski suits and jackets, the survivors of a band that had skied out of Austria and over mountain ranges to reach Spain. They said that two had second thoughts about continuing and had turned back; another, who had trouble with his skis, broke an ankle and had to be left in a town hospital; two others were intercepted by a border patrol and turned back. Not far from this group, two young women from Switzerland were sitting on their knapsacks, their blond hair disheveled, wondering what they were to do next. Squatting on a cot, a British officer from the Royal Air Force squinted through the barrel of a revolver that a Welsh lad had brought with him.

Everywhere in this subterranean, humid barracks, men talked of their determination and irreversible decision to come to grips with fascism. The many stories of the terror of Hitler's Germany aroused our anger. Men were here from the political jails of Poland, Hungary, Rumania, Italy, and many more nations. To the refugees, there was no road back till fascism in Spain spelled a defeat of reaction in their own countries. Victory in Spain would permit them to return home as free men and women.

We, the fifty or so new Americans, sitting on our beds of straw peeling off our socks, had become part of this. We had joined the International Brigades. Ninety-six of our countrymen had preceded us; more than three thousand were to follow.

Stretched out on my bed, my hands clasped under my head, my legs spread apart, and completely relaxed with a government-issue tin of wine beside me, I reviewed the dizzying pace of the past two weeks: New York City; then five days at sea, each day one of ease and pleasure; Le Havre; the southbound train to Perpignan; crossing the Spanish border; and arrival at Figueras at seven o'clock at night. What a surprise. Figueras was no feudal village, but a small modern city, dominated by this spectacular fort that covered hundreds of square meters, the Castillo de San Fernandez, with its distant view of the snow-clad peaks of the Pyrenees. We had no time to wonder what was next; the rapid pace continued.

After two days at Figueras, where we formed groups, drilled, marched, ate, drank, got acquainted with each other in that Tower of Babel, and strolled through miles of the sprawling fort, we were packed on a southbound train for Barcelona. On our arrival at the Barcelona station, we were greeted by a brass band and a mass of humanity. Thousands of men, women, children, and uniformed militia cheered as we paraded for nearly two hours through the broad boulevards. People waved from the windows of magnificent buildings that looked down on tree-lined avenues. It seemed as if the whole city was on holiday to greet us. We felt quickly at home, though in a city that did not understand our language, nor we theirs.

After an elaborate dinner at the Karl Marx Barracks, we boarded another train—south again. More hours of travel along the placid Mediterranean, more hours of breathtaking scenery and picturesque, postcard fishing villages, and more hours of warm greetings by a generous, gift-giving people. In the early hours of the morning we reached Valencia, and after breakfast we moved on again.

Sleepy and grimy from more than fifty hours of continous travel, our rail caravan arrived at Albacete, the base headquarters of the rapidly growing International Brigades. After a hot dinner in the Plaza de Toros, a good night's sleep, and breakfast at daybreak, we were on our way once more—this time by truck for hours of travel over bumpy, dusty roads. As we passed peasants walking alongside their donkeys or riding in their carts, they smiled and waved clenched fists. At Madrigueras, the British training base, we were greeted by the British commandant, who gave a welcoming speech and introduced us to forty or fifty Irish volunteers who, before we arrived, had voted to join the American battalion. On our way to the American training base of Villanueva de la Jara, we stopped only once—in a small village—for relief.

When we unloaded from our trucks on the crest of a hill commanding a clear view of the town of Villanueva de la Jara, we marched down the hill while children ran toward us waving flags and cheering. Another small group of children, singing their greeting songs and marching in organized formation, finally broke ranks and joined the rest of the children in a mad gallop in our direction. In the central plaza of the town, the mayor closed his welcoming speech by shouting, "Viva Rusia!" We couldn't figure out if the mayor thought we were Russians, or if he was a supporter of the Soviet Union. To us it didn't matter since we knew that if he mistook us for Russians, he may have gotten this misconception from fascist radio and press propaganda, which often stressed that all volunteers were Russians.

LA UNIDAD *del* EJERCITO *del* PUEBLO SERA EL ARMA DE LA VICTORIA

The unity of the people's army will be the weapon of victory

THREE

Training for Combat

Americans burst into Spain in January and February 1937, a powerful stream of determined and enthusiastic young volunteers, a stream that continued month after month, despite attempts by the United States government to prevent further exits from its shores. The French government cooperated by choking off its border crossings along the Pyrenees and along its southern seaports. Despite these government obstructions from both sides of the ocean, more than three thousand Americans found ways of getting to Spain.

Early arrivals and those who broke through the American and French blockades were sent to the quiet, friendly, sparsely populated agricultural town of Villanueva de la Jara—east of Madrid—a training base for International Volunteers. There we sorted ourselves out and by unanimous vote decided to name our unit the Abraham Lincoln Battalion. However, in the table of organization of the newly formed International Brigades, we were simply "International Column, 17th Battalion." Letterheads said so. With characteristic American ingenuity, our clerks typed "Lincoln Battalion" in parentheses alongside "17th Battalion" often enough that the memory of the numerals wore off and the idea of "Lincoln" remained.

When the Lincoln Battalion was finally complete, it consisted of two infantry companies of three sections each, a machine-gun company, a first aid and medical section (which included one whole, well-trained first aid unit from Holland), a kitchen staff attached to the supply and transport department, an armory section, and a headquarters and military staff. The political bureau and staff paralleled the military table of organization.

At the time the Lincoln was first ordered into battle, it numbered some 550 effectives. There were men from many parts of the United States and from Cuba, Mexico, Puerto Rico, and Canada (more than fifteen hundred Canadians made it across the ocean to join the International Brigades). We had one American Indian and several black Americans (between 100 and 150 black Americans were serving with the Lincolns by the time the battalion became a brigade). Special for many of us was Jack Shirai, a Japanese-American, who was to distinguish himself as a first-class machine gunner and battalion chief cook. Before he was killed in action, he proved that he was master of both skills.

The James Connolly Column of seasoned fighters from Ireland, already in Spain when we arrived, had voted to join the Lincolns. The Cuban column, the Centuria Antonio Guiteras, headed by Rodolfo de Armas, also formed a significant part of the new battalion.

When the Fifteenth International Brigade was organized at the end of January, the Lincoln Battalion became part of it, together with the British Battalion, which had just come up from the battlefields of Cordoba, south of Madrid, the Franco-Belgian Sixth of February Battalion that had been in almost continuous battles before our arrival, and the highly regarded, battle-hardened Dimitrov Battalion of Slavic-speaking volunteers—Yugoslavs, Czechs, Bulgarians, Poles, and a few Russians. By July, the new, completely American, Washington Battalion joined the brigade, but that very month the Washington Battalion suffered such heavy losses in the government offensive at Brunete, northwest of Madrid, that it had to be merged with the Lincoln, which then became known as the Lincoln-Washington Battalion.

In September, another newly formed battalion, the Canadian MacKenzie-Papineau (named for two Canadians who led a people's revolt against Britain in 1837), Mac-Paps for short, joined the Lincoln Brigade during the Aragon offensive, northeast of Madrid.

The brigade was fortunate and proud of having in its table of organization a Spanish-speaking battalion, the Twenty-fourth, (later named the Fifty-ninth). Many of its members were Cuban, Mexican, and Puerto Rican, and there were volunteers from Central and South America; it also included some English-speaking members of the brigade battalions.

Though the Fifteenth Brigade became known as the English-speaking brigade, Spanish government edict required each international brigade and its military units to include Spaniards. This clearly was to guarantee that ultimately the brigades would become thoroughly integrated.

In the meantime, the Fifteenth International Brigade was becoming popularly known in the Americas, Europe, and Spain as the Abraham Lincoln Brigade. Indeed, the American press, radio, and other information media referred to all American volunteers in Spain as the Abraham Lincoln Brigade. As used by the media, the appellation encompassed Americans in combat battalions, in various support units, such as postal services, armorers, and transport and auto park units, where Americans prevailed because of their mechanical expertise; the medical, hospital, first aid, and ambulance teams; radio and transmission units; and the John Brown Artillery Battery, in which Americans were more than adequately represented and whose political commissar was John Gates from New York, who later became political commissar of the Abraham Lincoln Brigade. Americans served in International Brigade Headquarters in Madrid, Albacete, and Barcelona, in radio and propaganda departments, and in brigade and government administrative offices. So it came about that the aggregate of Americans in combat battalions and in essential noncombat support services throughout Spain during the civil war was normally designated the Abraham Lincoln Brigade.

But to return to our arrival in Spain in January 1937, we trained for combat at Villaneuva de la Jara. We were quartered in an abandoned monastery, a two-story structure dominating the town and built generously of stone and solid concrete, its walls easily several feet thick; it was no problem for one to lie down on the upper ledges for a bit of sunbathing and still have room to twist and turn. Many inside walls had been decorated with graffiti—some crude and some artistic—by the French, who had preceded us. Americans, Irish, and British added their own. Prominent slogans of the Popular Front were scrawled everywhere—*Viva la Republica, No Pasarán* (They shall not pass), *Down with Fascism, Red Front*—and in as many languages as one could think of. The clenched fist of international solidarity was conspicuous among the slogans. So was the hammer and sickle.

The massive concrete monastery was cool during warm days but frightfully cold at night, and there were never enough blankets to keep us really warm. There was no running water. To wash we queued at the well in the courtyard each morning, and if we were lucky, we pulled up by bucket enough water to fill an old-fashioned porcelain washbasin. The icelike temperature of the water for washing and shaving was never welcome in those early morning hours. The building was unsanitary when we moved in, and it took us several days before it was made livable. The townspeople, mostly elderly peasants who worked the fields and orchards during the day, did all they could to make things comfortable for the *Americanos*. Affection and friendship grew noticeably between them and the men of the Lincoln Battalion. Language, at first, was a barrier, but it was surmounted with the aid of the Cuban volunteers, who never tired of helping.

One day Al Tanz, who came from New York City and was battalion quartermaster, phoned Madrid requesting a delivery of food items, including ham. *Jamón* is ham in Spanish. His diction as yet was far from perfect and he was misunderstood. An order was placed for a hundred pounds of *jabón*—soap. Luckily, somebody in Madrid had the good sense to call back to double-check. "Why do you need so much soap? You are in such a nice clean town. You can't eat soap, you know . . . " A Cuban got on the line and thanks to him we ate ham.

As in most armies, it didn't take us long to fall into routine. Breakfast at 6:30, followed by policing areas, making up bunk—in most cases simply a mattress or straw on a stone floor—then dressing for the eight o'clock drill and parade. This, too, was the time for all the kids in town to gather to watch the show.

Billeted and organized into squads, we got together with the men who had arrived before us. Drill—more drill—drill again! Form diamonds! Artillery formation! Spread out! Route column! Air raid, dive for cover! Military manual study classes! Political meetings: why are we here? New arrivals. More classes—always eagerness to learn. The number of rifles allotted to our infantry was too few for the number of men. Those without rifles used broomsticks or canes to train and march with. It didn't matter, though, for those outdated and prehistoric rifles were not serviceable anyway. If you had tried to fire one, you would have risked having your head blown off. Fortunately, no ammunition was available.

We selected temporary squad and section leaders by consensus rather quickly. Choosing political commissars took longer; sometimes it took several meetings. Because our high esteem for the Republic and our absorbing concern for the war were intensely political, it was natural for us to have frequent meetings, even during combat training, to discuss the course of the war and its politics. However important the military phase of training, we felt that the political aspects of the war were equally important.

Scribbled in French on one of our meeting room walls was a quote of what Talleyrand was supposed to have said: "War is much too serious to leave to the generals." Below it, in large block letters, repeated three times, were the words, "Viva the Political Commissar."

The political commissar, who ranked alongside the military commander except during combat operations, played an important role for the army and the government. Sometimes he was elected by his military unit, and sometimes he was picked by consensus, but most often he was selected by political superiors. Usually, his appointment meant that he was considered politically advanced, experienced, and stable, a person capable of instilling discipline and inspiring loyalty for the cause and one who could be expected to serve as an example of courage and fearlessness in combat.

Though concentrating on political education and morale, the commissar also concerned himself with the quality of food, clothing, incoming and outgoing mail, books, newspapers, magazines, state of health of his troops, and recreational and cultural activities, especially when his men were at rest or in reserve. From the moment he assumed his duties, his time and energy belonged exclusively to the welfare of his men. He knew he would be leaned on, so he was ever on the alert for problems, petty or major. A good commissar never hesitated to call meetings for resolving differences and disputes or for any other reason he considered important for maintaining morale and unity. He knew that as a result of the severities of combat volunteers soon became militarily and politically sophisticated. To be useful, the commissar had to come from the ranks and to have the confidence of his men. He would not last long in his post if he was not equally tough, straightforward, and honest in his dealings with those in his political command.

Even the U. S. Army during the Second World War recognized the validity of political commissars, although they were not called that. They were referred to as orientation officers and conducted an orientation program called "Know Why We Fight." Part of my three-year stint in the U. S. Army Air Corps and in the Infantry was spent as a noncommissioned officer in charge of orientation programs prescribed by the U. S. Army and supervised by the air base commander at Tinker Field, Oklahoma City. The syllabus provided printed outlines, brochures, film, lecture series, and instruction sheets about the war, fascism, and the enemy we were facing in Europe and in the Pacific. Detailed informational literature and films about our major allies— the Soviet Union, Great Britain, China, and France—were also made available to our staff. Washington regularly sent us instructions on how to increase the recruits' awareness of the political meanings of the war.

The orientation program was, of course, a great deal more circumscribed than what had been initiated in Spain and what had been expected of the political commissar; yet I couldn't help noting that the fundamental principle, political education of the troops about to go into battle, was there on every page of government outlines, in every film we showed on the screen with motion picture projectors provided by the army, and in every lecture we gave. We spoke to thousands of recruits each week, driving home political messages of the war and educating these young men as to why they were now in the army and what was expected of them. Those of us experienced in the need for political commissars and their role—orientation, if you like—saw this program as a sensible recognition by the army and the government that if men and women were being asked to lay down their lives for their country they should at least have the right to know the reasons.

The volunteer commissar in Spain knew that his life, the lives of his men, and the success or failure of a mission often depended on the depth of his conviction in the just causes of the war. The commissar was in the vanguard of keeping those convictions alive at all times.

Veterans of the Abraham Lincoln Brigade are still usually brazenly frank with each other. We know what skeleton, if any, is in whose closet. Some irreverent volunteers called their commissars "comic stars." I doubt, however, if you could find many volunteers who would have unkind words for their commissars. Standards for commissars were set so high that only the finest, as a rule, accepted the rigorous challenges of that post.

*   *   *   *

During a battalion reorganization, our small Philadelphia group held pretty much together, at least for training. Willi Frait, George Jacobs, Earl Leppo, Emilio Martinez, Louie Toab, Harry Wallach, and Martin Weiss were placed in Section One, Company One. I was already a member of the Cuban section, so I remained there. New arrivals from the Philadelphia area were dispersed. Among them were Sterling Rochester, a black American, fresh from eighteen months of Marxist studies in Leningrad, Martin Hourihan, Hy Rosner, John Simon, Si Podolin from Camden, and Fred Lutz from Moorestown, cities across the Delaware River in New Jersey and near Philadelphia.

Martin Weiss, at forty-six the oldest member of our group, who left behind a wife and three children to volunteer, stepped off the rear of a truck during training and had to be hospitalized with a bad back. That was the last we saw of him. Years later when I met his son, Stanley, I learned that after being released from the hospital his father had stayed on a while longer to drive an ambulance.

Companies One and Two were ordered to provide three cooks and ten KPs for the battalion. It was not easy. Several who were selected raised a storm. "We came to fight fascism, and I'll be damned if I'm going to cook, wash dishes, pots, and pans. I want a rifle, not an apron." Sort out the accents from Brooklyn, Boston, Chicago, the South, and the West Coast, and you have a cross section of dissent. It took some discussion, persuasion, and a pleading for discipline before a roster was agreed to and posted. Expressions of scorn persisted.

After supper, it was standard operating procedure (SOP) for company officers to assemble, discuss military problems and lessons of the day, and prepare the next day's training program and agenda, which they then discussed with their section leaders.

We spent our free time writing letters, reading, studying Spanish, listening to the news on the radio about the progress of the war and for bits of information on events back home. A few walked daily through the orderly local groves and jagged hills. I spent a lot of my free time with a family whose only son and daughter-in-law were serving with the militia on the Madrid front. Both parents reminded me of mine in age, appearance, manner of dress, and cultural temperament. Their white washed adobe house with a red tile roof was a short walk from our barracks. I could, from an upper floor of the monastery, look down the street and see what they were doing. Another couple lived with them in this single-room house, about twenty-foot square, with a floor of hardened clay. The room served as kitchen, dining room, and living room and converted to a bedroom at night. On occasion, when I accepted an invitation to dinner, we also had the company of other family members: a goat, a scrawny mongrel dog, and noisy chickens, none of them inhibited. All roamed undisciplined in and out of the room and around us but only rarely begged for food. A gentle lamb that ate out of my hand was my favorite.

For me this kind of living was not strange. When I was a boy and before I became a teenager, a distant relative of my parents, whom we called *lo caprare*, "the goatman," visited us on occasional weekends. I was always delighted to see him with his horse and wagon. Every so often my parents permitted me to ride with him to his little farm not far from where we lived. After he taught me to handle the reins, his horse seemed to know he was pulling for me. He'd stiffen his ears, give a quick turn in my direction and sound off to make sure I knew he knew he was trotting for me. I remember being so proud of myself.

In those days my parents' home was lit by gaslight, but the goatman's single-room farmhouse had neither electricity nor gaslight, just like the Spanish family's adobe house I was now visiting. Unlike the Spanish family's home, however, the goatman's was always cluttered with furniture, feed bags for different animals, vegetables, and plants and seeds of all kinds. I was at the impressionable age to be fascinated with the contrast between farm and city life, and I liked it. Animals strolled in and out of the frame house; my favorite was a Saint Bernard by the Italian name of Bertoldi, who was big enough for me to ride and seemed never to object to anything I did to him. Whenever I was visiting, he furloughed his routine activities and became my constant companion. Together we romped on the grounds, and when we tired, we slept together. His body was comfortably warm, but I slept with my head away from his because he slobbered so much that my ears and face were always wet and cold. I noticed, though, that when I was with him other animals—dogs, cats, goats—seemed to know better than to come near us. Even the chickens flew off in every direction. Only the horse ignored us.

Feeding time was a big event for me, because it was my chore to fill the big bowls and dishes with feed. The animals, of course, ate first; the goatman made sure of that. Bertoldi and I used the same dish, and when Bertoldi was through eating, the goatman refilled the dish and shoved it over to me. I don't remember if it was dog food or not. "Your turn," he'd say. It was always the same. And I don't remember either one of us washing Bertoldi's dish before I ate from it. But this farm experience is one of the few periods of my childhood that I remember with pleasure.

* * * *

For about a month we trained rigorously in military tactics and strategy, in field manuevers, and in handling rifles and machine guns. We had classes in street fighting, scouting, map reading, grenade throwing, and in the use of the bayonet. None of the brutalities of war was withheld from us. Lectures were often delivered from men in our ranks who, having read a book, were said to be familiar with methods employed in the fields of battle. We learned from each other. Each day we spent hours drilling and conducting sham battles as if the enemy were opposite us. It made war seem real.

Instructions, lectures, and drill techniques came entirely from our ranks. We had little professional direction. A few volunteers had ROTC training, several had served a hitch in the U.S Army or Navy, and a few like myself had been for some weeks in the CMTC (Civilian Military Training Corps), but for most this was to be their initial military experience, their first time learning to use weapons for warfare.

The training we received in this period did a great deal to prepare us for the events ahead. Above all, we learned the absolute necessity of working together. *Discipline* became our motto because we saw it as an imperative for success and survival. It can honestly be said that the American contingent demonstrated its caliber by molding a unified and efficient organization from a heterogeneous assembly of cocky volunteers.

Still, we were an incongruous fighting force. A veritable babel of English accents abounded: from Brooklyn, Boston, Philadelphia, Chicago and the Midwest, and a few Southern accents as well. The Cubans added unrivaled accents all their own to this mix. To my ears, the Irish sounded most melodious. Some distinctive British ways of speaking were more difficult for me to take to, but after a while I caught on. Then, of course, there were the European-Americans among Canadian and U.S. volunteers, and they brought with them a richly varied flavor of accents in fragmented English that occasionally defied comprehension.

Our baptism of fire came unexpectedly on 16 February 1937, much before we were ready and before the postage was dry on a letter to my family dated two days earlier. The censors had blackened out only the name and location of our training base, Villanueva de la Jara. The letter was addressed to my brother Dominic, and portions of it are included here to give a sense of the warmth with which we were received by the residents of this small, typical Spanish village.

14 February 1937

. . . We are spending our time at this training base either in drill or attending classes in military tactics and strategy. Last night we had a class in street fighting.

Tell mom and pop I am sorry I had to leave home the way I did, for I'm sure it hurt them a lot. For me it was also hard to leave home; I think of the family often, sometimes too often for peace of mind. You and Charlie can make up for me by being as kind and considerate as you can to both of them, and by doing all you can to make life easier for them.

. . . Since I've been in Spain I've gained about 12 pounds. We get plenty of fruit,

vegetables and meat. But we also get plenty of work and plenty of rest. I live most of the time in the outdoors and even our indoor quarters are like the outdoors. The air is fresh, clean and crisp, unlike Camden with its black smoke, black dust and heavy black crystal soot from the railroad yards and factories. Right now I bet you're freezing and digging yourselves out of snow. We, on the other hand, are enjoying mild, sunny weather, so much so that yesterday one guy stripped himself and took a bath in the stream near the town. The upper end of this stream is where we get our drinking water, the lower end is where the town's women gather daily along the banks and on hands and knees, washboards in front of them, dip the dirty clothes in the cold stream and scrub away like mad. Some even pound the wash on rocks. Can you imagine that happening in Camden along the Delaware River!

The townspeople are as warm to us extranjeros as the morning sun. Every family, by their own decision, gave up their mattresses so that the Americans can be comfortable. We protested our acceptance of this much hospitality, but if we persisted in our refusal, we were told, the people would feel terribly insulted. Every day the peasants bring us fresh eggs, bags full of freshly picked oranges from their local groves, fresh vegetables deliberately and carefully picked from their fields and gardens, and fresh meat killed just before delivery. They are so proud of their deliveries, and we are truly grateful. The best restaurants in America could never feed us as luxuriously as we are being fed here.

Tell all this to the rest of the family and tell them I am happy I'm here and that I'm sorry I left the way I did, that I love everybody, but that I had to come because I am doing what I believe is right. I have committed myself to certain principles and I cannot escape from them and still have self-respect. Life to me is more serious than just living to work, to eat, and to play without caring what goes on around me. Try to make them understand.

Because we were only en route through France and we were there for such a short time, I did not get the opportunity of visiting our aunt, uncle and cousins, but I hope some day to be able to do so. . . .

Without discipline there is no victory

They shall not pass! July 1936. We shall pass! July 1937

Part Two

THE JARAMA FRONT

February—May 1937

FOUR

Move to the Front Lines: Suicide Hill

The unexpected directive on 15 February to move to combat zones found the battalion willing but not altogether ready. Before we could say good-bye to our new friends in town, we were trucked to the small city of Albacete, the operation and administration center of the newly formed International Brigades, where we were marched into the town's only bullring, whose circular walls were splattered with blobs of blood. On the ground near the walls puddles of blood lay caked, but I was too busy searching out the strangeness of our surroundings and coping with the unreality of our presence there to be overly concerned about the blood of bulls. It was just about forty-five days since most of us had left the States for Spain, and for me the unbelievable speed of events, with the endless, abrupt changes, seemed to turn my world upside down. When someone whispered, "This bullring is famous because this is where spies, fascists, and traitors of the Republic are put up against the wall to face a firing squad," I remember feeling numb, not joyous. The thick, ugly blood suddenly looked human.

Before the stink of blood could affect us for too long, we were greeted over a public address system by André Marty, a principal organizer of the International Brigades and an important member of the Central Committee of the Communist party of France. His pep talk was followed by others. All the speeches focused on the seriousness of our situation and on the enemy we were facing, the unholy alliance of the Axis powers determined to dominate the world. Spain, because of its ready and abundant mineral resources, was a necessary step in their grandiose plans. The enemy came through to us sharply as being fascism and fascist rulers. People who supported the rulers and the fascist ideology were also the enemy.

Some of us felt uncomfortable in the bullring listening to what we felt we already knew while standing among the blood of fascists already executed. After the speeches, we were ceremoniously presented with our new bolt-action rifles, light in weight and well balanced, packed heavily with vaseline or grease, and in wooden crates that we ourselves had to break open. Russian markings disclosed their point of origin. With each rifle came a cloth bag stuffed with cleaning brushes and small tools. Without taking time to wipe the messy grease from our weapons, we climbed into waiting trucks and slipped away quietly without headlights from the sleeping town toward the front, without even moonlight to help guide the way.

We perked up, though, at the sound of a grinding hum of a light plane circling directly over us. Not knowing if it was *ours* or *theirs*, we inched along even more slowly and ever more cautiously, seemingly at a snail's pace. The ride was far from boring. Unlike the rest, our truck had neither tarpaulin nor windbreaker, and the icy mountain wind sliced through my uniform and cut the skin. Darkness was our only blanket. I worried about the driver, a Frenchman who knew no English, just as we knew no French, and with whom we communicated by hand signs and grunts. How could he see without lights? What if he flipped over the side of the road? Would we slide into a ditch or roll down a hill? Every second brought a new, sometimes unpleasant, thought.

In a way, the plane haunting us provided a distraction for the "generals" among us, who speculated on its purpose. Others just ignored it. Ray [Sylvester] Friedle, nicknamed "Chicago" after his home city, which he proudly boasted about, helped diffuse tensions and fears by raising his rifle high and swearing death to enemy "bastards." He kibitzed with the quiet ones, charged the moon and stars with being enemy agents because they were hiding, ridiculed the French driver for knowing no English, clicked his heels Nazi style, and with his arm extended in Hitler salute, shouted obscenities at storm troopers, blackshirts, and their cutthroats, wherever they were. His machine gun was going to take care of them all. We relaxed and laughed, even when he wasn't funny. We found later that his was not a false bravado, for he carried his determinations to the battlefield. He once said to me, "Don't worry about getting hit, comrade, and nothing'll happen to you." On the battlefield he'd often say, "Think only of your target, aim straight, knock off those fuckin' fascists." He was occasionally boisterous and just as often gentle.

We weren't alerted until afternoon that the flying night prowler was really an enemy scout plane monitoring our convoy's movements. We didn't have to wait long to find out if the pilot had done his job well, for as soon as our troop-laden trucks, some fifty of them, approached our destination near the town of Morata de Tajuña at the base of the Jarama mountains in the Madrid sector of the front, a group of about fifteen enemy planes surprised us from out of the clouds and dropped a load of bombs before an alarm could be sounded. We sprang from our trucks like jacks-in-the-box, spread out, and dashed for the best available cover, as we had been taught to do. A few fired rapidly and defiantly at the planes, though their targets were out of range. My rifle by now was wiped clean of grease and oil, and I, too, rolled over on my back and fired into space—mainly, I think, to get the feel of the weapon. The bombs did us no damage, for they fell in the fields, uprooting olive trees. As the planes returned to strafe us with their machine guns, a flight of Republican Loyalist fighters arrived and gave the bombers chase. We viewed our first aerial dogfight breathlessly. Four of our fast pursuit planes neatly cut off two huge clumsy Junkers and shot them down in exploding flames. The others fled. We jumped and cheered, blew them grateful kisses, and happily shook our uplifted clenched fists to our first encounter with la gloriosa, as the youthful and courageous, but meager, Republican air force was popularly called. This was our baptism of fire by aircraft. Our morale indeed flew high with our protectors.

We marched jauntily to a cookhouse operated by the British, where we were warmly welcomed for a hearty meal by volunteers who had preceded us and who were already veterans of combat. As we swallowed our last bits of chops and praised the British cooks, we heard the loud voices of authority: "Hop the trucks, get set for the last lap." The last time I heard this kind of "lap" command had been when I ran the Franklin Relays in Philadelphia for my high school. Then I had eyed the baton; today it was the rifle. No one knew exactly where we were going or what was expected of us. Johnny Parks, full-blooded American Indian from Philadelphia, who, with his sunken chest and stooped shoulders, looked older than he really was, suggested that the officers knew but were not letting us in on it. I noted a tone of resentment.

The sun had already set, the chill of the night replaced the warm breeze of the day, and the trucks positioned themselves for the short, final run. It was as pitch-black and uncomfortable as the previous night when we left Albacete, and we quietly bounced on wooden seats with the forward movements of the truck over the potholed road. The driver cheerfully whistled lively French tunes, but "Chicago" remained subdued. I watched others who, like me, were nervously fingering their rifles and tapping silent tunes. Our breathing was deep and heavy, either from the cold or from expectations, perhaps both. Someone broke the silence by saying loudly, "Soon we'll be hitting the fan and some of us are going to have to shit or get off the pot." Someone else said quietly, "It's cold as hell, but my hands are sweaty." We listened with ears cocked and parched lips to the distant sounds of artillery and small-arms fire, and we knew it wouldn't be long before we met the dreaded enemy.

At our destination, about four hundred meters behind the front lines, we were ordered to fall out and fall in to the side of the road. We snapped into section and company ranks, not without many rumblings of tanks crossing the road near us. I went over and touched a tank, the first time I had ever seen and felt one. Its size and power were awesome. With power like this, we would soon obliterate the enemy.

"Where's the Number One truck?" a voice out of the dark asked.

"Section leader Johnny Parks, where are you?" another asked louder over the din of tanks.

"Any member of Johnny Parks' crew around? Can you hear me?" Now there was anxiety.

There was no response. "Oh, my God," I heard someone say, "His truck didn't stop, didn't make the turn; it went straight ahead."

Yes, that's what had happened. Our lead truck, the headquarters truck with battalion records and even some passports, with Johnny Parks and about fifteen men, did not stop or make the left turn but drove unwittingly into no-man's-land and into enemy lines. Were they captured and summarily executed, as appears to have been the case? If so, what happened to the truck with its battalion records? Someday the Spanish archives may shed light for us on this incident. Our Number One truck was never seen again, nor were the men riding in it ever heard from. Some of us at the time speculated, and even feared, that the enemy may have infiltrated road guides and preplanned misrouting it. We discounted this theory later when we found problems of language communication to be real and sometimes, as on this occasion, fatally so.

Parks's earlier complaint that battalion officers were too secretive about destination and military plans, especially in withholding them from him, a section leader, appears in hindsight to have been justified. From this distance, it seems that the loss of the men and the truck might have been avoided had Parks, since he was on the point truck, been made aware of operational details and travel route.

Not much is known about Parks, the individual. We do know that he was an effective leader, Pennsylvania state organizer of the Unemployed Councils, that he was an active and leading member of the Communist party of Eastern Pennsylvania, and on occasion, by assignment from his party, came to Camden to help the fledgling party there solve some of its political problems. I knew he was an American Indian, but he was tight-lipped about his tribal background and never mentioned where he was born or if Pennsylvania was his home state. Unfortunately, he was lost to us before we got to know him better. I'm glad now that on the deck of the SS *Champlain*, on our way over, when I snapped pictures, one was of him—the only known photo of Parks. He was not an easy person to forget, with his deep-set dark eyes hardly visible behind prominent cheekbones, pale, drawn face, a cavity for a chest, and rounded shoulders. He looked consumptive and had that hungry look of so many in those depression years, especially of those who rode the rails. I considered him stoic, a stereotypical American Indian, and I'm afraid I felt that if he smiled the creases in his face would crack.

We also knew he was a serious student of political and social problems, well read in the theories of Marxism-Leninism. When he had lectured, which was often in Philadelphia and Camden, he tore into the capitalist system as outmoded, blamed it for the brutality of unemployment, poverty, and hunger, and for fomenting race conflicts and wars; above all, he condemned the system for "thriving on the destruction of dignity of race and ethnic minorities and, particularly, of the American working class." I remember once being very impressed with one of his many colorful speeches, which he closed by saying that he was dedicating his entire life "to doing my part in replacing capitalism with a humane system of socialism, where the individual is paramount, where human dignity will flower and cause all life to flourish."

The full impact of the loss of the men and the truck did not come till later. Company commanders, picking their way up a couple of rocky hills, led us to a crest of one of them, said to be strategic because it overlooked the far-ranging countryside, and after placing us in staggered diamond formations, told us to dig.

"With what?" came a chorus of shouts.

"Come on dig, dig in, dig with your bayonet, use your helmet."

Only a few of us had trenching tools. In New York City, we had been issued uniforms, collapsible spades, and shovels, but by now they were lost, left behind, or disposed of as weighty and impractical gadgets.

The order to dig did not have to be repeated. Streams of bullets whistled past and mortars exploded nearby; we fell to the ground and dug into rock and gravel. No Spanish earth in the next two years was as impenetrable as this rock on the lonely night of 16 February 1937. To spur the digging, we were warned to expect bombardments the next morning. "Your life will depend on the best shelter you can dig for yourself." Vigorous digging and chopping also helped to keep the body warm and the mind from wandering. Morning came, and those who dared sleep found themselves stiff with cold and without effective protection against the artillery barrages, which began at exactly six o'clock. Shells bursting everywhere were a terrifying introduction to the realities of war. Boom! A shell in front of us. Boom! One to the side, another behind.

"They are using heavy artillery! Chelebian just had his head blown off!" shouted Marty Hourihan, the Irish schoolteacher and seaman from Philadelphia, whose voice I recognized. Misak Chelebian, who came from the United States but was said to be of Greek background (although Chelebian is an Armenian name), was our first casualty—the first recorded in my diary.

We knew now we were no longer playing war games at our training base or marching at shoulder arms. For seven days and nights we held that hill, which we cursed as "Suicide Hill." Each day we dug deeper, constructing irregular trenches. Each day artillery and mortar bombardments pounded us implacably. Enemy planes visited us the first day with bombs that exploded nearby. The second day they paid two visits, both times emptying their bays close to our positions. At one point they succeeded in machine-gunning our trenches. They came at us several times every day, but the little Republican fighter planes did not let them do much damage. Often aerial battles took place right overhead, and then artillery bombardments would stop as both sides watched the dogfights. When one or two enemy bombers were riddled and went down in flames, enemy artillery and firepower resumed with telling vengeance.

Harry Wallach, a Philadelphia baker, affectionately noted for his rapid-fire manner of talking, told me and others: "Who ever said 'War is hell' must've been out of his cotton-pickin' mind. Hell can never be as goddam bad as this. Right, John?"

"Right, Harry."

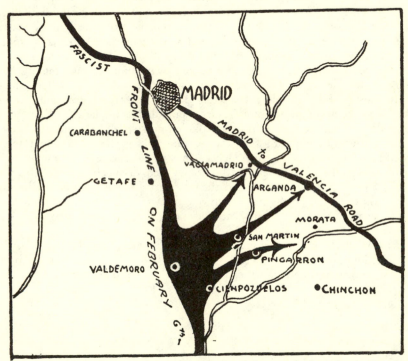

The three-armed fascist thrust moves toward the Madrid-Valencia Road.

FIVE

The First Battles

We withdrew from murderous Suicide Hill on 22 February and were ordered to occupy positions in second-line trenches. The next day we were shifted again, this time to right-flank areas, and after brief instructions, we prepared for frontal attack on enemy positions. The Lincoln Battalion, now in trenches previously captured by our predecessors after several days of severe and costly seesaw battles, could look over parapets between clustered olive trees and see the white sandbagged fortifications of the opposing forces four hundred meters directly in front of us. Their positions lay on the slope of a hill looking down on us.

It was late afternoon when the order came to get ready to go over the top. While we wiped our rifles and helped each other adjust munition belts around our bodies, a few guys relieved tensions with the inevitable wisecracks and jokes, often welcome in moments like these; but neither our nervousness nor our grimness could be easily camouflaged by well-meaning banter. Trench mortar bombardment of enemy lines now beginning was our signal to move to the offensive.

"OK boys! Get going!" The first section of the first company led the charge. The Irish followed, the Cubans next, and finally the second company to the right plunged swiftly toward the entrenched enemy.

At the outset, one of our tanks, about forty meters in front and to the left of my section, was hit and burst into flames; explosions followed. Riflemen who had been using the moving tank for cover split like wild rabbits in every direction. Flames from

41

the tank shot skyward, belching an awesome bonfire; my thoughts for a moment were of the crew trapped inside.

Our advance slowed. From tree to tree into open fields, with nothing but the roots of grapevines for shelter, we now charged more rapidly, vainly seeking cover, over the soft ground heavily raked by enemy fire. We had plenty of grenades, but they were useless unless we could get close to the enemy. To make matters worse, while we were charging and approaching enemy positions, a rapid and relentless machine-gun cross fire zeroed in on us. Nevertheless, a few of our men from an earlier wave of attackers, dodging from place to place like ducks in a shooting gallery, running, stumbling, falling and firing almost simultaneously, crawled close to enemy positions. Now grenades came in handy. We could see them being tossed. Men scattered over the broad, naked field, taking cover as effectively as possible behind stumps of grapevines, savagely digging in and throwing dirt on stumps in the hope of forming a bulletproof mound.

Rodolfo de Armas, leader of the Cuban section, was the first one killed. After rescuing a wounded member of our group, he had charged again, clenching his fist high into the air as he beckoned us to follow. I was alongside him, about twenty feet to his right, and felt secure under his leadership. To his left was the disabled tank, still exploding and shooting flames high above the few olive trees. We could almost feel its deadly warmth. At that moment, as I looked at Rodolfo, at the same time searching out where I would dash for cover in my next sprint, a bullet struck him in the right leg, and when he stooped to grip his leg with his hands, shouting obscenities toward the fascists, two more bullets hit him, one in the head and the other in the jaw. Instinctively, I ran to him, oblivious of whistling bullets, but I was too late. I stood over him in sadness and uncertainty, and in sudden loneliness, for the one person I had looked upon as indestructible, the one I had admired, lay dead.

Someone startled me out of my trance with a sharp slap on the shoulder, "Let's go, the medics will take care of him."

The losses of the Cuban section were heavy. Cries of "first aid, first aid" came from everywhere. Men fell in front, to the right, and to the left of us, dead or wounded. Enemy machine guns kept hammering away steadily, plowing up the ground around us. Bullets with their powerful thuds also dug into it, and if you were so inclined, you could feel around and pluck the bullets out of the earth.

The enemy, though, was waiting and was prepared to deal with us. I visualized their machine gunners peering down on us, firing joyously at beautiful targets in the open fields.

Stalled in our advance by the enemy's wall of fire, many of us labored desperately, chopping up the damp earth with bayonet and helmet to fashion some form of trench. Here again, too few had trenching tools. The lucky ones with shovels dug themselves out of the enemy line of fire quickly.

Not far from the enemy's sandbagged positions, I spotted a larger-than-average grapevine stump and sized it up as good cover if I could quickly pile dirt on it and pack a mound from where I could also fire my rifle. By now I had neither bayonet nor helmet with which to dig, so grasping long tips of unspent bullets I scraped the soft dirt and rapidly piled it in front of my head. My Russian rifle resting beside me was split and splintered by enemy bullets intended, undoubtedly, for me. Bullets came so fast and so close that the right side of my body felt momentarily paralyzed. I lay there, I don't know how long, a sheepish target in no-man's-land, with a developing sense of futility. I felt so useless that I wondered out loud, at the top of my voice, "What am I doing here?" But a quick glance around and I saw some of my comrades in even worse shape. A little guy to my right, whose face I couldn't see, was frantically churning the ground with his bare hands, ripping his skin and tearing off his fingernails. Another lay behind a stump clutching his rifle and trying to shrivel himself to nothing to avoid being spotted. It was impossible to advance further. A few, close enough to enemy positions, hurled grenades; but then they, too, were silenced, either killed or wounded.

I took heart in watching our company commander, Captain John Scott (his real name was Inver Marlow), an Englishman who had lived in the United States and had joined the Lincoln Battalion, as he walked erectly from man to man, disdaining the crashing of shells and bullets, offering encouragement to each of us, and urging us to lob grenades into enemy trenches. As the sun was setting, Captain Scott, who was looked upon with great affection and who did so much to give us strength, was himself killed by a burst of pinpointed machine-gun fire. He was promptly carried off the field by men who risked their lives to save him, though they knew that probably it was already too late. Paul Burns, of Boston, was one of those men. He, too, kept a diary and permitted me to quote from it when, in Madrid, during May 1937, I was preparing *The Story of the Abraham Lincoln Battalion.*

To the right was a company of Spanish and on the left across a road pelted by a rain of fascist bullets were the men of the Dimitrov Battalion.

The attack began late in the afternoon and continued into the night.

Over a field dotted by occasional olive trees with only the scant shelter of vineyard growth between, the advance was continued.

Given a withered grapevine, a mound of earth, or the more pretentious shelter of an olive tree, the boys dug in and opened fire on the fascist lines.

In one of these interludes beneath an olive tree I looked around—on my left was Charlie Donnelly. Beyond him the Cuban Section stretched between the road on the extreme left and the Irish Section. To the right of the Irish Section the American Section dug in and fired.

A few yards away in a little hollow of earth was Captain John Scott and with him Frank O'Flaherty, one of the three O'Flaherty brothers of Boston, who distinguished themselves by their heroic service and leadership under fire.

Donnelly joined me under the olive tree. We fired until our rifles burned our hands, with scarcely a word beyond the "Hi Charlie, how's it goin'?" and the reply, "Pretty good, how're the rest of the boys?" The infantry continued the advance. Explosive bullets split the air and the machine gun bursts raked the field. From behind a row of trees the fascists increased the fire.

Captain Scott, rising, had only time to shout "Continue the advance" when he fell with three bullets in his body.

MacDonald and Wheeler, company runners, had both been wounded. Eddie O'Flaherty, the other runner, crossed the field to call Bill Henry, leader of the Irish Section.

Bill Henry took over command. Captain Scott was moved from the field on a stretcher. Six men moved the stretcher forward.

At the edge of the field an eight-foot drop to the road exposed the stretcher to enemy fire.

A raking fire came from the fascist lines and four of the resuce party fell, among them Joe Mendelowitz, shot through the left eye. The others, whether killed or wounded, were unknown to Gomez or myself, the two survivors. We carried our badly wounded leader to within 100 meters of the first aid station, where we were assisted by two other comrades. At the first aid station, my arm with a bullet wound through it was dressed. Gomez returned to the battle with another rescue party. He was wounded later.

Many lay injured on the open field. Some rescue work was done by volunteers. Later we were shifted to first-line fortifications that had been built by others while we were on Suicide Hill.

George Jacobs and J. Lenoris, unaware that the battalion had retreated, remained under cover behind a tree not more than twenty meters from the fascists. They lay all night in one spot without a blanket. To keep from freezing, they dug deeper into the earth, but with each movement they invited sniper fire. In the morning, when they made the terrifying discovery that the battalion had withdrawn to its original positions, they began their desperate retreat. In leaps of three to five meters from one hole or tree to another, they moved anxiously toward us. They must have known that many of us were watching and urging them on while providing protective fire by peppering enemy machine gunners and forcing their heads down. Within clear sight of us, both made a fierce dash for safety. But Lenoris was riddled in the back. He lay motionless; no sound came from him.

It took Jacobs eight hours longer, waiting, crawling cautiously, and sprinting to within fifty meters of our trenches, where he collapsed. When we dragged him in, we saw how his shoes were nearly ripped from his feet. Bullet holes through his jacket along the arms testified to his narrow escape. Miraculously he was not wounded.

In the final history of the Lincoln Battalion, many brave deeds will be recorded; one in particular may be related here. This story of Robert "Slim" Greenleaf was told to me by Vincent O'Donnell, of the Irish company, a soldier from Slim's group, shortly after the February battles while he showed me how to cook stems of garlic over an open fire and how to enjoy eating them with hot, crusty French bread. I took notes for my diary, and later included this account in my booklet *The Story of the Abraham Lincoln Battalion.*

On the night of our offensive, February 23rd, Monroney, Slim Greenleaf and myself left the farmhouse at 6:00 P.M., as usual, with the battalion's supper on our truck. We had two kilometers of a hill climb to make, mostly in low gear, over a road eaten up by explosive bullets and occasional shrapnel. Slim was our driver. He was about six feet two inches tall, and twenty-four years of age. He had been in many seamen's strikes in Boston. Slim was a most abused comrade, since apart from being a sailor he could drive a truck, and each time our hot liquids spilled in the truck, rightly or wrongly we blamed him. But Slim could take it with a smile. Slim was OK.

We made the hill without a scratch, though rifle and machine gun bullets exploded on each side of the road as the truck neared our lines. He drew up as usual just behind the English munition dump. My fear that our comrades would be under so much fire as to make it impossible to leave their positions to come and draw their supper was justified, since we ourselves had to seek protection from the fascists' fire—they could not see us, of course—by keeping low. In fact we sat down with our backs to the stones which flanked the road.

An hour passed, and still we waited. It was then 7:30 P.M. Presently, a member of our General Staff came up and told us the position of the battalion. The hot food was useless.

Well, we made ready to return so as to fetch canned food when volunteers were asked for what turned out to be a particularly dangerous rescue.

A wounded Cuban comrade, heavily built, had been calling for help from the hollow of the road, three-quarters of a kilometer further on, round the bend, and had been lying there since the beginning of the attack.

Slim listened to the plan of rescue as it was unfolded. He seemed to be visualizing in his mind's eye the cross fire of machine gun, explosive, and antitank bullets, as they split the air, resounding on the stony bank of the road four meters above the body of our wounded comrade, whose appeals for water and aid were becoming gradually weaker and more intermittent.

Was the fascist fire weakening, or were they merely playing a cunning game? Was there a real chance of a successful rescue? Maybe there was. Maybe they would not be able to get within a radius of four feet of our comrade.

Whatever was passing in Slim's mind that night we shall never know. His thin and youthful face cleared as he said "Come on, boys, let's go!" Slim and Monroney were to join the other comrades of the rescue at the dressing station, one hundred meters further on, near the bend of the road. As the night closed around them, Slim appeared to be silent, while Monroney was doing the talking.

An hour passed at least when Monroney returned. He was alone. An explosive bullet had killed Slim as he crawled along four meters behind his companions.

The rescue was effected during that hazardous hour by the remaining three comrades. The wounded Cuban was saved from the fascists, but Slim died in no-man's-land on the Jarama front in defense of world democracy.

When the order came to retire, we did so in a soldierly and orderly fashion. The wounded were brought in. Several first aid men were wounded or killed while tending to the wounded still in enemy sights.

When we regrouped and took stock of our limited offensive, we found that our efforts permitted battalions on our left flank to move forward and to consolidate into more strategic positions.

Because we moved so much and because the kitchen staff was just beginning to get properly organized, we received little rations for three days. The next day, however, a welcome tub of hot coffee was sent through the trenches. Each took his share and passed the tub to others. When it got to our group, Bob Norwood dipped his metal cup into the coffee with great eagerness. Each time he did so, he drank it with his head tilted back and covering a hole between two sandbags facing the enemy. I warned him to get his head away from the unprotected hole, as did a chorus of others. Bob smiled and said, "Come on boys, dig in. I've got mine. This is my last cup." At that moment he was struck by a bullet in the head. He fell face down into the coffee—dead.

SIX

27 February

On 27 February we again went over the top, this time to face an even deadlier mortar, artillery, and machine-gun cross fire than that of the twenty-third. Sixty-six American reinforcements, many of whom had never held a rifle in their hands, went over the top and charged the enemy with us "old-timers" of the past two weeks. One lad went over the sandbags with a full pack on his back before anyone was able to advise him to drop it and leave it behind. We got him to come back and from behind a sturdy olive tree, amid the sound of crackling bullets, I taught him to load and unload his rifle and the elementary care of his weapon. He did not yet know how to use his grenades, so I took them away from him. Several other "old-timers" were also busy teaching the fundamentals of weaponry to new recruits, who were then released to continue the charge.

On this day, the Lincoln Battalion in particular suffered severe losses. Casualties were indescribable. Scores of dead, strewn across no-man's-land, could not be retrieved during the daytime. We could hear the groans of those not yet dead.

How I came across a wounded Frenchman, I don't know. He was in our forward positions and seemed to be there from nowhere. Much of his jaw had been shot off and all he insisted on doing in his semiconscious, bloody condition was to search his pockets for letters and pictures of his family, which he pressed into my hands, holding me tightly. I knew he wanted me to send them to his family.

Before the whole battalion had gone over the top, a wounded recruit made his way back almost to our trenches but was too sorely wounded for the last lap. Paul

47

Niepold, section leader of the Second Company, heard his call for help and planned a rescue. He motioned to me to follow. We crawled out to the recruit, and while Paul hooked his strong, muscular arms under the man's right shoulder, I did the same under his left. The weather was cool, but Paul's face was sweaty and grim; his square jaw jutted forward as we dug our feet into the ground and started to drag our man to safety. Paul's French helmet fell off his head. His sandy hair, which he wore long and disheveled and always looking as if he needed a haircut, blew in the cool wind and partially covered his eyes. Slowly pulling and tugging the big, heavy, groaning man the few feet to the trench under rapid, pounding enemy fire seemed in those minutes to be eternity. The past hour indeed was eternity. Nothing seemed to go right.

Suddenly, just as it was to be our last pull, Paul was struck in the chest. He let go his grip on the recruit and fell on his back into the trench. I dropped to my knees, grabbed him vigorously by the shoulders and screamed, "Paul!" At my outburst he lifted his head with a quick, involuntary jerk. It was his last gesture; his wide-set blue eyes seemed to blaze farewell. His head snapped back heavily. The butt of a rifle could have fitted into his chest, torn open by an explosive bullet.

Later, when I reflected on this traumatic experience, I was certain that my seizing his shoulders—violently, almost—my shouting to him, was in effect a frantic, useless plea: "Paul, please, don't desert me, not you too!"

Paul Niepold and I had been friends back in the States, not close, but close enough. I first met him while I was a student at Brookwood Labor College in Katonah, New York, a center sponsored and financially supported by labor for the training of promising rank-and-file unionists. Those of us who knew him at Brookwood and later in the Lincoln Battalion viewed him as someone special. An anti-Hitler German socialist who fled his homeland before the Nazis could close in on him, Paul came to the United States with his wife, Martha, accompanied by another antifascist German couple with the same first names as the Niepolds, Paul and Martha Koenig. The four refugees were employed as custodians of the Brookwood school grounds and buildings. However, they were more than just maintenance and handypeople; they also took part in the day-to-day student projects, participating in classroom activities and in after-class and evening bull sessions on domestic and foreign affairs. Niepold often addressed our classes about his experiences as a trade unionist in Germany and his role in the antifascist and anti-Hitler movement.

Paul Koenig, tall and powerfully built, was more reserved than Niepold but no less an antifascist. I always carried a special warm spot for Koenig. When I was learning the skills of ventriloquism from one of the other students—Conard Rheiner, a professional magician and ventriloquist—Koenig and his wife constructed a dummy for me. An accomplished carpenter, Koenig carved a head from two blocks of wood and glued together. For a mouth he used a piece of flexible leather and for eyes he used marbles, later replacing them with glass eyes he bought in New York City. The pitch-black, shiny hair, glued neatly on the dummy's head, came from a local horse's tail. By the time the head was finished and a heavy string hooked to the dummy's leather mouth so that it worked smoothly, Martha Koenig had completed a navy blue suit for it. The students, instructors, visitors, and sponsors—all of us— were proud of the finished product. Everyone referred to it as the "Charlie McCarthy dummy," associating it with the famous dummy by that name whose ventriloquist was the master, Edgar Bergen. But I named it Jerry. Later in the year, when Brookwood Labor College sent a labor chautauqua (nonprofessional entertainers—

workers and students—with prolabor messages) on the road from Virginia to Maine, Jerry and I were an important part of it.

Politically, however, Paul Niepold had great influence on us. Articulate and eager at every turn to present his arguments, he persistently impressed us with the need to learn—that it was not enough to be good trade unionists, that we had to be informed and good antifascists and masters of Marxism if we were serious about turning the world around toward socialism.

I was not surprised, therefore, when after leaving Brookwood I next saw Paul Niepold as a volunteer in Spain. It was natural, it was logical. But when he arrived and we shook hands, I still said, "Paul, how come?" His answer: "Well, isn't this the front line of world struggle against Hitlerism and fascism?" Our friendship, rooted back home, had grown and continued to the moment of his death.

At the Villanueva de la Jara training base, Paul and I had often taken long walks at the end of a day and discussed the lessons we were getting in military tactics and strategies. It was also natural for us to confide our innermost thoughts and to swap secrets of a personal nature. He told me how difficult it was for his wife, Martha, to see him go, but they had both agreed that he must, that he could no longer fight Hitlerism just in the classroom.

In our talks he marveled at the influx of Americans from all parts of the United States, Canada, and Cuba, and at the arrival of black American volunteers and a sprinkling of Orientals—Japanese- and Filipino-Americans. He was delighted when I introduced him to Johnny Parks, the unsmiling American Indian. They later spent hours together.

When Niepold spoke of his countrymen, the antifascist Germans who were at that very moment acquitting themselves so valiantly in hand-to-hand battles for every inch of ground in the city of Madrid, as well as elsewhere, he did so with a deep sense of personal gratification.

Though he felt comfortable serving with the American contingent, he aspired before long to be permitted to join the German columns then in combat. Nevertheless, he was not in a hurry to do so because he expected the U.S. Socialist party, of which he was a member, to make good its boast that it was organizing a column to be named the Eugene V. Debs Volunteers for Spain, which would join the Lincoln Battalion. It was to be a grand and well-deserved tribute to the memory of that great American labor leader of the early 1900s, the Socialist candidate for the presidency of the United States who got one million votes while in prison for protesting and opposing World War I as an imperialist war and who was the hero of the American left and of the progressive worker.

Paul wanted to be part of that column, at least for a while. He was never to find out that this promise from his party turned out to be an empty one and was never fulfilled.

Experiences on that memorable 27 February varied with individuals and groups. From Joseph F. Rehil's diary, which he let me copy that spring, we get a glimpse of the events he witnessed as first aid and stretcher-bearer.

I am sent with some other comrades on what is called a special detail. I wonder what it is.

I found out about the special detail bringing up supplies to the trenches, that is, food, water and ammunition. I hear we are planning an attack today. All the boys are at the front line trenches. Jeez, the bullets sure whiz by.

Never knew there were so many bullets in the world, and all of them seem to shoot around me.

Saw a few boys being carried down on stretchers. Most of them are French or Belgians suffering head wounds from shooting over the sandbags. Very fine, spirited men. They have their hands up in salute all the way down to the ambulance.

The signal is given to go over. The Spanish on the extreme right are scurrying for shelter. Then our boys go. I pass Jimmie, he smiles confidently and I give him a slap on the shoulder. The fire from the fascists seems incessant. Rat, tat, tat, a tat! It goes on for hours. I see another comrade who came across with me on the SS *Paris*. His gun was jammed, the poor guy was actually crying. I can understand how he feels. Like myself, he never saw a rifle before.

While there is no food or ammunition to be carried up, we carried down stretchers. Night is falling and it is raining very hard. The ambulance post is quite a distance away and there is a very slippery and narrow path up along the hillside. Christ, it is risky carrying the poor wounded. . . .

This goes on for hours. I just got back from one trip and there is another to be taken down.

I am almost exhausted. All of the comrades are doing their share.

Very few of us get a chance to eat and we're soaked to the skin.

At 5:00 A.M. we finally go to sleep—or fall exhausted I should say. There is not a dry blanket in the whole brigade, I think. Three of us get under a wet blanket and try to go to sleep.

The day had demanded maximum effort, and the maximum was given.

Centuria Antonio Guiteras, the Cuban section, fought ferociously, as if they were in hand-to-hand combat with their own fascist dictator, Batista. Their losses were heavy.

The few Canadians who were part of the early Lincoln Battalion acquitted themselves brilliantly alongside the Cubans and the Irish. Take the case of Francois Billedeau of Toronto, a little guy, close-lipped, but always with a ready smile. We traveled together on the SS *Champlain*, but I didn't know that our destination was the same until the last day of the voyage.

For three days Billedeau went over the top, three times each day, and each time he returned with prisoners. The brigade commander, Lieutenant Colonel Vladimir Copic, was so pleased that he decorated him with a Spanish government medal and presented him with a gold watch. Billedeau's luck finally gave out in one of his forays into enemy lines. He returned wounded and had to be evacuated to a hospital.

Black Americans also earned special merit. Oliver Law, who commanded the Tom Mooney Machine Gun Company, was highly respected by his fellow volunteers. He, too, was honored by the supreme command.

Then there was Sterling Rochester, a short, slim, wiry Philadelphian who, in hand-to-hand combat, proved to be worth several men. Though we had met for the first time on those blood-stained Jarama mountains, the fact that we were neighbors from back home and that we had mutual friends in Philadelphia and Camden made our friendship quick and natural. I remember the times we huddled together with one blanket between us during cold nights in the trenches, our teeth chattering because the blanket was often wet with rain. We remained close friends until he died in a Norristown, Pennsylvania, veterans hospital in 1978. Rochester was a student at the Lenin School in Moscow when the Spanish army officers' rebellion erupted, and when he heard Americans were volunteering for the International Brigades, he cut short his studies and came directly to Spain. He was fond of saying that he learned more Marxism with a rifle in his hands than he had from books or a classroom. After the Jarama front stabilized, he was returned to the United States for a nationwide speaking tour in behalf of the Spanish Republic and for the Friends of the Abraham Lincoln Brigade—the first such tour by a black American veteran.

Like many other volunteers of the Spanish Civil War, Rochester was repeatedly dogged by the FBI but remained to the end defiant of those he called "the boys in the light-tan trench coats." He paid for this defiance by losing more than one job after the "boys" paid his employers a visit. His last job was that of a stock clerk in a small supermarket that appreciated his honesty and sense of organization. He remained a member of the U.S. Communist party until he died.

Alonzo Watson, another black American, was killed in hand-to-hand fighting before we got to know him.

Douglas Roach, young and stocky, was evacuated to a hosptial with a wound of the stomach. At the training base in Villanueva de la Jara, Roach was forever surrounded by the town's children and was followed by them everywhere when they could get to him. He was the first black human being the children had ever seen, and they were fascinated by him, especially since he was affectionate toward them. One of the youngsters, holding and turning his hands, wanted to know why his palms were white while the rest of his body was black. He looked surprised for a moment, then teasingly said, "I've worked with my hands all my life, maybe the black just wore off."

Willi Frait, one of our Philadelphia spark plugs, wounded slightly on 23 February, was back in action on the 27th. Hy Rosner, an ambulance driver, also from Philadelphia, was taken to the hospital not too seriously wounded, while Earl Leppo* from Atlantic City was carried from the trenches in complete exhaustion.

But another Philadelphian was not so lucky, and it was hard on those of us who knew him to lose him. He was Emil Martinez. The Americans, the British, and the Irish who knew him and valued his aggressiveness in attacking the enemy showered him with warmth and admiration. He lost his life, though, when after wiping out one machine-gun nest with hand grenades, he went after the second single-handedly. This time he didn't even get close when he was spotted. His riddled body was dragged in later. Martinez was older than most of us and had left a family to come to Spain. In Philadelphia, he had been active in his union, in the organization of Unemployed Councils, in demonstrations for more adequate relief for those in need, and in strike and organizational picket lines. He took part in battles for social legislation—unemployment insurance, health care, social security—and for labor legislation giving workers the right to organize into unions of their own choosing without employer interference. Martinez said that he was a member of the U.S. Communist party for eighteen years.

---

*Though we knew him as Earl, official records of the Veterans of the Abraham Lincoln Brigade (VALB) list his first name as Ernest.

Many volunteers died that day, and sadly, we did not know most of them very well; our time together had been too brief. But Douglas Seacord, battalion adjutant, was one we had come to know just well enough to feel his loss keenly when he was killed leading a group determined to knock out a particularly troublesome enemy machine-gun nest. He was thirty-two. A Tennesseean, he had been union organizer of fishermen in Provincetown, Massachusetts.

During training, Seacord, who had also been an instructor at West Point, showed us how to take a rifle and machine gun apart and had us practice until we could put them back together in a matter of minutes. He conducted classes in attack and defense in practically every phase of military tactics and weaponry. But his talents had still greater range. At political sessions, we noted how well informed he was both about Spain's history and its current situation. I recall how he put the civil war in understandable perspective for us by writing on one side of the blackboard the names of organizations and factions making up the fascist alliance and on the opposite side listing the United Front, or government coalition. There were always lively discussions, questions, and answers about the conflicting sides of the war. During the day, we learned from him to be well-trained and disciplined soldiers; at night, at political meetings, he helped strengthen our understanding of the politics of being our kind of soldier in a People's Army.

Seacord organized and led the machine-gun company, and in battle, when the machine guns didn't work, he and his men picked up rifles. It was with rifle in hand that he lost his life.

By the end of the day our losses were staggering. The dead could not be counted, and many bodies were simply stacked into macabre piles to be burned. I was placed in charge of this body-stacking and burning detail against my loud protestations. "Somebody has to do it," I was told. It was weird, as I knew it would be, to watch those bodies burn—the bodies of men with whom not too many hours ago you had belly-crawled, maybe having shared a cup of cold coffee together, talked about family or union organization efforts back home, or even nervously joked with the ever so often repeated line: "When you can hear the whistling of the bullets and the sounds of exploding shell, it means death is already passing you by."

Many of the wounded had still to be evacuated. Stretcher-bearers were among the casualties. Morale took a heavy jolt. Auxiliary support we had been led to expect had failed us. Artillery to soften the enemy, scheduled to precede our attack, had remained silent; tanks to accompany our advance had not appeared; planes to bomb and strafe enemy positions, so that we could move ahead more easily and infiltrate those positions unmolested, had remained grounded; troops to the left of us and to the right of us—our flanks—had failed to give us adequate covering firepower. What had happened? We didn't know at the time. But we knew that our ranks had matured overnight and that a week of successive battles had turned raw recruits into seasoned fighters—if they had been lucky enough to survive.

Robert Hale Merriman, commander of the Lincoln Battalion, had led us into battle that fateful day. The attack was to start early in the morning, but when hours went by without the promised support, Merriman reached Brigade headquarters by telephone and, as we learned later, in several messages requested permission to call off the planned actions. Permission was denied, and he was ordered to initiate the attack. Even though Merriman was struck in the shoulder by fascist bullets soon after we began the attack, he refused to leave the field and continued to rally our troops and force the fighting. However, when orders came from brigade headquarters for his evacuation, he went. By the end of the day, he was removed to a base hospital, where he was treated for his wounds. Weeks later, while his arm was still in a sling and before he had fully recuperated from the damage to his shoulder, he trained troops at base camps until he was judged fit to return to combat.

Merriman was a striking figure—6 feet 2½ inches, 190 pounds, and 28 years of age—when he arrived in Spain among the first American volunteers. Promoted to major, for many of us, younger and smaller in stature, he was an awesome tower of strength, inspiring confidence in us by his competence, his calculated calm under battle conditions, his apparent fearlessness, and his genius for handling men. His ROTC college training—he had worked his way through the University of Nevada—served him and us well. His tenure as head assistant instructor in economics at the University of California must have prepared him to deal scrupulously with a multitude of details and military problems that forever challenge the battlefield commander.

Before Merriman pursued an intellectual career, he was a field and industrial worker. He worked in a paper mill, in log camps, in the Ford assembly plant, and in odd jobs as cement worker—wherever he could make a buck to help pay his way through college.

On the battlefield he grew into a magnificent soldier, every inch of him, and by the time of the Aragon offensive he had become the Fifteenth Brigade's chief of staff. As chief of staff and executive officer, Merriman was outranked only by the brigade commander. He had to supervise brigade administrative and military details, training, and promotions, to help prepare and execute battle plans, and to act as brigade commander in the commander's absence. Next to the brigade commander, his was the most responsible position. In effect, the chief of staff and executive officer was the workhorse of the brigade.

Except for the time required to recuperate from battle wounds, Merriman led the Lincolns from their first days of battle until he was captured and executed, along with Dave Doran, Lincoln political commissar, and others, in the 1938 spring retreats at Gandesa.

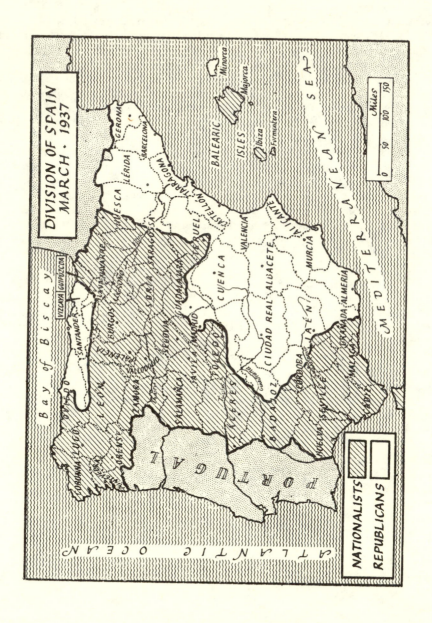

DIVISION OF SPAIN
MARCH · 1937

NATIONALISTS
REPUBLICANS

SEVEN

Consolidating

To a number of Americans in the Lincoln Battalion the planning and execution of the recent battles seemed ill advised and poorly conceived. They carped about the division and brigade leadership and complained that not one American was included in this headquarters staff leadership. There was bitterness and disenchantment; rumblings and rumors abounded. "Maybe there was a fascist officer at the top conspiring to get the Americans decimated" before they became an effective force, some said, a thought that also crossed my mind. One particular target of a rumor was the brigade chief of operations, Lieutenant Colonel Hans Klaus. "Look, isn't he a German? Wasn't he a Prussian officer in the Imperial Army during the World War? Look at his uniform, how immaculate, see how tall and stern and aloof he stands! He's got to be a Nazi." Others contended that they could not believe any volunteer on our side could be anything but antifascist, and someone warned that we may be developing a vigilante mentality to conjure up a scapegoat. Of course, as we got to know the impeccable colonel better, such unfounded and ugly rumors soon disappeared.

The heart of the matter was that many of our foot soldiers, including myself, were simply groping for answers and explanations for what appeared to us to be rank confusion, absence of auxiliary support, inexplicit orders, and wasteful expenditure of lives. What kind of high-ranking officers do we have, the question was more than once posed, to send greenhorn troops into such sophisticated battles so poorly prepared? At least some of us were privileged to have fired five practice rounds of ammunition into the side of a mountain from our new grease-packed Russian rifles before charging the enemy. New arrivals, however, experienced no practice shots. They came right off the boat, brimming with enthusiasm, with packs on their backs and rifles in hand, though some of them did not know a butt from a barrel.

Divisional and brigade headquarters heard the clamor and got the message, for not long afterward the battalion was summoned for a meeting in the courtyard of the brigade cookhouse, located on a slope at the base of the mountain. Streams of men walking silently down toward the meeting grounds, rifles slung across their backs, ammunition belts and grenades dangling from their hips, looked like a tired army in slow, orderly retreat. We were pleased we had gotten the ears of the top officers. Now we knew we were part of a true People's Army, a great democratic force. But it didn't take long for the obvious question to pop up: what army in the world would abandon its front lines to have a meeting in the rear? Surely, if the enemy knew about this foolish mass exodus of rank-and-file soldiers for a meeting with their officers, they would unquestionably have mounted an attack in our absence and perhaps, together with an artillery barrage and aerial bombardment, finished us off neatly once and for all. Luckily for us, they did not know. Looking back on this episode, we saw it clearly as a reflection of the inexperience and naivete of the men of our battalion and of the headquarters officers and staff as well. Yes, we did learn never again to pull this idiotic stunt, which we soon recognized as betrayal of our front lines.

The cookhouse and the courtyard were jammed with sullen-faced members of the Lincoln Battalion, with many British and Irish, and with members of flanking battalions and services, the concerned and the curious. I climbed for a seat on the courtyard wall offering a panoramic view of this tense gathering. Among the top officers who spoke there were no Americans, but we hung on every word of translation from the French as the importance and the successes of the battles were outlined for us, along with the many insurmountable problems of supply, the effort of coordination of services, the loyalty and bravery of unavoidably inexperienced men and officers, but above all the political and military importance of holding the present battle lines at all costs. We achieved a better understanding of the urgency of keeping control of the Madrid-Valencia road, which we could see from where we were positioned. It became clearer to us that the loss of this lifeline road out of Madrid to the eastern part of Spain would have meant encirclement of Madrid—the heart and core of Spain's resistance to fascism—and would also have led to entrapment of hundreds of thousands of hard-pressed Republican forces defending the city. Without a doubt, such a catastrophe would have resulted in a quick victory for Hitler, Mussolini, and Franco's invading troops. We understood; we were impressed.

By the end, the foolhardiness of chancing a meeting under those battle conditions hit us between the eyes. We were now anxious to rush back to our positions. Morale took a giant leap forward. We returned quickly to our lines, singing on the way up, joking, whistling, cursing the bloody fascists, and pledging revenge for our fallen comrades, proud and secure in the knowledge that our efforts and our losses were not in vain. With the end of the meeting and a cool wind buttoning us down, a new spirit and determination swept through the ranks. We knew, too, that though the past month had been tough on us, the ever-increasing number of troops, tanks, artillery, bombers, and materiel from Germany and Italy could turn our lives into a living hell in the coming months.

The outdoor meeting satisfied us as to the whys and wherefores of our role in those hills, but in the days and weeks to come we looked for and found ways to keep ourselves better informed.

The whole line now concerned itself with consolidating the gains made. With the fascists prevented from wresting control of the Valencia-Madrid road, a regular system of zigzag trenches was constructed with sandbag supports and peepholes to fire from. Communication trenches leading out of the main trenches provided an intricate network of narrow passageways fairly safe from stray bullets. The fascists, too, arranged a systematized line of trenches.

Martin Hourihan, a former Philadelphia schoolteacher and seaman, succeeded Merriman as battalion commander.

Light exchange of rifle and machine-gun fire continued at all times between both sides. It became more or less a battle of sniper against sniper, except that our artillery shelled the fascists almost every day. Morning, noon, and night, around their mealtimes, the fascists received a disturbing barrage. They did not often respond with their artillery. Trench mortars, however, were showered upon us on numerous occasions.

Finally, on 14 March, the fascists made a desperate attempt to break through our lines. They concentrated their heaviest fire on the battalion to our left, consisting of recently enlisted young Spanish troops. It was a sulky day; it rained in jerks. Enemy tanks fired into our trenches and charged toward the young troops.

From my diary and journal notes I reconstruct the events as follows:

14 March

Despite fresh setbacks and casualties, American, British, Irish, French, and Slavic volunteers hold fast. The fascists, in a suprise move, attack our left flank, occupied by recent Spanish recruits. As enemy tanks approach, these raw and uninitiated troops wildly desert their trenches, retreating 200 to 300 meters. The American first aid crews, from their field hospital tents and ambulances at the base of the hill, see the young men fleeing downhill, some throwing their rifles to the ground in what looks like panic. Without hesitation, the first aid teams, led by John Simon, medical student from Philadelphia, fan out and halt the retreating soldiers. After some stern lecturing by our doctors and first aid men, the recruits are encouraged to return to their abandoned positions. Later, our line is grateful to the first aid teams and doctors, especially Simon, for their quick thinking and bold actions under a sudden mortar and artillery fire.

In the meantime, the Lincolns, aware of the dangers of enemy breakthroughs, promptly spread out along the deserted fortifications, to cover as wide an area as possible. The Moors capture part of our trenches, but we prevent them from making a decisive breakthrough, which at this sensitive point could be devastating, leading to a severance of the Madrid-Valencia road and resulting in the complete encirclement of Madrid, where the stubborn resistance of the last six weeks, with the loss of hundreds of lives, must not be made meaningless. Our understanding of the importance and crucial nature of this part of the front keeps us on edge, day and night. Now this unnecessary crumbling of a part of our lines adds to the tensions. Not helping much is brigade headquarters' repeated harangue that we not give up one additional foot of our treasured ground.

A few of our men on the thinned-out left flank hand-grenade their way until they confront, face to face, the aggressive Moors. Moors are killed, the rest flee; but farther down, to the extreme left, the fascists succeed in holding about 150 meters of our trenches.

J. Robert Raven, who had returned to the front lines a few days before this battle, after having recovered from a wound suffered during the attack of 23 February, was one of the first to dash to the left flank following the enemy penetration. He was seriously injured during a charge to rout the enemy. A letter he wrote from a hospital to his friend Lieutenant Phil Cooperman tells his story. That letter, entrusted to me by Cooperman immediately after he received it, is still in my possession.

Dear Coop,
Just writing to let you know what happened to me after you left. I rushed up about 350 meters of empty trenches bringing up all the Spaniards I could rally around. Then I met a Canadian. The trenches had been filling up gradually at our exhortation of "No pasaran." Suddenly we ran into four soldiers whom we thought our own at first, but their helmets and clothes proved them to be fascists. They tried to capture us. We tore away from them and ran back thirty meters and grabbed some grenades. My Canadian comrade opened the lever of his grenade and handed it to me, which he should not have done. However, I crawled up towards the fascists under cover of the Spaniards' fire who had just come up, and was about to toss the grenade when there was a terrific concussion in front of me and I felt my face torn of. Naturally, I dropped the grenade from my hand, having been knocked out. My own grenade exploded at my feet filling my legs with shrapnel.
My comrades must have retreated again and I kept crawling blindly, dragging my body through those trenches over all kinds of obstacles calling, "Comrade, Comrade." Words cannot describe the agony, the exhaustion with which I dragged myself through those narrow trenches. Finally, I felt somebody near me and he touched me, and an hour or so later somebody was carrying me and I landed at the hospital here. Most of the shrapnel in my legs has been removed, also both my eyes. They were too bad for repair. Tell my comrades I said, "No Pasaran" and I hope we didn't lose those trenches.

After the events of 14 March, we spent many feverish days constructing stronger and more defensible fortifications. We had learned the bitter lessons of how easy it was to pay with your life for shallow and carelessly built trenches. Light rifle and machine-gun fire and occasional mortars kept us on our toes.

Following through with the policy of keeping us better informed, headquarters issued regular information bulletins. One was called *Our Fight, Organ of the Front of the XV Brigade*, a single sheet mimeographed on both sides. It offered, as previous ones had, briefs on the progress of the war, the active fronts, domestic problems, and government decrees, and gave synopses of world events, emphasizing CIO organizational drives in the United States, which were of particular interest to the many trade unionists among us. Sometimes *Our Fight* was two pages and carried letters and poetry written by the men in the front lines. I was surprised, though pleased, when issue Number 18 printed one of my two poems. The second poem was printed in issue Number 25. Naturally, I sent copies to my brother, who kept them in good condition to this day.

Easter Sunday, 28 March
 The Irish not only respect their dead, they honor them: both those who gave their lives in this war against fascism and those who gave their lives in the battles against British domination and imperialism.
 Many of us, rifle in hand and eye on the enemy, witnessed today the Irish Easter service, held in the frontline trenches, facing the fascist enemy less than two hundred paces away.
 The Connolly Company, as spic and span as is possible under battlefront conditions, fell into line on a slope behind the sandbagged trenches. Kelley, a volunteer, was the first to step out to speak. When he spoke of our recent dead, whom he honored profusely for having given their lives knowingly and unselfishly in this war against world fascism, he did so loudly but solemnly. But when he spoke of James Connolly, leader of the 1916 Irish Easter Rebellion, he spoke buoyantly and with eloquence, in a beautiful Irish brogue.
 He paid tribute to the Lincoln Battalion for naming one of its companies the James Connolly; he considered it appropriate that we should have done so, and he was proud of this fact. He likened the struggle of the Irish to that of the Spanish people, who were accomplishing today what the Irish find still as unfinished business, their aspirations for freedom and dignity and their war against the forces of darkness and colonialism. He concluded in a ringing voice that the certain victory of the Spanish people over Franco, Hitler, and Mussolini would lighten the hearts of the Irish back home and would inspire them to intensify their struggles for ultimate freedom from British imperialist clutches. The presence of the Irish on Spanish soil and in the International Brigades was not only appropriate to show international solidarity with Spain in its war against fascism, but also to serve notice on the British that as long as Ireland is not free and independent, the British colonial masters will remain in fear and chained to their own oppressive policies.
 Though there were occasional bursts of mortar and the persistent crackling of swishing bullets, not a man moved nor did an eyebrow flicker during the brief ceremony.

That Easter, newspapers carried the story that thousands of Italian troops, fully equipped, had landed in Cadiz, and that Mussolini, aboard one of his warships on his way to Libya, wired his Italian command at Guadalajara, "Inform legionnaires I am following hourly their fight which will be crowned with victory."
 The Spanish government announced that Italian prisoners captured by our forces at Guadalajara declared that the Mussolini Blackshirts and the professional Littorio Division of the Italian Army were independent units not under the command of General Franco and answerable for their military actions on Spanish soil to Mussolini alone. Mussolini's touted army of "volunteers" once again proved the Non-Intervention Pact to be ineffective and a farce. The pact, proposed by Britain and France and signed on 25 August 1936 by the major European nations, including Germany and Italy, pledged to stop the flow of arms and troops to both sides of the civil war. The Soviet Union also became a signatory. A Non-Intervention Committee had been set up on 2 September 1936 to supervise the terms of the pact.

"Nonintervention" worked out very nicely for Franco. While for the legal Spanish government the French border was sealed to the transport of legitimately purchased supplies, arms, and equipment and the admission of the genuine, antifascist volunteers, Franco with impunity regularly brought in completely equipped combat soldiers with a full complement of officers from Italy and Germany.

The British foreign secretary, Anthony Eden, questioned in the House of Commons, admitted that an unknown number of troops had disembarked from Italian ships at Cadiz on 5 March in violation of the ban on volunteers imposed by the Non-Intervention Committee on 20 February 1937.

5 April

The battalion again went over the top supporting an advance movement on the left flank. The Garibaldi Battalion of antifascist Italians, fresh from their victories over Mussolini's Italian regular troops at Guadalajara, led the attack. The Dąbrowski Battalion of Polish volunteers, to the right of the Garibaldi, charged next; then came the Spanish units, followed by the Lincoln Battalion. The enemy bombarded our lines intensively with hundreds of trench mortars, heavy artillery, and rifle grenade bombs. A sweeping machine-gun and rifle fire ripped open our sandbags. One of our tanks charging clumsily ahead of our thrusts was incapacitated by antitank shells. By a few bold encircling maneuvers, the indefatigable Garibaldi Battalion recaptured the trenches lost to the fascists on 14 March and rounded up some 150 prisoners.

Davey Jones, acting Lincoln Battalion political commissar, was wounded in the upper right arm while rescuing a wounded comrade. Casualties, painful even when we lose only one man, were comparably slight.

Major Allan Johnson (his real name was Allan McNeil), Lincoln Brigade staff officer, in September 1938, while in Barcelona preparing for his return to the United States, sketched for me this map of the events of 5 April 1937. His map shows that the Polish Dąbrowski Battalion remained in position during the action. Later, when I compared my notes and diary, written in the evening after the battle, I found this map at variance with my written record, which indicates that the Dąbrowskis did indeed engage the enemy until they, too, ran out of ammunition.

6 April

Although today is my 23rd birthday, there is little to celebrate after yesterday's needless casualty. I almost became one myself. In preparation for the attack, Liam Tumilson, a serious but cheerful Irishman, who in the last few days had been arguing that we were not aggressive enough in our assaults on the fascists, stood up straight, with head and shoulders above our parapets, defiantly examining enemy positions and calling for us to follow him. His khaki beret, which he preferred to a helmet, was tilted to the side and almost covered his eyes. I was not more than ten feet from him, with my head low, my feet dug into the ground in a track runner's position, ready to dart forward; I shouted to him, "Get down! Keep low!" At that moment a sniper's bullet struck him in the center of the forehead. He fell back and off the mound where he had perched himself. Two of us put him on a stretcher and hurried him downhill, but the ground was wet and the narrow, rocky lane was slippery. A mortar shell exploded almost on top of us and we lost our footing. I don't know who fell first, the other guy or me, but down we went. The Irishman slid off the stretcher and everything in his head fell out.

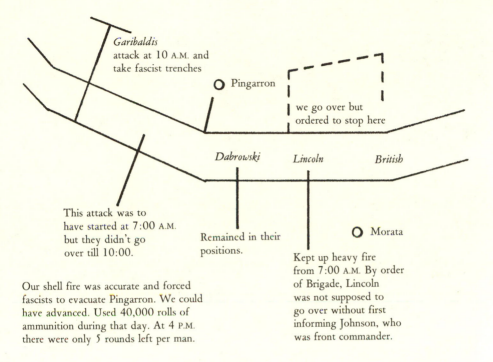

Garibaldis
attack at 10 A.M. and
take fascist trenches

O Pingarron

we go over but
ordered to stop here

Dabrowski   Lincoln   British

This attack was to
have started at 7:00 A.M.
but they didn't go
over till 10:00.

Remained in their
positions.

O Morata

Kept up heavy fire
from 7:00 A.M. By order
of Brigade, Lincoln
was not supposed to
go over without first
informing Johnson, who
was front commander.

Our shell fire was accurate and forced
fascists to evacuate Pingarron. We could
have advanced. Used 40,000 rolls of
ammunition during that day. At 4 P.M.
there were only 5 rounds left per man.

* * * *

Reports from the French frontier say that the bombing of the defenseless Basque country town of Durango was witnessed by the Dean of Canterbury and his British church delegation 31 March and that they were horrified. Sixty planes took part. Bombers were piloted by Germans and pursuit planes by Italians, according to a captured pilot. The churchmen witnessed the bombing of a hospital and a mental asylum, whose inmates were machine-gunned.

EIGHT

Life in the Trenches

When the front lines stabilized somewhat along the Jarama mountains, the need for activity and diversion became important. Frederick Lutz, agronomist and engineer from Moorestown, New Jersey, now political commissar in place of the wounded Davey Jones, initiated several ideas. One was the setting up of a canteen where we could buy essential items, such as candles, flashlights, writing paper and envelopes, and other small, but to us necessary articles during that period. Our mail went post free—for that we were grateful—but we had to buy playing cards and shaving supplies. Though the canteen was a help, it couldn't come close to meeting demand. And the one thing that most of us wanted, American cigarettes, couldn't be had at all during those first weeks.

Then came a welcome library, with books by Jack London, Sinclair Lewis, Fannie Hurst, John Dos Passos, and many others. Here, too, the supply failed to meet the demand. Magazines and newspapers of many languages were passed around until they wore out from use.

A barbershop was improvised by our digging a hole deep enough to shield us from stray bullets. I became the battalion's first barber and filled that role until I was replaced by an experienced professional, Steve Troxil, a Californian. I have no doubt the frontline patrons welcomed the change.

Next, Political Commissar Lutz bought a radio somewhere and hooked it to three loudspeakers spread out so that all members of the battalion could hear the music and listen to the news. When the news was good for our side, we turned it on as loud as possible in the hope that the enemy would also hear.

Then Lutz dreamed up an idea that appealed to me. He asked me to set up a wall newspaper. We had no walls, so we accomplished the same thing by stretching an army canvas shelter half between two iron posts in a dip of ground reasonably protected from enemy fire. We named it the *Daily Mañana*. It caught hold instantly and became popular and important to us. It was our link with the outside world. Often, letters from home, even personal ones, were posted for all to read. Letters from our wounded, in base hospitals got special attention, particularly letters from those we thought had been killed or just didn't make it because of serious wounds. Each letter from a friend or comrade who had been presumed dead restored a part of us. We pinned onto the *Daily Mañana* clippings as they arrived enclosed in personal letters from back home. Many dealt with the recipient's hometown news, labor struggles, sit-down strikes, and the progress of the great unionization upsurges led by the still new CIO, often satisfying our need to know what was going on back home. Accounts of the revolutionary struggles in China, the fortunes of the Eighth Route Red Army, and events in the Soviet Union drew keen interest, often sparking late evening discussion.

Before long we encouraged men to write accounts of their experiences in Spain. Many of them did, and a few of the accounts were preserved and can be found quoted in newspapers, magazines and in books about Spain. A surprising number of poets flowered in this period. There was also room for varied humor, for biographies of those who died in battle, for drawings and cartoons sketched by our talent in the trenches. The canvas bulletin board became not only a source of news and opinion, but also an avenue of creative expression for those so inclined. We posted everything, including daily progress reports on the war. Government communiqués were always overbearingly on the optimistic side, and we learned to read between the lines. For instance, we knew that when a communiqué announced, "We shortened our lines to more effectively meet the onslaught of the enemy" it really meant that we had retreated to avoid defeat or encirclement.

After all, our volunteers were of unusually high political caliber and thirsted for accurate news of what was happening in Spain, Europe, Asia, and above all in the Americas. They learned early of powerful world pressures on the peoples of Spain and their government. They were prepared for the worst, for they had transferred themselves voluntarily from the political and trade union battlefields of America to a parallel struggle in Spain, except that here the volcanic military conflict resulted in the spilling of rivers of human blood. There was no substitute for the truth; they saw through phony rhetoric and rejected it. By now they had learned to take defeat without whimpering and victories without having their heads tuned to illusions of instant triumph. Tampering with reality led to cynicism and to our impatience to get to the bottom of a snow job. Our *Daily Mañana*, that eight-foot piece of canvas, met and passed daily the challenging test of reality and truth.

An annoying problem that almost overwhelmed us was that of lice, the crawling vermin entrenching themselves in our clothes and on our bodies and engaging in their own little wars. Of course, a battle against the louse ensued, and its initiator and supervisor was Dr. William Pike, a feisty New York physician who did a great deal to raise the general health level of our ranks to high standards. He was assisted by John Simon, a medical student from Philadelphia, who had left school to be among the first to join the Lincoln Battalion. After his return from Spain, Simon continued his studies and got his medical degree. If a medical degree, like a military officer's commission, could have been earned on the battlefield, Simon, cheerful and tireless, with his accumulated experience and dedication under the most primitive and difficult of war conditions, would certainly have been awarded at least one doctor's degree and, together with Bill Pike, a chestful of honors. Their greatest reward was the affection of the men of the battalion they so loyally served.

Dr. Pike was a strict disciplinarian when it came to regulation-size spacing and digging of latrines and very strict about our keeping them clean. It wasn't a laughing matter at the time, but I laugh now when I am reminded of the Cuban who missed the hole, his pile landing on the latrine's edge. Dr. Pike caught him walking away from his mess and let out a spirited tongue-lashing.

"Don't you know where to shit?"

"Yes I do, but it's too late now," said the culprit, chagrined.

"The next time you have to go, let me know and I'll show you where," the doctor scolded.

"OK, Doc, what you can do now is show me how to put the stuff back into my ass," the Cuban answered and walked away chuckling, proud of his retort.

On 10 April, rain came at sunset and poured mercilessly till sunrise, and then continued intermittently throughout the day.

11 April

The trenches are ankle-deep in water, dugouts impossible to enter, and there is no part of me not soaking wet. I am not only wet but cold. Equipment is a mess: rifles, machine guns, all need drying and cleaning. We can't worry that maybe the enemy is having the same trouble, so we spend a good part of the morning working like beavers to get our weapons in shape for any surprise attack.

Because my shoes soak up the rain like a sponge, I get permission to go to the cookhouse for a good pair of boots. While there, I gather armfuls of books and magazines and trek back to the battalion with them.

In the afternoon, I am delegated to attend a political meeting at the first aid hut, presided over by Lutz, the commissar. Among others present is Bert Williams, a political commissar for the British, who also is a member of the Central Committee of the British Communist party. We discuss fully our many grievances, some petty and some not so petty. Williams offers a number of suggestions to help adjust our sagging morale. Apparently, the British and Irish have plenty of beefs of their own.

Sitting next to an alert young Spaniard, I find him dexterously rolling cigarettes. He helps me roll mine. After we become friends, he confides that he belongs to the left wing of the Spanish Republican party but that he prefers to serve with the extranjeros *(literally "foreigners" but in his context it is his affectionate term for International Volunteers).*

The front is quiet, and in rare moments when the sun smiles I grab the brigade camera and take pictures, many of them, for lack of anything better to do. In the evening I bring the exposed film to brigade headquarters for developing. Oliver Green, and Englishman, walks me back to the lines and promises to get the developed film back into my hands. I had gotten to know him earlier and found him to be trustworthy, companionable, and helpful. [These pictures came in handy at a later date when Green worked with me in doing the book of the Fifteenth Brigade.]

13 April

The dawn peeked early this Tuesday. The town of Morata de Tajuña at the foot
of the mountains behind us lay slumbering and quiet. Seven of us squeezed into a
secondary dugout to share hot coffee when, in rapid succession, enemy shells exploded
around us. Surprised, we sprinted to frontline trenches and better-constructed dugouts for
greater safety and to look through the peepholes of sandbags to see if the enemy was
mounting an attack.

After lobbing more rounds than we could count, they quit as abruptly as they
started.

The enemy knows, as we do, the devastating effects surprise bombardments have on
nerves. Nothing is so terrifying as nearby bursting shells, and if you are so close that you
feel the earth rumble, your body rumbles with it. You imagine each exploding shell
having your name on it, each seeming to say: this is for you. As the earth is torn
apart by explosions, your stomach also convulses, and the more rapid the shelling, the
more rapidly your heart beats. There are times I seem to feel no heartbeat at all.
Nerves are taut and your head feels like a clutter of over-tightened guitar strings, and
you are aware that with one more twist the whole damn works may snap.

The shelling comes to a halt and the gripe sessions begin. Morale drops; we've
been in these mountains for two difficult months with frequent promises of relief that
remain just that, promises. It is not uncommon to hear expressions of wanting to go back
home. A few say they're fed up and quietly whisper that they're thinking of deserting if
relief doesn't come soon. One guy said that after we get relief he won't come back even
if he were put in chains. Another warned authoritatively that he knew for a fact that
many will never come back to the front after we've been pulled out. We sympathize
with the low morale of the British Battalion and, by contrast, we conclude that ours is
higher than theirs. But we also know that British and Irish volunteers had arrived
many weeks sooner than Americans and have been in action, without relief, longer and
often in more severe battle conditions. Their casualties have been extraordinarily high
and proportionately more numerous than ours.

Fierce shelling by the other side keeps us keyed up. Then heavy fire, initiated by
our side, continues through the afternoon. According to reports passed down the line,
our Madrid army has three thousand fascists encircled in University City, and our job
is to keep this sector very busy to discourage the enemy from even thinking of
withdrawing troops facing us to reinforce their besieged.

Late evening, after fireworks taper off, I make my way to the cookhouse to pick up
some flashlights, bulbs, and batteries. About halfway down the slope a mortar barrage
strikes here and there, but I find good cover behind a solid rock. When I pass First
Aid Station No. 4, I am told damage was done by fragments with an almost direct
hit, but no one was hurt.

Ten Americans arrive to rejoin the battalion; eight, returning from base hospitals,
now are almost recovered from wounds suffered in these same mountains less than two
months ago.

Wednesday, 14 April

This day finds us noting the sixth anniversary of the birth of this Spanish
Republic. Around this time in 1931, King Alfonso XIII abdicated his throne, after
overwhelming popular electoral victories for candidates committed to the establishment of
a republic. Supporters of the monarchy were decimated by the nationwide results. Fascist

and profascist candidates were also swept aside. The Catholic church, where it widely advised its followers to vote against republican candidates, was just as widely ignored. Thus this Republic was born.

Rich and powerful agricultural landlords (many of them absentee owners), industrialists and bankers, the hierarchy of the Catholic church, and the former political representatives of these groups, stunned by the scope of the people's march to Western-style democracy, were temporarily disoriented. However, they were soon to catch their breath, reassemble their loose coalition for a concerted drive to undermine the Republic, and turn loose on a peaceful people the violence of fascist-minded army generals and their followers. For to them it was better to ruin than to permit the elected representatives of the people to rule.

Newspapers detail stories of the day's significance. Political meetings of the parties of the Republic are reportedly taking place throughout the country to commemorate this important anniversary. Civilians—la retaguardia—*and soldiers are called upon for even greater effort and sacrifice to* aplastar el enemigo, *crush the enemy.*

Meanwhile, we drag on in these hills from day to day, our ranks getting thinner. It is cold, damp, and windy. Nothing seems to stay in place for long. Strong winds often blow the khaki beret off my head—I can't stand wearing a clumsy and ill-fitting helmet, World War French issue—and I chase it downhill. Sometimes it is stopped by the trunk of an olive tree.

I'm edgy. My nerves are about to give. If others feel as I do, I don't know what keeps the line together. Last night, for the first time, I slept uneasily. I twisted and turned, half awake. I sat up terrified when an explosion in my head awakened me. I found myself looking into and studying the dark for a stealthy enemy solider wanting to slip a knife into me. And I knew I wouldn't be the first so nicely and quietly taken care of. Not even my playing poker with the 147 pesetas I got in pay today can shake off a bad case of nerves. I do need rest; all of us need relief, even if it's just for a week or two.

15 April

After days of hiding, the sun finally reappeared, and though windy, it was warm. All morning I fought the wind while cutting hair, then I gave up because every time I opened my mouth fresh-cut hair blew into it.

Following lunch, I dug for a half hour around the posts anchoring the Daily Mañana, *to drop the canvas closer to eye level. Then I walked along the line asking for articles from each who cared to write, especially about current labor events in the U.S., "your participation in them, your impressions and analyses." I asked several for their experiences and also their impressions since their arrival in Spain. Of those who had been in more advanced political activity in the States, I requested articles reflecting their political views. The response, though hardly overwhelming, wasn't bad. The poets were especially shy about showing their work. When I asked for poems I knew had been written during lulls, I received them reluctantly. I was handed personal letters, though, and newspaper clippings. Lucky for me to be making the rounds after mail delivery.*

While collecting this material, I also recruited volunteers to help dig deeper the underground canteen. Immediately, a few sharp tongues interpreted my project to be a sure sign we were digging for a longer stay, maybe even for the duration of the war. "Fuck the canteen, how about relief instead?"

For me, a high point today was the letter I received from Harry Wallach, a

Philadelphia baker, wounded in February. In the evening, right after supper, I was given permission to walk down to the cookhouse to show the letter to Willi Frait, also a Philadelphian. Frait cried while reading, and when he finished it, sat down with his head in his hands. They were good friends back home.

Harry's letter was short. He wanted us to know that after we carried him down on the stretcher to a first aid stop, he was transferred to the frontline hospital unit near Morata de Tajuña, where he was left in a room with many wounded. A bullet had entered his right chest and exited his lower back. He could not talk, but he could hear and had not lost consciousness. He heard the moans and appeals of the less seriously wounded and could tell when they were brought in and taken out. He could hear doctors working in adjoining rooms, and it gave him hope to feel that sooner or later they would get to him. Night fell and still no one had worked on him, but someone walked into the room and covered him with a sheet. In the morning he heard a voice say: "OK, let's get all the stiffs out of here." When they came to get him and removed the sheet, he rolled his eyes frantically and grimaced. He welcomed the new voice, a high-pitched one: "Hey, Doc, this stiff's alive." Harry was immediately on the surgeon's table and his life saved. He said he expected to be sent home as soon as they were able to stop the drain of pus from his wounds. [Harry was to suffer a drain in his back for years before he was finally cured.]

While I was at the cookhouse, the Cuban on duty, Juan Hernandez, agreed to take me to visit a couple of truck-driver friends, Sam and Al, who were somewhere near Morata. When we found them, they told me to pass the word that they were driving night and day moving troops out of Morata and that the Lincoln Battalion and the entire brigade was due for relief soon.

But when I returned to my sandbagged position, I found a letter for me from home with the demoralizing question: "When are you coming back home?"

16 April

Rumors of relief kept me busy cutting hair all morning. Everybody wants to spruce up for town and the girls. There is excitement, exhilaration.

The news was so good that we canceled a scheduled board meeting for the Daily Mañana. *So, after supper, we played blackjack with matchsticks by candlelight in a well-protected dugout until midnight, with no interruptions from the other side. We didn't disturb them either.*

17 April

Again I cut hair all morning. Some guys exasperate me by acting like they're in a barber chair back home:

"Let me look in the mirror," or

"Cut off more here, but leave the other side alone," and

"How about trimming the hair out of my nose and ears?"

Next one: "Not too much off the top." He had a fresh scar straight across the top of his head from front to rear where a fascist bullet had torn his scalp in early February. "And leave my sideburns long, just taper the back."

To the pests, I say: "For free you get what I give you. Too many around here need haircuts. I have no time for style." I didn't tell them, though, that I didn't know style A from style B.

The chatter during haircutting keeps backtracking to the same tune: When will relief come? Where will we be sent? What will we do? How long a rest do they plan for us? Will we be allowed to go home if we ask to do so? In the midst of all this, MacDonald, an Englishman attached to brigade headquarters, strolls in to announce that rumors of relief are false. The bubbles burst, the spirits drop to another low.

At a subdued editorial board meeting, one guy was so pissed off at the latest news that he proposed changing the name of the wall newspaper to The Bullet Board. *Another sarcastically suggested that it be called* The Bullshit Board. *Tempers were short.*

* * * *

Forty Americans arrived today fresh from base training camps. They are like we were a couple of months ago, full of piss and vinegar, enthusiastic, confident, and spirited, anxious to face the enemy. Like some rookies, their mouths talk big while their eyes show anxiety and fear. We look beat to them. However, they will find out before long that we are hardened, seasoned, and surefooted, experienced in the attack, the counterattack, and in the art of trench warfare, but fatigued—physically and mentally—and impatient for a change. They have only recently arrived from the States, received the kind of professional training we had not been lucky enough to get, and want action. We, instead, are ready for peace. Although they look like a hell'uva good bunch, they can't see being sent to the front and immediately leaving for a rest camp. If they listen, they're going to learn a lot from our old-timers—and live longer.

* * * *

It took a lot of walking before I found the brigade estado major *[head-quarters]. From a distance I could see this elaborate, beautiful, castle-like estate perched like a bird's nest on the side of a carefully cultivated hill of vineyards, fruit and olive trees, and several shade trees I'm incapable of naming. It overlooks miles of surrounding terrain, including the main Madrid-Valencia road and the town of Morata, perfect for brigade headquarters.*

While waiting for Oliver Green, a Briton, who is in charge of gathering material for the 15th Brigade Book, I engage Primo Camino, a Spanish soldier, in conversation. He tells me that this estate and all these farmlands, as far as the eye can see, a la redonda (all around), were formerly the personal property of a wealthy marquis, who had fled with his family and fascist friends when the military rebellion failed in this area. He says the peasants who work these fields from dawn to dark live over there, and he points to a hill. Through binoculars I see holes dug out of the side of a hill, and on the ledges of the cliffs women and children and burros meander. There the peasants and their families eat, sleep, marry, and propagate—and die. I remember the stories in our own history books about the cliff dwellers of prehistoric times.

Before we begin our discussions, Green takes me on a tour of the grounds. The entire estate is fenced in. To get to the main house, now turned into quarters and offices, we climb a hard-surfaced road lined on both sides by gently arranged flower beds. The flowers are about to bloom and spread their varied and colorful spring beauty on a world tormented by fear and hate. To the left of the main house are other buildings, probably used as servants' quarters in the old days. But now the one to the left is a jail house with a kitchen and dining room, barred on all sides; the one next to it is now an armory and sleeping quarters for the military police, photographers, and visitors. Green's room is on the second floor. In the back of these buildings is an immaculate flagstone beer garden with an occasional marble-topped picnic table, a delightful family-sized swimming pool, an outdoor fireplace—all beautifully landscaped. Unlike peasant dwellings, these buildings are supplied with electricity, spacious kitchens and modern conveniences, Spanish tiled bathrooms with the most exquisite plumbing fixtures, mosaic tiled floors, a library, and fine imported furniture. The marquis didn't miss a trick.

This life of splendor enjoyed by those who owned the land contrasts sharply with the life of those who tilled the land. I thought of Villanueva de la Jara, our first training base, where, together with a Cuban, I became friends with the peasant family with whom we broke bread. I compared their life in their whitewashed, adobe home of not more than twenty square feet, with a red-tiled roof. Though the inside was clean, the floor was of hard earth and the fireplace was their cooking stove. Four people lived in this room, as well as their goat, dog, chickens, lamb, and other animals, roaming in and out of the house. For furniture there was one old wooden table with four chairs just as old, and not enough eating utensils for six people. The men with their burros worked the fields, the women did their wash at the stream by pounding the clothes on rocks. There was no school, no electricity, no social hall, no movie, no bathtubs, and certainly no swimming pool. There was, however, a church and a monastery. What land the marquis did not own the church did.

On the way back from the estado mayor, *I stopped at the battalion's halfway cookhouse. Farina, a Cuban, invited me for a cup of tea. "Cuba" Hermosa, who was on guard duty, joined us, and we swapped stories and experiences and lamented the comforts of home. They're both wonderful guys. Hermosa said he has learned more English here in Spain than he did in the U.S. I can believe it. Hermosa's name, translated, means, "Beautiful Cuba," but his first name is really José. About 5 feet 8, boyish looking, magnificently proportioned, erect, and strong, he is beautifully jet black, with a mouthful of pearls for teeth and black, glistening eyes that are always smiling. Like other Cubans a refugee from Batista, he is anxious to go back to his home, family, and a free Cuba. He took the death of Rodolfo de Armas very hard.*

After leaving the Cubans, I stretch out in my dugout, and as I write by candlelight, enemy artillery and trench mortar shelling begins on our right flank. The British are catching hell again. Why the shelling? The day has been quiet on our part as well as theirs. Even our tanks make no noise. It's so now that every time there's an explosion my heart beats faster. I can't seem to get used to the unexpected explosions, shellings, bombardments.

18 April

The day is warm and all is quiet along the front. For part of the morning, I am able to cut hair without having to dive for cover. I collect material for the Daily Mañana *and for the proposed 15th Brigade Book. When I go to* estado mayor *to work on my material in Green's room, I find Earl Leppo, now brigade orderly. Earl is from the Atlantic City area in South Jersey, and though I didn't know him back home, we met on ship and have become fast friends. He whispers to me that with what he's seen and heard around headquarters we are really scheduled to be replaced soon, maybe as quickly as within a couple of days. Because of the many false alarms and disappointments, I put little credence into what he has to say.*

I wonder at the quiet of these hills on this day; except for the hustle and bustle of brigade headquarters, the war seems unreal and distant, so I stop for coffee at the halfway cookhouse and enjoy visiting with the hardworking and friendly staff. Jack Shirai, a Japanese-American volunteer, now chief of the cookhouse, is always pleasant and has excellent organization among his crew despite serious shortages of equipment and supplies.

19 April

After gathering more material for the Brigade Book, I fell in with an ongoing poker game following noon chow, and during an unusually quiet hour I won back all that I had previously lost, almost anyway. But I resolved never to play poker again, a game that seems to me to waste so much time and emotions. At night I was to break that resolve, and though I lost 35 pesetas, I had the satisfaction of companionship of true comrades, each of whom would give his all to the next guy. We exchanged frank views about ourselves, our families, our friends back home, the war and its politics, the current military situation, and before we knew it we were in a bull session helping to untangle each other's nerves. We parted fresh and hopeful.

Davis, newly appointed brigade photographer, whom I had been expecting for days, finally showed up and blamed the delay on receiving poor equipment and no film. He was directed by brigade headquarters, at my request, to take photos for use in the Brigade Book. I requested photos of the Irish and their various positions, of those in performance of their duties, whether cleaning a rifle, examining sandbags, looking over the enemy through binoculars, or any other interesting shots. I got a group to pose for pictures around our field radio; a picture was shot of the Tom Mooney Machine Gun Company and their crews; two pictures were taken of a disabled tank straddling our trenches to the left. Finally, I asked for individual and group pictures, and he shot a whole roll. But when I asked for pictures of the Daily Mañana, he balked, until I insisted. He said he didn't think that was important.

20 April

Dawn is early, the sun warms quickly, and the day becomes one of those beautiful days in Spain that makes one feel good to be alive. It is so peaceful that I cut hair in the trenches all morning stripped to the waist. The hot sun is soothing and bakes my body under a soft breeze.

I cut Yale Stuart's hair. A tall, athletic figure, with broad shoulders, he tells me he is transferred to liaison between battalion and brigade, a task well suited to him. He's a runner, a scout, and is here and there and everywhere, like a bouncing basketball. He has no doubts about the final outcome of the war and is certain the Republic will defeat fascism. He is also optimistic about developments to establish a Republican army with a more unified command, with all political and military units, including the International Brigades, under that single command. We agree on the desirability of this, but we also know that the areas where the Republic will meet the greatest challenges to centralizing the army command will be in Aragon and in

Catalonia, where the anarchists and their trade union syndicalist organizations have prominent strongholds. [Yale Stuart was to lose an arm in combat along the Ebro River in Aragon in July 1938.]

In the early afternoon, I again go to estado mayor *to work on the Brigade Book until early evening, and on the way back to my unit, I stop at battalion headquarters, where Fred Lutz has me read a letter from his friend Shirley, from Philadelphia. [Not too many months after his return from Spain, Fred and Shirley were married in a private double wedding, for by then I, too, had met my wife-to-be. May and I witnessed for them and they witnessed for us. Between us we have four children, two for them and two for us.]*

21 April

Another warm day, but another day of disappointment as far as replacements go. Ran around urging men to write more for the Brigade Book. Typed several pages this afternoon, then went over materials with Marion Greenspan, reporter for the New York Daily Worker, *who helped me sort out some of them. I gave him several pages of stuff I had typed to be used in stories he was sending to his paper. With more time, we can get more contributions. After that I ate with Pat Long, guard of the night, at the halfway cookhouse—a swell supper of a delicious piece of meat with potatoes. I lay in the kitchen and tried to sleep but didn't until 3:00 A.M. Between coffees I wrote a poem to be posted on the Bulletin Board.*

22 April

The night was cold, but the day is sunny and warm. Firing on both sides is light. Our men are spreading newspapers on blankets to make a pattern indicating positions to our planes expecting to do some bombing to the other side.

Davis is replaced by Lerner as Brigade photographer. Thrilled with his new assignment, Lerner took four rolls of pictures this morning and appears to be experienced and competent. I, too, am excited over this new book project and am still running around collecting articles. Paul Burns is a big help and contributor. He seems to have more writing experience than the rest of us. I wish I had more time to work on the material before we go on leave. Once on leave, the distractions of behind-the-lines activities may reduce the interest, and the effort.

In the afternoon, I again worked in Oliver Green's room, typing articles already submitted in handwriting. Material looks good and is beginning to roll in nicely. I stopped at the cookhouse and washed myself thoroughly. Green says he's going to Madrid soon to line up a printer.

News of an unfortunate accident: a truck carrying a detail of our men and driven by Jack Steele and Daniel Sugrue collided with another on the Morata road. The driver and his helper were not injured but seven to twelve others were, including Johnny Perrone, a volunteer from Northern New Jersey.

Ground newspaper layout was good, but not one of our planes showed up, so no bombings. To avoid being attacked by our own planes, we employed prearranged newspaper layout signals for our pilots to spot our locations.

23 April

To Fred's suggestion that a new barber replace me I concurred happily, and I handed over my tools to a professional, Steve Troxil. With that responsibility off my mind, I lay in a dugout all morning working on more material for the book without interruption, except for Macdonald, the Englishman, who came to object to Al Tanz's article on Captain John Scott, also English, killed in February. He said the description was too brief, too incomplete, that it failed to properly acknowledge this unusual and superb military commander, one who took extraordinary risks to inspire others to continue the attack. Paul Burns has agreed to rewrite it.

While continuing my work at brigade headquarters until after dark, I detected activity which may mean we'll be leaving soon for the long-awaited rest.

24 April

While I was at brigade HQ transcribing copy from script to type, lightning and thunder shattered the quiet. The fascists must have mistaken thunder for guns; they let loose a savage barrage on our lines. Our artillery, in turn, responded just as savagely. A few of us thought this sudden exchange of artillery fire might be a prelude to an enemy charge on our battalion, so we sprang out of HQ and headed for the lines when suddenly the sky opened up with a torrent of rain. We ducked into the cookhouse for shelter and after a while the firing stopped, the word got to us that it was all a false alarm—just jagged nerves on both sides. However, the rain did not stop.

25 April

The rain continued without letup. I covered the canvas Daily Mañana *with more canvas, but the wind and rain had already ruined much of the stuff on it.*

In the dugout, waiting for the rain to let up, I read articles and stories to others and was offered interesting and constructive suggestions.

In the afternoon I was called to brigade HQ for a conference on the makeup of the book. Leading the discussion was Jean Barthel, the French brigade commissar, and present also, besides myself, was Oliver Green, the Englishman. We were satisfied with the progress we were making, but both of them gave me hell for writing notations on the backs of pictures. They claimed writing could scar the face of a picture. After examining a couple of pictures, I had to agree.

Dinner at brigade with Phil Cooperman, battalion staff officer now attached to brigade, who has read much of my stuff and feels we're on the right road. He also thinks it wise to consult broadly and involve as many individuals as are interested. Later he made some good criticisms.

On my way back to the lines I stopped at battalion headquarters, where I noted much activity, as if big movement was to take place soon.

My mind, instead of concentrating on the direction I intended, must have wandered to a dozen other things, and I discovered to my consternation that I had lost my bearings in the dark, and it was such a black night that I didn't find my way back to the dugout till after midnight. My fear of ending up inside enemy lines, or shot at by our own guys, was too real for me not to have worried.

26 April

I spend a long and productive day editing and rewriting. Before leaving for brigade headquarters to do this work, I spot a poker game under an olive tree, where a couple of Spanish recruits are being taught the rudiments of a card game they find perplexing, though profitable. For the kibitzers their playing is hilarious—they just don't get the hang of the game. Each of the lookers gives pesetas to our guys to lose to the Spaniards. I'm tapped for 10. We enjoy watching them win, and they are delighted with the easy pesetas they are picking up, which undoubtedly they'll be sending to their families. They believe us when we assure them they are gifted with beginners' luck.

On my way to estado mayor, *I stopped to visit with the Irish, who were, as usual, roasting stems of garlic over an open fire in a dip protected from direct enemy view. Who would guess burnt garlic and stale bread could be so tasty? I took some extras with me to Green's room, where I was to work. Two visitors I had offered a chunk of bread and garlic to left quickly; oddly, I had none of the usual interruptions for the rest of the day. After having supper with officers and staff, I continued working into the night but quit when my mind kept flipping back negatively to the better-quality food served at HQ compared to that served the line soldier. This bothered me.*

Earl Leppo, from Atlantic City, who was assigned to KP duty at officers' mess today and who was our waiter for evening chow, joined me for a short visit after cleanup. We talked mainly about volunteers from our home states. To get a figure of how many came from the Philadelphia–South Jersey area on our ship, the SS Champlain on 5 January, we counted by name each person we could remember and came up with 43. Of this figure, 22 were Cubans or of Cuban background, 21 were North Americans, including 1 or 2 Canadians. Of the 43 total, 10, we concluded, were from the Philadelphia–South Jersey communities, a figure we were not displeased with. Of course, following us, scores more arrived from our areas in even broader spectrum in late January, February, March, and they are still coming.

Language is still a problem at brigade headquarters. There are only thirteen staff officers, yet eleven translators are required.

27 April

We ate our breakfast during a cold, mean, and cutting wind, then I served on a cleanup detail of the trenches and grounds. There is hardly any shooting taking place, except that of the bull about Spanish troops scheduled to relieve us soon.

28 April

It is official! *We are to get ready to move to the ancient town of Alcalá de* Henares, near Madrid, *where Cervantes wrote* Don Quixote.

The order of the day, signed by Marty Hourihan, battalion commander, is loud and clear. The 14th International Brigade of French and Belgian volunteers is to relieve the 15th, our brigade, sometime after midnight. Officers of the day are responsible for leaving trenches clean and sanitary in every respect.

Order of movement is listed in the Order of the Day:
Men and arms, including machine guns and crews go first.
Armory to follow with written inventory of arms and equipment.
Next comes Quartermaster, ditto orders.
All trenches and communicating trenches and grounds will be policed.
No passes; no exceptions.
Telephone section will prepare immediately to accompany battalion.
We will be supplied with trucks and be responsible or our own transportation.

We had been in the front lines of the Jarama mountains continuously since the middle of February, seventy-three days of trench and combat life, with no breaks, no relief of any sort, our best comrades killed almost every day, and we were under artillery fire that often drove us underground. It was a steady diet of ground and aerial bombardments, and of bullets that whined and crackled incessantly, craving the flesh rather than the bark of a tree. It was battles, blood, work, and sometimes hunger. Despite the hardships, the men of the battalion and all auxiliaries carried on.

The experiences of the battalion under the most unequal conditions and the ability of the Lincoln volunteers to resist, to fight the enemy to a standstill, and to paralyze his will in spite of his numerical and material superiority filled us with renewed confidence in ourselves and in the officers promoted from the ranks. As noted earlier, Martin W. Hourihan, Philadelphia seaman, had replaced Merriman, who was wounded, as battalion commander; George Jacobs, also from Philadelphia, had discovered, as Lincoln Battalion observer skills that he didn't know he had before. Fred Lutz, the unflappable Moorestown, New Jersey, agronomist, had become battalion political commissar.

The changes, promotions, and reshuffling in the sections and companies improved the quality and caliber of officers because the tested and the best were advanced to the most responsible posts. The men of the Lincoln Battalion had earned the short rest they were about to enjoy.

NINE

On Leave

Though the next day, 29 April, I went to brigade to do some work, I accomplished little because of preoccupation with our leaving. So I returned to the lines, loaded the political commissar's truck with materials, books, and magazines, stripped the wall newspaper, gathered everything that belonged to us, and then left with great anticipation for Alcalá de Henares.

After our arrival in Alcalá and before unloading the truck, a group of us walked the streets and alleys at random to get acquainted with the town. At first we were cautious, but when we found the people welcoming us graciously and hospitably, we felt at home. As others rolled in from the front, they were greeted by some of our comrades who were already tipsy from visiting the wine stores now doing a holiday business. They told of storekeepers who gave them free bottles and who refused to take any money when they found that some of our guys didn't have enough to pay for one bottle.

The challenge was to find a whorehouse, and I went along, but I found the scene distasteful when we did locate one. After paying my fee, I left together with Alfred Ripps, Sol Lerner, and Joseph Mesada, who also kicked in, all of us wondering aloud why the government had not yet wiped out prostitution.

"It is unbecoming for volunteers to come into town and right off the bat look for a woman joint," said one of my companions.

"I'll bet you're married," retorted one of the others.

"It happens I'm not, but what's that got to do with it? Suppose you get diseased, you're out of circulation. That's as bad as desertion."

Later a Cuban told me of his experience after he found a house where he was well taken care of. The woman he was with even refused money. She said, "If you can come all the way from America to help us, this is the least I can do for you." Pepe added that the house is a respectable place with high health standards because "it is unionized and collectivized." He promised to take me with him next time.

We had been looking for the new brigade *estado mayor* and finally located it a couple of miles outside town in a big, elegant, well-cared-for white house, formerly the residence of one of the wealthiest landowners this side of Madrid. Here we ate *lentejas* (lentils) mush, and the coffee was better than we had ever had at the front. Our bellies full, we walked back to town to share the warmth of the locals. When we failed to find *posada* (lodging) in town, we slept with the British, using Steve Daduk's (commander of Lincoln's Company Two) blankets, which we found still neatly packed in the truck.

30 April

Friday. The frantic search for the political commissar's truck that disappeared with our equipment and supplies while I was asleep, took me back to the new brigade estado mayor *outside Alcalá, with no success.*

When I started my walk back to town, I was joined by a dog that kept pace with me as if we had been lifelong friends. A truck stopped, offering me a lift into town, and I asked that the dog be included. The driver said emphatically, "No dogs." When I boarded the truck, my new friend whined, stretched his body on the side of the road, and put his head with large watery eyes between his paws.

All Americans from Jarama are now here. We are quartered in one of Alcalá's largest churches, of which there are many, though a number of them have already been gutted by bombs. We consider this offering of the least bombed-out church for our accommodations, with good clean straw for bedding, another proof of the generosity of the local people. Despite the punishment of being bombed by air almost every other night, the morale of the people remains high. However, rubble has not been cleared, a reminder of what aircraft can do, even to churches.

Bombed-out homes are a pitiful sight. Rows upon rows of what were once houses are now one big pile of mortar and stone. Who knows how many are buried beneath this mess, along with their possessions! There is not a house in town whose windows have not been shattered by the aerial blasts. Countless women and children, and men who appear to be grandfathers, now live in underground tunnels, and hundreds more walk every night to holes in the hills outside town for rest and sleep.

Fred Lutz, Dan Kramen, who is a photographer, and I locate the political commissar's truck parked near the church, which is now our barracks. Al, the driver, said he was ordered by a brigade officer, some Frenchman, he says, to go back to Jarama to pick up additional equipment we had forgotten. We were too happy to see the truck to pursue our suspicions further.

The three of us continued our stroll down the main street, our minds at ease, then leisurely through the side streets and to the outskirts. This small but old city must have been a beautiful and prosperous town before the war, and a corker for its citizens to be receiving so much fascist vengeance from the air. Everywhere you are greeted with "*salud, salud,*" *smiles, and offers at every turn to do something for you. We decline, of course, but are pleased with all this attention. We feel honored, but people talk and act as if they are the ones who are honored.*

We asked a teenage girl who was limping badly what happened. She said she was hit by falling stones from a bombed building because she didn't run fast enough to the refugio.

The local population turned out by the thousands to greet the 15th International Brigade in our parade through town; we were led by a loud-playing Spanish band. Camaraderie, gaiety, wine and kisses and cheers, Viva las Brigades Internacionales, Viva la Republica, No Pasarán, *were the order of the day. Large banners with slogans and greetings to the Internationals were stretched high across streets and tied to buildings. A few of our guys were missing from the parade; they were drunk.*

* * * *

I lend Vic (the driver of the brigade quartermaster truck) 50 pesetas. He lost his money in a stupid poker game.

* * * *

Jean Barthel, the French commissar, went to the International Brigade Headquarters in Madrid to discuss the publication of the book we're readying. I am to go mañana *and join him there.*

Moving to Alcalá, I packed the Daily Mañana and related materials, planning to continue, wherever feasible, what to us was an important service. Brigade headquarters, however, had other ideas. Barthel asked me to pack up for a trip to Madrid and to report to the International Brigade Political Commissariat, where I was to be assigned to write the story of the Lincoln Battalion's first months in Spain.

The task picked for me could not have been more exciting or more challenging. Though I had studied for six months at the Charles Morris Price School of Journalism in Philadelphia, I mildy protested that I was not an experienced or professional writer, that there were others more qualified than I to do this job. It didn't matter. One of the political commissars said, "Neither were you an experienced soldier before you came to Spain, so take off."

Frankly, I hated to leave my comrades and that cordial antifascist town, but I accepted the job, for I did want badly to visit Madrid, the city of No pasarán, the city that already was a legend in the first months of the war, the city that had checked Hitler's and Mussolini's professional troops and Franco's African mercenaries.

When in October 1936 Franco's Moors and legionnaires hammered their way into the outskirts of Madrid, into University City, and into sections of working-class districts, La Pasionaria rallied the Madrileños with the cry No pasarán, "They shall not pass," perhaps even demanding "Don't let them pass." Citizens and militia responded by rushing to the suburbs and erecting barricades in the face of the advancing enemy troops. Molotov cocktails suddenly appeared and stopped fascist tanks from entering the center of the city.

In the first week of November, International Volunteers arrived and, marching *through the streets of Madrid armed with rifles and other weapons, electrified the citizenry. The people of Madrid, buoyed by this display of international solidarity and chanting, "No pasarán," stopped the fascist breakthrough. Madrid's citizens, the militia, and the International Volunteers paid a frighteningly high price in lives lost, but Franco, who had boasted that he would soon be having coffee in Madrid's main square, la Puerta del Sol, never got there that year. And for two more years fascist armies did not pass.*

May Day

Everybody said so. Alcalá de Henares never had a May Day like this.

Thousands of soldiers paraded through the streets, International Volunteers as well as Spaniards, militia in their monos *with rifles or side arms, many young women in unorthodox uniforms, including* monos, *proudly handling their weapons as expertly as the men beside them, and children dancing around everyone, singing their praises and seeking attention like children everywhere.*

Americans, British, and Irish, the tallest, singled out to lead the main parade, stood out prominently in orderliness and discipline as they marched smartly with rifles at shoulder arms down the avenue to the Plaza de San Diego amid wild cheering and clamor of the townspeople. All businesses were closed, including the wine stores.

The infantry was in the lead; next came the Tom Mooney Machine Gun Company, followed by a company of Spaniards; then the first aid crews, ambulances, and the medical corps, which received special and prolonged applause.

At the very head of the parade, almost apart from it, a large wreath with a red ribbon streaming from the bottom of it was carried slowly and solemnly by an American and a Spaniard. The wreath was huge enough to seem to cover both men. It was hooked between two rifles in vertical position; horizontal cross sticks, one above and one below, provided sturdy support. Across the top was a board half a meter wide decorated in colors of the government flag—red, yellow, and purple—with the inscription En Memoria.

By groups the Machine Gun Company fired five of their guns that had served faithfully at the front. The first gun was decorated with colors of the government flag, the second was done up with wreaths and colorful flowers, the third had a sign jammed into its muzzle which blazed the popular slogan: PASAREMOS *(We shall pass).*

Neither for the Lincoln Battalion nor for the Fifteenth International Brigade was this the end of their role in Spain. It was another beginning. For another year and a half, the men and women of the Lincoln Brigade were to continue battling shoulder to shoulder with the Spanish people and with additional thousands of volunteers from all over the world in a glorious though bitter crusade to head off the holocaust being prepared by nazism and fascism and visible on the horizon for all those who wanted to see.

Among my notes of the day I found the following:

Today was like May Day back home: parades, speeches, band music, drinking, and dancing. George Aitken, British Battalion commissar, in a short but eloquent speech to an attentive and respectful audience, paid tribute to our fallen. I took written notes and under a clear sky snapped several rolls of pictures. Then without warning, almost immediately after the parades and ceremonies were over, the clouds darkened, thundered, and burst into a heavy downpour.

When the hour came for me to leave for Madrid, I found it difficult to get transportation, but I hopped an *intendencia* (supply) truck, whose driver was kind enough to drop me off at the Puerta del Sol. Destination: Hotel Florida.

Departing aboard the *S. S. Champlain*, 1937.

This is the only known photo of Johnny Parks, an American Indian, who disappeared with others when his truck accidentally drove into enemy territory.

Rodolfo de Armas in Barcelona, January 1937. A Cuban exile, he was killed only a month later leading a charge on fascist positions.

Fraternizing with a peasant family at our training base, Villanueva de la Jara, February 1937.

Frank Ryan (left) and "Shorty" Robinson, October 1937.

Lieutenant Colonel Vladimir Copic, 15th International Brigade Commander.

Robert Merriman, October 1937.

Robert Raven, blind and on crutches as a result of the events of 14 March 1937, visits with Norman Duncan, also wounded.

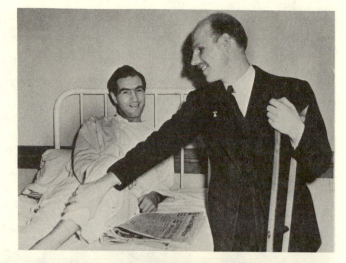

Robert Merriman, Umberto Galleani, Ernest Hemingway, and others.

Lou Secundy (left) and Abe Lewis.

Alvah Bessie (left)
and Ed Rolfe,
Corbera, August
1938.

Milton Wolff,
April 1938.

The editors of the *Volunteer for Liberty* at brigade headquarters in Barcelona, October 1938. From left: Seweryn Ajzner (Polish), Mario Fernandez (Spanish), the author, and Giacomo Callandrone (Italian).

Ed Bender, November 1937.

Deyo Jacobs, the brigade's prolific artist. He was later killed in action.

The author (on mule) and comrades in Jarama, May 1937. Also pictured are Cuba Hermosa (with helmet), Louie Taub (with beard), and Harvey Hall (carrying binoculars).

Dave Gordon, December 1937.

The author and Lieutenant Fred Lutz look over the latest issue of the *Volunteer for Liberty*.

Paul L. Robeson, speaking to a gathering of the Veterans of the Abraham Lincoln Brigade, 21 September 1946. Robeson was a supporter of the Spanish Republic and had visited brigade battle fronts.

The Eighteenth of July, 1936–1937

Part Three

MADRID

May—November 1937

TEN

The City of No Pasarán

At the Hotel Florida in Madrid, where my friends of the Lincoln Battalion recommended I stay, I was not doing too well in my still faltering Spanish in conversation with the desk clerk when a tall, heavily built, mustachioed man listening to us quickly translated and got me accommodations. I thanked him. He stuck out his hand and introduced himself: "My name is Ernest Hemingway." Though I knew he was in Spain, I was startled, but delighted, by the unexpected encounter. He invited me up to his room for a drink, then supper. With a three-month scrubby beard and feeling dirty from the hot and dusty trip to Madrid on the back of a Ford pickup, I wanted first to shave, shower, and buy some clean clothes. The tight-fitting short khaki jacket I was wearing I had retrieved from a dead comrade during one of the battles in the Jarama mountains. It had a bullet hole in the sleeve, and it was still bloodstained. Hemingway suggested, however, that I should first have my picture taken in my present condition. He accompanied me to a photo studio he knew, and now I'm glad I followed his suggestion, for the picture is a vivid reminder to me of the Spanish Civil War, May 1937.

Neither Hemingway nor the desk clerk warned me that my hotel room faced the direct path of enemy artillery. The Madrid front, where the fascist columns were stopped dead in their tracks, was not far off. That night I slept well—that is, I thought I had slept well. The room was spacious, the bed soft, the sheets clean, the pillows downy. This unexpected comfort, however, was too much too soon, for when

I woke up in the morning, I found myself stretched out on the floor alongside the bed. My trousers were wrapped around my shoes and nestled under my head for a pillow, and the blanket from the bed was tangled about my feet. When I came down for breakfast, Hemingway and others were astounded that I had slept in my room all night. Most of the hotel residents, they said, spent a sleepless night in the *refugio* in the basement because of severe artillery barrages. One of the shells, a dud, hit close to my room, one floor below. I heard nothing. I was a sound sleeper then as I am today. Had the shell exploded, someone quipped, it might have been the last bit of noise I was ever to hear.

Hemingway hosted me generously—as he did later other American and Canadian volunteers—and introduced me to a number of English-speaking newspaper men and women then in Spain. Their names escape me after so many years. I do remember Martha Gellhorn because we had dinner together on several occasions in the basement of a fancy hotel—I believe it was the Gran Via. Though I found Gellhorn to be engaging, striking in looks and dress, I was shy and reserved in her presence, but I liked her. Besides, she wrote sympathetically of the Spanish cause and of American volunteers for *Collier's* magazine. On the other hand, with blustery Hemingway I was always comfortable. He was too much one of us for me to feel otherwise. During my occasional associations with them, it became obvious to me and to others that Gellhorn and Hemingway were intimate; later they married, following a divorce from his wife.

When I told Hemingway that my mission in Madrid was to complete my *Story of the Lincoln Battalion*, an account of our first months in Spain, January to May 1937, and to continue, with others, the work on *The Book of the XV Brigade*, he volunteered to look over what I had written and make suggestions. I appreciated the offer. In turn, he got to look at a lot of material that few journalists knew existed. He let me use his typewriter as often as I needed it and wouldn't let others disturb me while I was working.

At times, as he read my material, he'd say, "Not bad, but you need more detail." If I had had a keener sense of history, I might have recorded these discussions better. I do remember his insistence on details about each incident or person. "How tall? How old? The color of hair, eyes? Was he able to speak after being struck by bullets? How did the tank get on fire? Who were his friends? What were his politics? How well did you know him? Was he liked? Time of day?" On and on. Superfluous, I thought, but I provided details anyway. Hence, I was able to give a better description of the Cuban leader, Rodolfo de Armas, in his last moments, and that of Paul Niepold, and of others.

It was easy for some of our guys to be buddy-buddy with him because he had genuine affection for the American volunteers and the International Brigades, and a continuing love affair with the Spanish people. Our friendly but casual relationship was to last until the very day Barcelona fell. He drove north with Herb Matthews of the *New York Times* to the French frontier while I sweated out several more weeks in Catalonia, moving north from town to town before reaching the same border.

The next day, 2 May, I spent the morning with Josephine Herbst, correspondent for the North American Newspaper Alliance and free-lance writer, whom I had met and had spent time with at Jarama during one of her visits to the front. Nearly everybody called her Josie. We went over some material for the Brigade book, sorting out the best stuff, editing, and discussing the merits of each story.

When she started suggesting more details, I told her she was beginning to sound like Hemingway. She laughed. Hemingway permitted me to use his typewriter for part of the morning and afternoon, then Herbst and I had dinner together at a place where we ran into Lincoln Battalion's Dr. Bill Pike, Herb Klein of the *New Masses* (a Communist party monthly magazine, and published in New York City), and Melvin Anderson, from my rifle company, who was traveling with several men of the British Battalion. They got a bang out of my story about sleeping last night in a room facing enemy artillery and of the artillery dud that almost went to bed with me.

Back at the hotel after dinner, together with Herbst and Hemingway, I went over the pile of articles, stories, and anecdotes I had brought with me. But at ten o'clock, tired from my first full day in Madrid, I excused myself and left for bed.

I tried probing my memory for more detailed information of encounters with Ernest Hemingway, but I have not yet found what I was looking for. I found instead, frustration, a feeling that perhaps my memory fluids were drying up.

True, images of Hemingway and of his aristocratic-looking lady friend, Martha Gellhorn, of hard-working free-lance journalist, Josephine Herbst, better known to her friends as Josie, and of others, have stayed with me over these many years. But it is the substance of conversations and of discussions and descriptions of incidents and stories I had brought back with me from the battle fronts that have so cruelly evaporated into mist.

And I must admit that when I come across a cryptic phrase in my diary, such as, "had a conversation with Ernest today," I want to shout out loud, "Idiot, that's an empty phrase. What the hell did you talk about?" If this sounds flippant, I don't mean it to be.

I do remember one story I told Hemingway and others in his hotel room, an incident I have never forgotten. It had to do with Josie's visit to the Lincoln Battalion battle lines on a warm day in April, 1937. I escorted her through the trenches and introduced her to our guys. I told her that during lulls some were learning Spanish from the recruits, and in turn they were tutoring the Spaniards in English, a fair exchange. She agreed. She greeted each volunteer pleasantly, which was good for our men and, as she reported in a story she later wrote, gratifying for her.

Her lanky body twisted through a narrow part of an unfinished trench when, unexpectedly, she faced a Spanish recruit stripped to the waist, cleaning his rifle. Though surprised, he gave Josie an amiable grin, and a big hello in English. Pleased, Josie addressed the lad in her accented Spanish. "I understand you are learning to speak English from the Americans." The young man, with disassembled rifle in his hands, jumped up and proudly said, "Si, si, fucky, fucky!"

From Elinor Langer of Chicago, who was researching the possibility of writing a biography of Josephine Herbst, I received in February 1976 a verbatim copy of the following entry she said she found in the Herbst journal:

Hugh Bonar & Charles Connelly (poet) 26 years univ. grad. killed Feb. 27. Body found very close to fascist lines. Body stinking after 10 days. Brought in. John Tisa one of the bearers. Face fresh and naive looking.

Langer adds the following: "Your name appears in the corner of the page previous to that, but with nothing specific. Her overall heading for the page and the next is Notes on the International. I guess it is not much, but it is something."

There appears to be a typographical error in one of the names. It should have read Charles Donnelly. Five years before the discovery of Josie's journal, I had received a letter from Joseph G. Donnelly, dated 6 April 1971, 2 Longford Terrace, Monkstown, Co. Dublin, Ireland, requesting information about his brother, since he was writing a biography of Charles:

> I understand that his personal papers and effects were given to the Battalion Commander, Robert Merriman.
> These would have included some correspondence with my brother Tom, a letter from his girl friend, Cora Hughes, together with a letter of commendation from the late Sir Basil Liddell Hart regarding a thesis on military strategy which my brother had submitted to him. Most important of all, however, would be his own observations and writings, including some poems. I am hoping some of these may have been preserved by you and are amongst your papers.

I was saddened to inform Joseph that there was nothing in my possession that referred to his brother.

3 May
As I opened my bedroom door to go to the hotel's coffee shop, I literally bumped into Norman Duncan, a Lincoln machine gunner on leave, who looked silly wearing a bright red kerchief around his neck like an overgrown boy scout. I muffled a laugh. With him were P. Stanley and Tony De Maio. Though I had just seen them a couple of days ago, we had a grand reunion over hotel coffee, cheese, and canned sardines they had brought with them. They accompanied me to the Madrid International Brigade Headquarters, where I took notes on their experiences and typed out a story, which they checked out and, after some corrections, okayed. It was good being with them.
We laughed at how our tempers at the front sometimes get the best of us. We curse, ridicule, shout, argue, blame others unjustly, and call each other harsh names. Because our comradeship and the cause that brought us together are deeper than the tongue-lashings we give each other, these unpleasantries are soon forgiven and forgotten.

4 May
Am now quartered at I.B. Headquarters, 63 Calle Velazquez, where I am to live and work until the book is completed—which must be done before the batallion goes back to the front.
I took time out to shop in the Puerta del Sol, to have more pictures taken before I shave off my two-and-a-half-month beard, and to visit with J. Herbst, who was not in when I called.
Marion Greenspan, New York Daily Worker *reporter, came to spend an hour, and we talked about the material I have on hand. He wanted copies, but I told him they were not yet ready and as soon as I had* The Story of the Abraham Lincoln Battalion *in shape, I would give him a copy to send back home. George Brodsky, a New Yorker, who had been Albacete base commissar and was now in my rifle company, dropped in. He said he had heard where I was and wanted to visit. We plan to explore Madrid while he is on leave.*
Ralph Bates, English author, a war commissariat representative attached to the

15th Brigade staff, arranged for an office worker to teach me Spanish; I'm to teach her English. Our first lesson was from 10:30 P.M. to midnight, by candlelight.

5 May

After working all day, having started before breakfast, I was glad to accept Greenspan's invitation to see a Soviet film. We found J. Herbst there and afterward walked her to her hotel. As we made our way through the crowded streets and the thronged Puerta del Sol, we agreed that Madrid does not look like a war city. Except for difficulty in finding anything to buy, for the stores are bare, life seems strangely normal.

Greenspan and Herbst know their way around. They took me to a restaurant and had no trouble getting a full-course meal, starting with macaroni soup, followed by steak, vegetables, bread, and wine. [Milt Wolff has recently told me that this restaurant was a black market center. I'm glad I didn't know it at the time. I might not have enjoyed that dinner.]

The building occupied by the International Brigade headquarters at 63 Calle Velazquez, to which I was assigned for my temporary work, was orginally the palace of enemies of the Republic. Its concrete and marbelized facade was not impressive and deceptively hid the ornate interior. The ceilings were high, the rooms large, the mirrored doors wide. Shuttered full-length doors opened onto a narrow balcony overlooking the tree-lined street. Windows were numerous and oversized, making artificial lighting unnecessary during the day.

On the first floor there was a well-stocked library and adjoining it a social hall that appeared to have been used frequently before the war. The original elegant furniture, tables and chairs, many with hand-carvings adorning their legs, small and large famous paintings, sculptures, wall hangings, and decorations, which seemed to belong in El Prado or some other art museum, remained in place just as the previous tenants had left them, except that a magnificent grand piano had been pushed into a corner to make room for the new occupants' needs. Hand-painted, rich-looking vases, from knee-high to shoulder height, seemed to be everywhere; one or two were used as door stops. Amid this tasteful lavishness, matching heavy plush rugs stretched across the floor, inviting care and clean boots. Every floor had colorfully tiled, spacious bathrooms with big tubs and enclosed showers, and all the toilets worked.

The building combined modernity and antiquity, the past and the present. Modern home conveniences, stainless steel, and marble kitchen with well stocked pantries, spacious bedrooms, and living and dining rooms confronted you throughout the building. So did hundreds of years of Spanish history and the awesome atmosphere of past royal, landlord, military, and religious power.

The contrast between such opulence and the hovels and homes and buildings I had seen in small towns and in the countryside dashed any hopes that the elements who possessed all this wealth would stop fighting so brutally to retain it.

Extensive land reforms, as well as reforms affecting education, housing, industry, the military, the relation of church and state, and the political processes—planned and already initiated by the new Republic to correct the disparity between the haves and the have nots—were interrupted by the generals' rebellion and the civil war. Yet despite this violent interruption, many reforms, except those in housing, picked up speed and continued throughout the war, earning the government the fierce loyalty of the average citizen and soldier.

6 May

Am still in Madrid. Weather is dry and mild. Work is taking longer than I had expected. Spent some time writing letters. The longest one was to John Green, old-time socialist and head of Local 1, Industrial Union of Marine and Shipbuilding Workers of America, Camden, New Jersey. I told him if he wanted to he could print the letter in the union newspaper because I wanted all Camden to know what was at stake here.

I ran into Irving Goff, who is now a driver for Brigade. We walked downtown looking for a place where I could buy a camera. We found none, but the walk was pleasant. We had a couple of beers; then he headed for Morata and I headed back for more typing. [Irving had dragged a wounded buddy and a dead man from no man's land during the night of 27 February. By serving on the frontline details together, we got to know each other well and became friends. In World War II, Irving was assigned by Donovan's OSS (Intelligence) to be liaison between the Allied forces and the Italian partisans led by Luigi Gallo (now Longo). When I was in Italy in 1950, I visited with Gallo during a dinner reunion of mutual friends, and he gave me a medal to bring back to the United States for Goff. Irving, and especially his son, treasured that medal.] Work is thinning out and I'm beginning to get bored with this place. If it wasn't for Celia, who is teaching me Spanish in exchange for English lessons, I would take a powder and go back to battalion. She is proficient in French and promises to teach me that language after I've mastered Spanish.

No bread at any of the meals today, but we did have a rationed supper of macaroni soup, meat, and wine.

I get a message that Steve Nelson has arrived, sent by the political bureau of the U.S. Community party.

7 May

Today, like yesterday, pleasantly mild. Oliver Green returns from Alcalá de Henares with more material for the book. We do more writing, editing, and typing, and I'm to get more biographies of the officers of the Lincoln Battalion.

Jock Cunningham, captain of the British volunteers, carefully reads and comments favorably on stuff Green brought in.

O.A. Succar, volunteer from Peru, visited headquarters to introduce himself and admired Celia, my Spanish tutor.

8 May

It is again sunny, but breakfast coffee was cloudy. I am told that it was made of roasted barley but it tasted like one-week-old brown, soapy dishwater.

The printer who's putting the book together told me it will be done in 8- and 10-point type.

Walking back from the printer, I stopped for a beer and handed the bartender a 50-peseta note, which he handed back to me saying he had no change. I pulled out other change, but he refused. I learned these bartenders often do that with the Internationals, even offering them a drink on the house. I stopped at another store and bought a bottle of ink and three pencils.

Mailed out my poem "Famous Flyers" to New Masses.

Found a picture of King Alfonso in the wastepaper basket, thrown out by one of the Spanish secretaries, who said she didn't want to see his face around here. These headquarters formerly belonged to royalty, she explained.

Celia told me that the University of Alcalá was founded by Cardinal Cisneros in 1508.

For my information: *Movies have one daily showing, 5:30 to 7:30. Then Madrid is blacked out and it is best to stay off the streets.*

For supper: *Watery lentil soup (I can count the* lentejas*), a sliver of tuna fish, a glass of wine, a slice of bread with cheese. Though we leave the table hungry, no one complains.*

Another language lesson till late into the night.

9 May

While I was at the Hotel Florida to pick up an article written by Josephine Herbst on Pablo de la Torriente Brau, Cuban writer, poet, internationalist, and friend of Hemingway's, who fell at Majadahonda, near Madrid, on 19 December 1936, I got an emergency phone call ordering me back to the 15th Brigade Headquarters immediately. When I got there, I found Ralph Bates, Bill Lawrence, Harry Haywood, and several political commissars in a session with James W. Ford [chairman of the U.S. Communist party], who had just arrived from the States. Our job was to help him plan the speech he is to make over the Spanish radio. When there was common agreement on the content, I typed it.

When I got back to HQ just before supper, Barthel, the French political commisar, Etienne Sacco, the Frenchman working on the French edition of the book, and two Italians invited me for a walk to a cafe for a drink. It turned out to be a book-planning session.

At the dinner table Celia read my palm: "You have a big heart, will live long, have a promising future, will marry soon, will be happy, have one child, and get disillusioned once in a while." I liked the part about living long.

Since Oliver Green can't type, I worked late into the night typing twenty-seven pages for his part of the book dealing with the British Battalion.

10 May

Monday. Sunny, pleasant and mild. I was about to go out to buy some clothes but did not because I had to retype J.W. Ford's radio speech after he had made a number of changes.

Gave Celia an English lesson but had no time for my Spanish lesson because I had to do more typing for Green's part of the book.

When it came time to go to sleep, I found an Englishman in my bed, stone drunk. I pushed him over and got into bed anyway. He snored, he rolled, he grunted, and when he vomited, I grabbed my pillow and blanket and went one flight below to sleep on the office floor the rest of the night.

11 May

The weather today was like yesterday. For the past eleven days that I've been in this beautiful city, I have not seen a dark cloud—except for this morning's enemy artillery bombardment. Shell after shell poured in, arriving so fast and exploding so rapidly that they sounded from where we were like a series of loud firecrackers set off accidentally.

Going back to the front to collect biographies of the officers and political commissars, I rode on the back of a large camion *(truck) carrying seven members of the British Battalion, with three in the cab. The dirt roads were dry and dusty, and by the time we got to brigade there were no parts of our bodies, mouths, ears, or clothes that were not covered with sand and dust.*

The trip, however, was profitable. Besides collecting the biographies I came for, visiting with comrades was refreshing. Morale is high. Moreover, the Brownie box camera I had brought from the U.S. and lost during the battles of February had been found and the film developed by someone at headquarters—to discover, I suppose, if the camera belonged to an enemy spy in our ranks. When the pictures proved the camera to be mine, someone thoughtfully put it away for safekeeping for the day I returned.

I slept on straw at the cookhouse after hours of catching up on gossip.

Dr. Pike announced a campaign to fight diarrhea. There will be a load of clean sand to be used to scrub the dishes and utensils, followed by rinsing with water treated with a disinfectant. Latrines will also be covered with sand. Lectures by him and his assistants on health care will be instituted immediately. Pike means business.

After returning to Madrid in our battalion's small Ford camion, *I stopped downtown to buy some underwear, socks, and a shirt; I have a lot of work to catch up on for the printer before I can continue writing.*

14 May

Yesterday, I returned to the front to gather further material for the Volunteer *and for the proposed Brigade Book. Also brought back American candy caramels. Teresa's birthday (teenage daughter of a member of our Spanish staff); she'll like them. Heavy bombing of the city in the early morning. Got proofs from the printer.*

Attended sad funeral this morning and am downcast. The bodies of two Bulgarian officers, killed on the Gran Via by an enemy shell, were placed alongside each other in crude pine boxes at Madrid International Brigade Headquarters. On the wall behind the corpses was a six-foot poster picture of Azaña, the president of Spain. Antifascist posters and slogans decorated the walls around the room. Standing at the heads of the dead volunteers was a group of imposing, but somber, Bulgarian officers and four Bulgarian guards on each side of the boxes. At the feet of these dead soldiers was a group of civilians, obviously personal friends. I stood among them. I was stunned, for it was just a few days ago I had met, talked, and had dinner with these same officers. One of them spoke fluent English. Now they're being buried.

The highest ranking of the Bulgarians made a brief speech, which was translated into Spanish. He spoke simply and slowly in a hushed, broken voice, tracing the dead men's lifelong struggle against fascism in their homeland and now in Spain. He did not waste many words of praise, but I was touched with his expressions of warmth and affection. Flowers of various hues arrived from all parts of Republican Spain and were placed at the foot of the pine caskets. The Spanish flag was wrapped around the bodies, and I wondered what the Bulgarian flag looked like and why it wasn't displayed.

When the speeches ended, twelve men, six to each nailed box, carried the bodies in reverential procession. The pallbearers were led by uniformed guards with rifles, the shining bayonets at the fix, pointed to the ground, moving slowly through the building's iron gates to the street in the direction of two black clean limousines, while the crowd saluted with raised clenched fists. Twenty guards paraded in front of the cars and, as these limousines cut a path for their exit, the crowds shouted, "Viva los Bulgaros! Viva las Brigadas Internacionales!" I could not help comparing, though not bitterly or in envy, our fallen at Jarama, where we had no time for such honorable burials. Our dead were too often stacked in one big pile and burned.

15 May

Smoked cigarette in the afternoon, another at night. Good thing I'm only an occasional smoker, for I would not want to get like some of the others—pissed off and cranky when cigarettes are hard to come by.

Party going on in hallway downstairs. It's a celebration of the unexpected return of a Spanish militiaman who was seen captured and was presumed dead. They tell me that while he was being interrogated by fascist officers in a small room of the town's church an emergency developed for them and the fascists abruptly left him (Enrique) with an armed guard. As the guard, with his back to the prisoner for a second, closed the door after the departing officers, Enrique seized him in a stranglehold and knocked him unconscious. He changed into the upper part of the guard's uniform—most importantly, the pointed cap with the falangist emblem and tassel. Since he knew the town and countryside intimately, he found his way back to the government side without too much difficulty. His main fear was of being shot accidentally by his own comrades.

We see colorful posters with colorful slogans everywhere: inside private buildings, schools, hospitals, offices, plastered on the outside of government buildings, banks, retaining walls, restaurants, and erected on billboards in the squares:

No Pasaran!
Madrid Shall Be the Tomb of Fascism!
I'd Rather Die on My Feet than Live on My Knees!

17 May

Ralph Bates said to me, after reading The Story of the Abraham Lincoln Battalion: *"John, I could not have done better myself." Ralph, a skilled writer with several books under his belt, is not in the habit of overstating his opinions. Naturally, I was pleased.*

In the evening I had dinner with Bob Minor, a commanding, tall Texan, formerly a newspaper and magazine cartoonist and now a member of the Central Committee of the U.S. Communist party. But he is hard of hearing, and a conversation with him is indeed trying. In the restaurant I had to speak so loud that all eyes and heads around us seemed to be glued in our direction. At his request I gave him a typed copy of The Story of the Abraham Lincoln Battalion *to take back home, while advising him that I had already given a copy to Greenspan of the* Daily Worker. *I also gave Bob a five-page, double-spaced story about how Paul Niepold was killed, to be delivered to the* New Masses.

By the end of the day I was feeling flushed and hot, not feeling well at all, which depressed me.

Today, more than forty-five years after my diary comments about Minor's hearing affliction, I too have developed serious nerve-loss hearing problems in both ears, and I am sure not a day passes that a member of my family, a friend, or an acquaintance does not declare aloud, or at least think, how carrying on a conversation with John is "indeed trying."

*   *   *   *

It rained hard, on 18 May, a welcome relief from the steady oppressive heat of the previous two weeks. From Madrileños I learned that the real blast of a Castilian summer was yet to come, so I decided it was a good day to rush off a letter to my brother. Later I found out that for some inexplicable reason the day of the month and a couple of innocuous sentences of the letter were blacked out by censors. Neither in Spain then nor later during the Second World War when I served in the U.S. Armed Forces could I fathom the incongruous and often autocratic mentality of a censor and his seemingly limitless and unquestioned power to ink out at his sole discretion what was frequently public knowledge the world over.

Anyway, in my previous letter I had told Dominic that I was now assigned to the propaganda section of the International Brigades in Madrid and that I was working directly under Ralph Bates, the British writer and author of several books. Now I wrote:

> *. . . he spent many years in Spain and knows it well; he speaks Spanish fluently and writes beautifully and writes always in longhand and in small script. Such style and talent, I wish I had it. He either does not know how to type or doesn't like to. He says he can think better when he writes with a pen. So he shoves these handwritten sheets under my nose and asks me to type them for him. When I do so, I feel as if I'm typing poetry. For a while I found his handwriting hard to decipher, but in time I got the hang of his peculiarities. Sometimes it is hard for me to understand his English. He's Welsh, I believe. Every time I ask him to repeat what he's saying, he gets mad, as if I'm the one who speaks with an accent. I once made the mistake of telling him that I didn't think he spoke clearly and that he chops his words. But I learn so much from him—about writing and about the politics of Spain. He seems to be grooming me for work with him on the* Volunteer for Liberty, *our frontline newspaper. It's more of a tabloid; I'll send them to you as they appear. Ralph said, listen to this, "For a young chap you've got a quick knack for writing." He commented favorably on my* Story of the Lincoln Battalion, *which should be in the States by now for publication. Of course, he's exaggerating and is just trying to be encouraging. . . . Bates insists I learn to speak and write Spanish better, because, he said, my Spanish accent is awful.*
>
> *. . . Bates must have known what he was doing to have picked such a charm to teach me Spanish. She looks to be about only 17, but acts a lot older. She is small-bodied and elastic. Often I wonder if she gets enough to eat. Even on a hot day her hands are like icicles. She has brown eyes, black straight hair, bobbed in front and cut down just below the ears to longer in the back, the kind of haircut you and I have often given American girls. Occasionally she wears horn-rimmed glasses, which seems to blend with her personality. The red tint on her cheeks is natural, which accentuates her soft, pale face and small chin. She walks rapidly with her arms raised and out from the elbows as if she's about to push somebody; her body seems so fragile that I expect*

*any one of her limbs to just drop off. She smiles readily with a clean set of even teeth. I
love being her student and teacher. But you can't make headway with Spanish girls
unless you promise to marry. She's strictly on the up and up—no false modesty—and
talks about men, women, and sex in the politics of the revolution. When one guy chided
her with being cold, she flushed and said she is not cold with anyone she loves. She says
she's in love with a brigade political commissar, who is right now in Asturias
(northwest Spain). She says she finds it hard to like the Germans or the English
because they seem to her to be aloof and snobbish. Oh yeh, she has a small wart below
her nose which she thinks objectionable and is trying to remove it with nitrate. She is
brilliant and serious about her work—sometimes, I think, too serious. A pronounced
Communist, she belongs to a Socialist-Communist youth organization, which she wants
me to join.*

*As you can see, I'm intrigued with the headquarters, the many important people
who come through it, and with the work I'm doing. Please save everything I send
you—posters, books, pamphlets, letters, cards, etc.*

My work desk at the Madrid International Brigade Headquarters was on the
second floor by a floor-to-ceiling window, which opened out like doors onto a
balcony. From this vantage point I could scan the neighborhood, and sometimes,
while daydreaming or during moments of leisure, I would doodle with the keys of the
typewriter and then put the results away. From yellowed, mice-eaten notes I decipher
the following:

A DAY IN MAY

People hang from the back of a trolley. A newsboy hops off the moving car
while another, hawking his newspapers, jumps on. The old, prewar commercial
advertisements are still on the outside of the streetcars. A big sign promises "the
height of fashion" for *señoras* and *caballeros* at a *sasteria* (tailor shop) on Calle
Mayor.

Across the tree-lined street with a grassy center promenade, some women
and children are sitting on stools and chairs on their balcony, while others are
leaning over railings and looking down on the hustle and bustle of people below.
Laundry is stretched across makeshift clotheslines marring the beauty of the
neighborhood. Many of the sons and husbands and relatives of these women are
at the front or participating in the defense of Madrid in one way or another.
Some will never come back and will be buried by their neighbors and friends.
These thoughts and fears must be crossing their minds, too. But they are patient
people. They fervently believe La Pasionaria's cry: "It is better to die on your
feet than to live on your knees."

People are coming from work; shoppers are returning from the Puerta del
Sol with packages under their arms.

Siesta is an old custom, almost a ritual, here. They open their *tiendas* (stores)
in the morning at nine, and close them at one o'clock, then reopen at four or five
for a couple of hours more. True, there's not too much to sell or buy, but the
routine of better days continues.

There is a stream of automobiles passing by, some driven by civilians; most are military cars and many are *camiones*. There goes the British Embassy car. It stops down the street in front of a large building where the British and American flags are rippling in the warm breeze.

A little red mule cart, with four smiling children standing in it, is leisurely passing by; the old man is holding the reins of one of the donkeys while walking beside it. I wave to him and he responds with the clenched fist.

The street lamps along the promenade are not being used and haven't been used since fascist planes started to bomb the city. At night the city is ink dark. If one doesn't know one's way around, it is better to stay inside. I've heard of guys getting shot at, either on purpose or accidentally, especially if they didn't know the password.

21 May

I awake at daybreak and stepped onto the second-floor balcony and into a cool, invigorating breeze, feeling alive and lucky to be in this great city with its wonderful inspiring people in this momentous war for dignity and freedom. The dawn was clear, the sky crystal blue, and the air crisp. The sun was not yet hot, but it unfolded like a warm blanket. I shed my flannel uniform for light khaki. What a morning! What a red sky! No sound of artillery. No shells exploding. I wondered if artillery would ever hit this magnificant building, which not too many months ago, I'm told, belonged to those related to royalty, hostile to the Republic, and counterrevolutionary to boot. I reflected on what happened the other day when an enemy shell went through a window of a building in the Puerta del Sol and exploded, killing a group of people taking cover from a bombardment. It's funny but one loses fear of shells after a while, even when he realizes one may explode in his lap anywhere and at the least expected time.

Many say Spaniards are foolishly fatalistic. Outsiders are often amazed at how the peasant nonchalantly goes about performing his chores, working the fields, walking the donkeys, saluting with clenched fists while tanks rumble past, artillery thunders, and enemy planes roar overhead, some dropping their bombs indiscriminately, while troops fire their weapons and are being fired upon. Is it fatalism? Or is it scorn and defiance of the fascist? Or is it refusal to accept the fact that anything can really happen to them?

An event I saw the other day is an example of fatalism, fearlessness, or bravado; I don't know which, and I can't understand it. When a shell did such damage in the Puerta del Sol, instead of scurrying for cover, as I and many do, with the expectation of more shelling, Madrileños simply gathered around the shelled building scrutinizing the activities of cleanup and salvaging gangs, just as crowds at home might push and shove to the scene of a huge fire. The difference here is that this same group could be blown to bits in the next few minutes. This seems not to faze them; they continue walking, conversing, and shopping in and out of stores, which remain open, in utter disregard of danger.

23 May

Today I finally wrote a letter to Catherine Gabrielson in England. She came across with us on the SS Champlain *and was a friend of Milton Rappaport's. When she disembarked near the coast of England onto a small ferry, which was to take her to Plymouth, she shouted to him, "Don't forget to write." I told her I was sorry to have* to tell her this, but Milton will never write. He had been killed 27 February, just within reach of hand-grenading enemy trenches, and his body was never recovered.*

I also told her of the death of Rodolfo de Armas, whom she knew, and about the wound in the stomach Douglas Roach, American Negro, received, and that he was being returned to the States. She liked him because he was always so cheerful and politically knowledgeable.

27 May

Returning to the front several days ago, I startle at the captivating beauty of the Jarama Valley. The well-cultivated fields, close up or from afar, make red patchwork quilts. When I comment to a Spaniard walking with me about the peculiarities of the fields, he expresses shock at my ignorance. "No, hombre," he points out, "those are poppy fields." He said that poppies are grown and treasured by the farmers for their seeds and oil, but not for opium.

During our months in battles on these hills and mountains and valleys, we were not much captivated by the charms of the surroundings. We were too concerned with survival and with doing the job we came for. It is hard to appreciate the beauty of vineyards with their gnarled stumps and earth that we found hard and soft, cold and wet, resisting our diggings, resenting our intrusions.

In my travels along the trenches, I ran into Fred Lutz, who took one look at the clothes I was wearing and promptly got me a whole new uniform that was ridiculously big but better than the rags I had on.

For a bad night's sleep, I flopped in the frontline supply room, where the flies buzzed my nose and ears all night. During my disturbed slumber, I kept hoping for a bombardment to scare off the little bastards.

For breakfast the next morning we had not only unusually good coffee, but an exceptional treat of four crackers per man.

* * * *

This morning's sun is very hot, making the long walk to Sepu (name of department store) very uncomfortable. I deliver a note for Bob Klonsky—another Philadelphian—who's back on the line, to a couple of his girlfriends that he recently met and has flipped over.

At Sepu, who do I bump into? None other than Louie Taub from Philly, the guy we nicknamed "Nifty." We talk, we treat each other to beer, and we shop together through the half-empty store. He says he has blown two thousand pesetas in the first two days of his leave and is enjoying every minute of it. He shows me a phonograph apparatus with records he had bought and asks permission of the storekeeper to play several of them. When he is through, each saleswoman comes from behind the counter and thanks him. This place, Louis confides, is great for meeting girls.

*After I had sent this letter to Gabrielson, it came to my attention that Rappaport's body was recovered by a patrol a couple of days after he was killed, with rifle in one hand and an unexploded Mills bomb in the other. I recorded this, and it is in *The Story of the Abraham Lincoln Battalion* (New York: Friends of the Abraham Lincoln Brigade, 1937).

We see women, some with children, sitting for hours along the sidewalk chopping small blocks of wood. We don't know why, nor do we ask for reasons.

While we're in Sepu, heavy enemy shelling pours on us. People clear pavements as fast as one can blink an eye. Women grab their children and run hysterically. One girl runs from behind her store counter, puts her head in my arms and cries; others stand immobile, faces fixed, worried, perhaps too stunned to panic.

I'm glad I'm with International Brigade Headquarters, for it gives me time and opportunity to record these happenings while they're still fresh in my mind. How quickly the mind blots out the hardships, heartaches, and tragedies of February and March, and of the weeks that followed!

But Dr. Pike made those memories vivid for me again during our joint trip from the front at the end of May.

Dr. Pike, who was also chief of the frontline medical units at that time, and I drove together to Madrid, he for medical supplies and I with a stack of unedited materials for our frontline tabloid, the *Volunteer for Liberty*. On the way, he told me about an event that took place in February, and I wrote up the story and, with his permission, planned to use it with his byline. I found it among my personal possessions years later and have long forgotten why it missed being printed in *The Volunteer*. I offer it here under its original title.

SAGA OF AN AMBULANCE

A quiet morning, a calm, peaceful countryside—hardly a time for an attack. We had just left the truck at the point where our narrow, winding, hill-climbing road joined the main cement road. We were stationed there to bring our wounded to the first hospital station while our one ambulance labored between this point and the first aid station. One hundred yards away from the trench, the enemy bombardment began. We were bringing supplies to the first aid posts: bandages, dressings, splints, and stimulants in preparation for the sad processing of our wounded.

Shells and shrapnel exploded all around us. After only a few minutes of this terrifying shelling, the driver fled with his truck. We cursed and went on up the trail. Mentally, subconsciously, I noted the ghastly rhythm of the madly exploding shells, five, six explosions, then a breath-saving pause. During each pause we ran forward, then dropped flat on the ground when the shelling resumed. At times loose dirt and small stones struck us. We took refuge in an abandoned dugout and saw two duds strike the hillside, not more than ten to fifteen yards from us. It was madness, but we went on.

The enemy was shortening its range, the shelling pursuing us all the way to the halfway kitchen and then to our first aid post. There we found our ambulance, and I could not help a momentary feeling of pride in work well done. This was to be our first effort with our ambulance in transferring the wounded two hundred yards from the front lines, a matter of five minutes to the main road. We were to abandon our old painful stretcher-bearing route, which was an hour and twenty minutes long. But that congratulatory feeling was short-lived. In ten minutes a piece of shrapnel tore through the side of our new ambulance, flattening a rear tire, while flying stones punctured another two, and we had no spares. I ordered the ambulance driver down the hill. The driver argued that the wheel frames would be ruined, but finally agreed to take it for repairs. He disappeared and was not seen again.

Message after message went down, but there was no news of the ambulance until I got a report that an ambulance was at the foot of the road, several miles down, and that the driver refused to ascend because of the heavy shelling and, by then, aerial bombardments. I sent a messenger with orders to the driver to return with the ambulance, but the messenger returned with the news that the driver and the ambulance had fled. Our bleeding wounded were beginning to arrive, and they had to be treated first and carried, by hand stretcher, down the long, difficult path. Munitions and food trucks were arriving, adding to the confusion and congestion of the road. An official car was commandeered. A volunteer was asked to search for and bring back the missing and much-needed ambulance. Hy Rosner volunteered. He had just returned from a rear hospital after two sieges of illness. He was weak and pale, yet he was volunteering for this dangerous task: traversing a road that for hours had been under heavy shell fire, and now there was the added danger of rifle and machine-gun fire crisscrossing the entire area. His orders were simple, yet extremely difficult: bring back the ambulance.

"If I bring it back, can I drive it, can I be your driver?" he eyed me anxiously, eagerly.

"Yes."

Half an hour later the ambulance appeared, the same ambulance that others said couldn't make the trip.

"I saw this ambulance on the road," Hy said, "jumped in it and drove it off."

A mild-mannered man, faithful, and courageous, Hy has driven that ambulance ever since—succeeding while three others, physically superior, had failed. There is still much work to be done, work which Hy discharges efficiently and bravely. I am proud of my ambulance driver. He is one of the most valuable men in the medical unit and in the whole Lincoln Battalion.

After spending ten days in a hospital mending his wounds of 27 February and though not completely recovered, Hy Rosner returned to the front lines to remain with the brigade until the end of 1937, when he was sent back to the States by Dr. Pike because of an ear infection that could not be properly treated in Spain. In a letter to me he said, "When I came back, I went to a hospital and they fixed me up."

Until Pearl Harbor, Hy worked at odd jobs and then responded to a newspaper advertisement seeking employees for an army post hospital. After filling out his civil service questionnaire truthfully, especially about his having been an ambulance driver in Spain, he didn't have to wait many days before two men in slick raincoats appeared at his place of work, questioning his employer. The employer spoke well of Hy and assured them that he was a very responsible person. Hy told me, "Later, I got a letter from the two slick raincoats saying that I wasn't accepted because I was in Spain."*

---

*FBI agents in the 1940s and 1950s traveled in pairs and wore slick (shiny) tan raincoats. To those harassed, "slick raincoats" meant the FBI.

His troubles were only beginning: "I was called by the draft board and everything was OK until I admitted I served in Spain. That finished my talk with that army officer. He said he was sorry but I couldn't be accepted."

Hy, working for a friend in a drugstore, announced that he was quitting and registered for the merchant marines. He was on the high seas for about six months. During one of his trips, his ship delivered a cargo of gasoline to a European port. "After unloading the fuel, we joined a convoy on our way home," he related. "The first day out at sea we came in contact with Nazi planes. There was a terrible fight that lasted about six hours. In the fight I took over a 20 mm gun." And in this veritable theater of war, Hy was shot in the leg, which later had to be amputated. Hy Rosner spent a year in U.S. hospitals because of injuries received in his zeal to combat fascism and in the service of his country.

Rosner's experience was not unusual. The disease of McCarthyism was present in our land long before McCarthy made it infamous. Upon my return from Spain, I, too, was thwarted at every step in trying to serve my country, and the reader interested in that part of my story will find it described in the final chapter.

Madrid, November 7, 1936

ELEVEN

Settling in at Headquarters

The shelling of Madrid continued. I described it in a letter to my brother Dominic.

28 May 1937

. . . In answer to your questions as to what effect the burning of the Hindenburg has had here: not a ripple. There was simply a small news reference to it, period.

Madrid sits almost in the center of Spain and almost in the heart of a wide valley, skirted by rolling hills and peaked mountains, some of which are still snow-capped. When you look at these distant snow-tops, the intensive heat feels even more oppressive, especially when you imagine your mouth and fingers sunk into that cool, clean, white snow. From the outskirts, you can look down into the city and, since the fascists control the hills of Ciudad Universidad (University City) overlooking Madrid, they have command of the city with their artillery and can, at will, shell any part of it with deadly accuracy. This they do regularly, to cause not only casualties, but panic as well.

. . . The other day, after I walked out of a department store on the Gran Via, an enemy shell hit not more than twenty feet from where I was window shopping, smashing a hole in the concrete sidewalk. In seconds the crowded street was clear of people. I, too, quickly retreated into the same department store I had left. More shells

111

exploded against the building. A falling brick hit a man squarely on top of his head as he was running for cover, and it made his head look as flat as the brick that had hit him. Back in the store I saw a woman trembling from the top of her head to her feet while she crossed her arms in front of her chest and pressed herself tightly as if trying to hold down the shakes. Another stood pale and silent, except for her teeth that chattered like a typewriter. When the shelling abruptly ended, her teeth stopped chattering just as abruptly, and she smiled to those around her, bid them salud compañeros, *and walked out straight and proud. Another woman, while holding her little girl firmly with her right hand, kept repeating the sign of the cross with the other. A counter clerk buried her head in her hands and cried loudly with each bursting shell and with each occasional shattering of glass. Men hid their nervousness by making silly jokes about the uselessness of fear: "Why be afraid? When your turn comes, you won't know it anyway!"*

Exploding shells don't frighten me as much as they used to, but the scene of people in terror does unnerve me.

On the outside later, I watched together with a sullen crowd as stretcher-bearers carried a mother and her two little boys, victims of a shell that had hit their fourth-floor apartment.

Obviously, the frequent surprise artillery bombardments are aimed solely at terrorizing the population, but the opposite often happens—the people refuse to be intimidated. After the temporary pain of terror passes, they carry on as if nothing happened.

There has not been an enemy air raid lately. This is due, I think, to the effectiveness of the government's antiaircraft batteries, for whenever the enemy planes appear, at least one or two are brought down . . . .

29 May

A government communiqué refers to our plane bombing the German battleship Deutschland, *anchored at Ibiza Harbor (Balearics), killing twenty and injuring seventy-three of its crew. According to our information, the* Deutschland *fired first. What was a German battleship doing in a Spanish harbor, a patrol area assigned to the French by the Non-Intervention Committee? Could it be that both the French and the Non-Intervention Committee are blind, or is this another example of collusion with the Germans against the Republic?*

(30?) May

Very sunny, really hot. I'm just not used to this kind of heat this time of year. Fred and I took pictures yesterday of statues, cultural centers, and areas in El Prado damaged by enemy artillery. We walked and talked and walked. University City and the railroad station look a shambles. It was near here that Oliver Green got a stray bullet through a soft muscle of his leg—he felt a sting, then saw blood.

I went for a paseo *[stroll] around the Puerta del Sol. Whoever said that it is the Times Square of Spain surely knew what he was talking about. Thousands circulate on the square day and night, some on business, others for pleasure—it looks to me mostly for pleasure. They mill leisurely about in cafes, wine and liquor stores, small shops, restaurants. Just as at home, thousands are window shoppers, not buyers. Soldiers on leave mostly looking—just looking—for what, who knows? You can easily go mad trying to pick two identical Republican uniforms. Ralph Bates explains it this way: the bulk of the regular army sided with Franco and therefore controlled the arsenals and* uniforms. *The Republic had only the people who made up their own uniforms and grabbed whatever weapons they could find and are still in the process of building a new army—a People's Army of the Republic. It is supposed eventually to be a unified army. Militarily, I would say it is not yet so—only in spirit, comradeship, and common cause.*

Streetwalkers are still around, and I am told that a fairly safe one would cost about 25 days' pay—150 pesetas and up. My impression from this busy, exciting, populated square is that one wouldn't know there was a war on. Yet, if one watches long enough, one sees uniformed men bandaged, arms in slings, and an occasional soldier on crutches.

It is enriching to be among such wonderfully warm, affectionate, and considerate people, who have such supreme confidence in themselves and so much trust in each other. I feel it in my bones and see it in many ways. Even when I ride the noisy trolley car. The conductor keeps his eyes on the road and the trolley on the track, looking always for an obstruction, and seemingly ignoring passengers. People—uniformed, nonuniformed, young and old—jam the trolley, sometimes chasing it, hanging from its railings, or riding on the car's running board, but never getting off without first elbowing their way to the front of the car to leave their fares. I wonder if others miss their stops, as I have, before reaching the conductor to pay the fare.

Another excerpt from a letter to my brother Dominic:

Madrid, 3 June 1937

. . . It is getting hot, beautifully hot. Indoors it's cool, for the Spaniards over the centuries have learned how to erect buildings that resist and deflect the blazing sun.

Soon I shall be speaking from the Madrid radio E.A.Q. at midnight each day for two weeks on a program beamed especially for the United States audiences. Figure out the time difference and if you are able to pick up our program, let me know immediately . . . .

The meaning of E.A.Q. remained obscure to me. The station must not have been powerful enough, because no one in the United States, as far as we were able to determine, had ever reported hearing our program. Naturally, it was discontinued. The series was made available to the press, and so we were not surprised when a staff member of the U.S. Embassy stationed in Madrid requested copies—a request that, of course, we were pleased to grant, since we were most eager to get our message across, especially to the United States, which, because of the Embargo Act, was denying the Spanish government the right to purchase arms. We had no way of knowing if the Embassy or the State Department made any use of these copies aside from adding more clutter to their files. Reporters who asked for copies also received them.

Some of my June diary entries, while stored in my garage, were chewed by mice. From the first half of June, only the next two paragraphs (except the date) remained legible.

Mid-June
. . . the three young Anarchist militia women I talked with wore Anarchist emblems

and colorful red and black kerchiefs around their necks. None looked older than twenty-one. They had healthy tans from being on the Madrid front for several weeks. Their exuberance was contagious, but it gave way to seriousness when they spoke of their experiences in the combat zones. They did not make light of the enemy, nor of the many tragedies they witnessed, and condemned the fascists as beasts who must be defeated if the human race was to be spared another long dark period of conflict and self-destruction. They spoke in generalities about the dark ages—Spain will never go back to them, Spain has unfolded a new vision of herself—freedom, love, life. "We are fighting to open the gates for all to see this new future." Exploiters will disappear; government will no longer be the oppressor, and the people will govern themselves.

They peppered me with questions about the attitude of the people in the U.S., about Roosevelt, the Embargo Act, and Non-Intervention, as if, because I was an American, I had the answers. I could not explain the intrigues and betrayals taking place in London, Paris, and Washington. I could not explain why these great capitals could not see that by denying the Spanish Republic the right to buy arms they would lead Spain to its defeat and hence the world to a greater war. Of the U.S.S.R., which they pronounced "uurs," they had nothing but "oohs" and "ahs." Our conversation ended with an invitation that I visit their juventud *(youth) headquarters.*

17 June

British newspapers report that General O'Duffy, with 633 Irish volunteers fighting on the Franco fascist side, returned to Ireland defeated and disenchanted with their role in Spain.

Il Popolo d'Italia, *in an article on Guadalajara attributed to Mussolini, denounces the British press for allegedly exaggerating the defeat of il Duce's troops in those mountains. At the same time, Mussolini warned, as reported in the article, that the defeat caused by "hyenas in human form" would be avenged and that the defeat had been caused by bad weather.*

The same Italian newspaper hailed the overwhelming advances of the Italian Black Arrow Brigade on the Bilbao front in the north. Simultaneously, the Franco communiqués from Salamanca announced that the attacking forces against Bilbao were "totally composed of Spanish forces."

The same Italian newspaper announced an official casualty total of 2,000 of their dead and wounded while boasting of the many thousands of "reds" killed. There was no mention of prisoners. But our Garibaldi volunteers inflicted casualties on Mussolini's troops many times greater than these false figures and captured thousands of Italian prisoners by propaganda sound truck alone. It is revealing to see the extent to which the Italian and Franco newspapers lie to their constituents. The Germans seem more discreet; we glean no detailed reports on their activities.

20 June

On the fall of Bilbao, a blow to the Republic, Franco wires Mussolini: " . . . most enthusiastic greetings of this army, proud of having shown itself worthy of trust placed in it by great Italian people and Duce."

It is hot, unbearably sticky-hot. Madrileños tell me this is just a summer sampling, that it will soon get worse. I suffer with this kind of heat. I like what I'm doing and I would hate to have to ask to be transferred.

RUMOR: A War Department order is about to be issued requiring soldiers to have their heads shaved. If true, how do they expect to enforce this order? There must be something to this rumor because some officers already have baldies. There are heated discussions on this question wherever there are gatherings, with resulting resentment and protest. The order is labeled arbitrary and illegal, and those with the most hair seem to be the loudest in its condemnation. They claim they were not consulted, nor were they given a chance to vote on it.

27 June

I forgot today was Sunday, so when I went to the Puerta del Sol to buy film, I sat at a sidewalk cafe waiting for the store to open, drinking one hot chocolate after another. Naturally, the store didn't open.

However, riding back to headquarters on a trolley, I spotted Oliver Green and Phil Cooperman [now a member of battalion headquarters staff] walking in the opposite direction. In my haste I hopped off the car without paying my fare. They invited me to have lunch at the Hotel Florida, but by the time we got there lunch had already been served. "Coop" went into a huddle with the manager of the hotel and talked us into an excellent full-course late lunch of garbanzo *soup and* arroz con pollo. *For dessert, "Coop" walked us around to another hotel which, he said, was an exclusive joint catering to well-to-do foreigners. I didn't want to deflate him, so I didn't tell him that I had been there several times before with Hemingway and others. We had ice cream—at least it tasted like ice cream. It was ice covered with chocolate. I liked it. By now anything that looks like ice cream appears to taste like it.*

We were haunted by prostitutes on our heels. They charge high prices, and if you show no interest, their prices keep coming down until they think they've got you hooked. One of our guys, who on board ship often boasted he'd never have to buy his sex, is now under treatment for V.D.

(?) June

With the hot, sticky summer coming up, the fascists plan, according to rumor, to use gas to terrorize the Madrid population. I hope it's only rumor, for I haven't seen a gas mask in all of Spain. It wouldn't only be terror or murder, it would be genocide.

Today I went to a hospital to visit a Greek-American volunteer by the name of Solonick (as close to the spelling as I can get). He is suffering from T.B. and is not expected to live. I had heard of his whereabouts from one of the medics at brigade headquarters. The ward of about fifty beds had only three patients. Solonick was one of them. Unlike the warm greetings of the past, as soon as he saw me he covered his head with the bed sheet, and in spite of my offering him fruit, water and comfort, he would not come out from under. The nurse said he was very sick and was suffering great pain. I feel there is more to it than that. I shall try to get to the bottom of it, and maybe revisit him; there must be something more we can do for him. [I guessed he didn't want anyone he knew to see him in the sickly and shriveled condition he was in. He died before we could arrange to get him back to the United States and into a sanitarium.]

When I asked the nurse why there were so few patients, she said the ward is more than full during battles, and when patients are well enough to be moved, they are transferred to other hospitals, east of Madrid, or to convalescent centers on the coast. It makes sense! The ward was immaculate, and a bookcase at the end of the room was full of interesting antique-looking books, but all in Spanish.

From the hospital I wandered leisurely through streets thronged with shoppers. Street vendors with their pushcarts and donkey wagons displayed and hawked their wares. There is much prewar unsalable merchandise; however, there seem to be quick buyers. Good thing I'm broke or I might end up with some of this leftover junk. I'm sure many people buy just because they have nothing else to do with their money.

In a liquor store I ordered what I thought was soda—horrible—I left half of it on the counter. I could not complain because, as so often happens when the storekeeper knows you're an International Volunteer, he refuses to accept money.

After a few minutes' walk I saw a block-long line of people at the ticket office of a theater featuring Charlie Chaplin in Modern Times. *I've seen it about half a dozen times and when I can afford it I plan to see it again.*

On the grassy promenade of a street intersection, I was attracted by a crowd around two angry men; one was accusing the other of being a fascist. The accused man denied it and tried to apologize if his remarks, he said, made him sound like one. He claimed to be a captain in the Republican Army. The accuser refused to believe it, and when the accuser stuck his hand into his back pocket as if reaching for a weapon, a civil policeman stepped in and seized the accused to take him in for questioning. A Spanish officer, in a captain's uniform, intervened and spoke in behalf of the accused. I don't think half the crowd believed the captain, but no one interfered. When the captain and the accused walked away, several in the crowd loudly muttered colorful Spanish curses at them, including "quinta columna" (fifth column). From what I could gather, the argument started shortly after an enemy artillery dud struck a fourth-story window of an apartment building. Who said what to whom I couldn't figure out—too much excitement and too many speaking rapidly at the same time.

The term *fifth column* was first introduced by the fascists to describe the active presence of their supporters, undercover agents, spies, rumormongers, infiltrators and provocateurs, behind the government lines and among Republican Loyalists and armed forces.

As Julio Alvarez del Vayo points out in *Freedom's Battle* (New York: Knopf, 1940, pp. 38–39), "Everything was being prepared for street fighting. The Fifth Column, with understandable haste, had begun to show its head and could now be seen at close quarters. Mola [one of Franco's top generals] himself, in his blind assurance, had given the alarm when he declared that, besides the four columns advancing on Madrid, there was a fifth waiting inside the city to cut off the Republican retreat."

6 July

At Ralph Bates's suggestion and in accordance with his arrangements, I was able to attend the Congress of Writers, held in a local movie house with a large stage. Many of the world's finest and best known writers sat with La Pasionaria and André Malraux, who were on stage. We listened to hours of speechmaking and some florid rhetoric. While endless and tedious translations were taking place, I made notes for their possible use in the Volunteer. *As I looked around at the many notables, I remained seated and inconspicuous, because I knew I was among literary giants. Malraux seems afflicted with a tic: his head moves uncontrollably from side to side, in short jerks.*

The electrical high point of the Congress was the speech by La Pasionaria. As she started to speak, the screeching sound of an air raid siren sounded. It almost seemed as if the fascists had gotten the signal that she had taken over the speaker's microphone and were deliberately causing this interruption to silence her. Although the lights went out and the meeting hall was so darkened that one could not see the next person, this incredible woman did not stop speaking for even a moment, nor did her voice waver, nor did she betray a note of concern or fear. Writers and scholars from all parts of the world sat transfixed. No one stirred, no one got up, no one made a move toward the exits. If anyone had the urge to run or panic or gasp with fear, the darkness kept it a secret. I'm sure the audience, some coughing nervously, others breathing heavily, sat uneasily; nonetheless it listened intently as her rich voice rang across the theater, sharply and clearly; at the close of her speech, again as if the fascists had gotten the signal, the all-clear sirens sounded and the electric lights came back on.

A letter to Dominic:

Madrid, 11 August 1937

Dear Dom,
I got a letter from C. Rheiner the other day. He expresses hostile views towards Russia. If you see him, tell him that if he were here he would see for himself that it is the only major power which is giving substantial aid to Spain and that the people of Spain have a high and dear regard for the Soviet Union. Ask him what the democracies of the United States, Great Britain, and France are doing for Spain, other than clamping an arms embargo (the U.S.), closing the border to the Spanish Republic (France), and doing a lot of double-talk on nonintervention (Great Britain). With the U.S. embargo and with the nonintervention farce, the democracies are consciously and deliberately aiding the victory of Franco, Hitler, and Mussolini, and helping to strangle the young Spanish Republic.
Also ask our dear friend Rheiner where is that Debs Column his Socialist party has been broadcasting to the world it would soon send to fight in Spain? To fail to do so, as is apparently the case, is to defile the name and the great heritage of Eugene V. Debs.
On the other hand, the International Brigades are composed of a great many communists and members of the Young Communist League. The number of socialists here is few, but those who are here are wonderful, dedicated, and staunch antifascists. I guess I told you about Paul Niepold, the Socialist we knew at Brookwood Labor College, dying in my arms. . . .

Though I saw Russian rifles, weapons, supplies, tanks, and planes, along with similar supplies and equipment from Mexico and France, and even smuggled supplies from the United States, I never met a volunteer I could positively identify as having come from the Soviet Union. this did not surprise me because I knew I could not distinguish Russian from Polish, Bulgarian, and other Slavic languages. But I knew we had Russian volunteers because my Polish comrades told me so. They were not there in great numbers, but they were there, and they kept a low profile. Even at this writing, in 1984, there is a functioning chapter of Russian Spanish Civil War volunteers, with an office in Moscow.

When in 1983 I visited Leningrad's Friendship House with a tour group after viewing the May Day parade, a General Yamanov was introduced to me as a volunteer of the International Brigades. We shared experiences, and I learned that he had served as a rifleman with the Dimitrov Battalion until he was struck in the back by a bullet. As he was being carried away, he was hit by shrapnel, near a road not more than a hundred meters from our positions on the Jarama front on a day we both knew too well, 27 February 1937. When he recovered from his wounds, he joined the Soviet Air Force, became a pilot, and eventually, during World War II, which he called the Great Patriotic War, was made general of the air force, Leningrad sector, charged with the defense of that city. He explained further that it was his air force group, with his bomber in the lead, that inflicted the last bombardment on Berlin on the day just before it surrendered. He was now retired with a chestful of medals and ribbons and obviously proud of himself and his country.

15 August
   Sunday. Green has discovered a swimming pool in Madrid. It is little used because it is often raked by enemy fire. He has asked me to further explore it with him tomorrow, a way for us to beat the unrelenting Madrid sun—the hottest in the world, so it seems to us.
   The people of Madrid are as bright as this sun.
   In between work schedules, I have been translating Spanish poetry into English.
   Ralph Bates is leaving for the United States a week from now for a propaganda tour. I told him I had written my brother about his trip and that before he arrives in Philadelphia he should notify Dominic and try to meet him.

In the meantime the war was not going well in the northern regions of Spain. My notes record that despite the Republic's bold July Brunete offensive, west of Madrid, designed to relieve the isolated northern coastal provinces by forcing Franco to withdraw troops and rush them to central Spain, and to free Madrid from partial encirclement, fascist forces drove deep wedges into nationalistic Basque territory, into toughly defended Asturias, and into industrial Santander.

These northern coastal provinces, along the Bay of Biscay, were cut off from the central government by Franco-occupied areas and Italian troops. There were too few planes to have an effective airlift. Getting help by sea was equally difficult because of Italian submarines sinking merchant ships approaching the Spanish coast, no matter whose flag they were sailing under.

As if these difficulties were not enough, modern German bombers constantly blackened the skies of the defenseless northern coastal provinces and spread death and terror. On the ground, artillery and tanks were just as brutal. The final offensive against Santander began on 18 August. Three Italian divisions—Black Arrow, Black Flame, and 23 March—attacked. Each division had at least five thousand soldiers, equipped with the best arms and supported by fifty tanks and ample artillery units of its own.

By 25 August Santander fell. The fifth column surfaced, and together with the Civil Guards and Carabineros, demanded that the Basque government surrender. Those in government who refused were summarily shot. The government militia was disarmed, and the city yielded to Franco forces. President Aguirre and members of his Basque government escaped to Bayonne, France, in fishing boats.

27 August
From today's Spanish press, we learn that the fall of Santander is celebrated in
Rome with parades, flags and speeches. The Italian press (Tribuna) exalts the
"Italian victory." It states that the victory is essentially and typically Italian, obtained
in collaboration with the forces of General Franco.
Franco and Mussolini exchange congratulations on the capture of Santander.
Referring to the participation of Italian legionnaires, Mussolini telegraphs that
"brotherhood of arms" will guarantee victory. General Terruzi, commanding Italian
forces in Spain, telegraphs Mussolini that "the Duce's orders" have been carried out.

8 September, Albacete
With Lieutenant Durward Clark, of San Quentin, California, first commander
of the all-American unit of the Primero Regimento de Tren—First Transport
Regiment—and a Polish officer who needed a ride, we pulled into Albacete after a
fast and reckless drive. The driver, a young Spaniard, hit every hole on the road at top
speed. Without slowing down, when he approached a peasant leading his donkey and
cart full of hay, he would blow his horn and speedily swerve around him, scaring the
wits out of the peasant, who held onto the reins of his frightened animal. More than
once Clark warned the driver to slow down. "Take it easy. Give that peasant a chance
to move over. What's your hurry?" It was as useless as talking to the wind; he
pretended not to understand.

I looked up Sandor Voros, who was on leave from the battalion; when I found
him, we went together to Dennis Jordan, headquarters clerk, from whom I got a pass
to sleep at the Guardia Nacional—National Guard. Because I didn't like it there, I
slept at International Red Cross headquarters. I had run into a couple of our guys
who invited me to flop with them.

Ed Bender, personnel cadre attached to International Brigade Headquarters in
Albacete, whom I was to see about transit and travel arrangements for several British
visitors, was not in town. While I strolled about, I met a lot of the Lincoln fellows
who had been wounded and who were recovering and waiting for repatriation.

Internationals of all descriptions were here, and almost every language in the
world could be heard. Between the civilian population and the influx of volunteers,
the town had become overcrowded, and it was now too small for the big job it was
trying to do. It was here on the night of 15 February in the town's bullring that we
first received our greased-packed Russian rifles and set off to the mountains of Jarama.
I didn't like Albacete, and I had not found one American who did. The people were
fine, but when it rained, as it continued to do for my entire stay, the town became one
big mud hole. I borrowed ten pesetas from Lieutenant Clark and looked for a good,
dry place to eat and to kill time while I waited for Ed Bender.

9 September
Bender not in town because he, Bill Lawrence [a recently arrived volunteer], and
Dr. Busch [Irving Busch, of the American medical team] had rushed to a hospital to
visit Steve Nelson, brigade political commissar, who had been wounded in the neck and
groin at Belchite. I had nothing to do but bum around town. During that time, I
talked with several Americans, Canadians, and Cubans who were expected to return
home. I made notes on their experiences: where wounded, what hospitals they were

treated in, and other items of possible interest for the Volunteer. *I spent a lot of time talking with Vincent O'Donnell, the Irishman who taught me to roast stems of garlic over an open fire and how to enjoy eating them with bread; he was with his friend Sam.*

10 September
    Eddie Bender has not returned yet, but he is expected tonight. I sat around his office at the estado mayor *chewing the fat with Americans assigned there. Brodsky is one; Ed White, an American Negro, another; the third is a guy who's in artillery and knows Si Podolin, from my hometown, well.*
    There is little to do but walk around, and there are few useful things to buy, even if one had the money to spend.

13 October, Madrid
    The first anniversary of the International Brigades' participation in the Spanish Civil War is being celebrated throughout Republican Spain. The press, radio, governmental organs, and the Spanish people, through small and large meetings and other festivities, are over-generous in their lavish accolades of the International Volunteers. No matter where you go, it is common to see on walls, of both public and private buildings, the large painted slogan, viva las brigadas internacionales.

10 November
    A surprise visit from Si Podolin. He, along with Fred Lutz and myself, were the only three from Camden to come to Spain. Needless to say, we had a happy get-together. Though we had kept contact with each other by mail, this was the first time we had seen each other in ten months, mainly because Si has been attached to the artillery and has been active in Extremadura. He had his red mustache shaved off and looks younger and more serious, but, as always, he is still a first-class kibitzer. He gave me permission to quote part of his last letter to me in the Volunteer for Liberty.

    The portion of the letter mentioned above appeared on page 2 of the issue of the *Volunteer* dated 17 November 1937.

ALL SIX FOOTERS, TOUGH MOUNTAINEERS

    A significant highlight on our rearguard activities against the fascist invaders is revealed in a letter written by an American now active on the Extremaduran Front.
    "The other day," he writes, "I spoke with . . . members of a band of guerrilleros who had just come out of the mountains on a short mission. They carry on constant partisan warfare behind the enemy's lines. With the band was a very business-like and attractive young partisan girl. She carried a big gat [gun] on her hip. The entire band was the finest-looking group I've seen in all of Spain. All six-footers, tough mountaineers."

    Later that month I wrote my brother, pestering him for American chocolate.

Madrid, 24 November 1937

. . . lots of men are receiving packages from home containing candy, chocolates, and other things. Packages are sent through the Friends of the Lincoln Battalion and if you can afford it, arrange with them for a box of chocolates to be addressed to me. I sure miss American candy. Another way to do it is to get a nickel bar of Hershey's chocolate and put it in the next letter you send me, but write often. Pass the word on to others to do the same and I'll reimburse them when I get back home . . . a piece of American chocolate in my mouth makes me feel like I'm at home. . . .

One of the most unusual men I got to know in Spain about this time was the Italian Giacomo Canapino. From the hardcore antifascist and anti-Mussolini underground of Italy, he came to Spain early and helped organize the Garibaldi Battalion. Many of the Garibaldini came not only from Italy, but from France, Switzerland, England, and a few even from the United States, where they lived as political exiles and planned for the time they could push Mussolini out of power. Some, like Canapino, traveled in and out of Italy consolidating the antifascist forces and organizing new groups. These Italian antifascist political refugees never lost contact with their homeland, even when some became active in their host country's left-wing and trade union movements. In Spain they joined early in the defense of Madrid with the stalwart German, French, and other volunteers. These early Internationals had played a decisive role in the early part of the war in repelling Franco's African mercenaries, Hitler's mechanized units, and Mussolini's ground forces.

Canapino was not only among the first in combat, but also among the first to be seriously wounded. He didn't like talking about it, but one day after a strong cup of coffee made from who knows what, he told me what happened. He had been leading a company of men at Guadalajara, attacking and counterattacking day after day and suffering heavy losses. Then, with the few men left him, he decided to hold a high ground, overlooking a bridge, while an enemy fleet of Junkers bombed them over and over. Finally, one bomb seemed to make a direct hit in the middle of his back, but it was really only a few feet away. Anyhow, by the time he was carried off the field, he said, his body was punctured by innumerable bomb fragments. Blood seemed to pour from a thousand holes. What made it worse, he was conscious through it all.

The sound of aircraft, friendly or otherwise, was to affect him for the rest of the Spanish war. To me, the experience he related explained his supersensitivity to the approach of planes.

Catalans! It is better to die on your feet than to live on your knees!

Part Four

ARAGON AND CATALONIA

December 1937–September 1938

TWELVE

Teruel

By the end of December 1937, the weary and depleted forces of the International Brigades were delighted and thrilled at the capture of the important fascist salient of Teruel and its environs by the all-Spanish troops of the Republican Army. The Internationals did not play a role in the planned offensive, nor in Teruel's capture. To most it came as a welcome surprise. No one, however, kidded himself into thinking that this meant the end of the need and usefulness of the International Volunteers. It did point to the great strides the Republic was making in forging a regular and unified army out of the early street fighters, militia, and irregular volunteers consisting of workers, peasants, students, and others.

This new Republican Army, taking the rebels completely by surprise when it launched an attack on the morning of 15 December, had like clockwork for seven days carried through the plans of the General Staff. Most dramatic of all, perhaps, were the operations during the first day when, having just ten hours of daylight at their disposal, the two columns entrusted with carrying out the pincers movement, simultaneously from the northeast and southwest, established contact with one another. This movement, which enclosed the rebel soldiers in a circle of iron, sealed the fate of Teruel. The planning of operations was no less brilliant than the way in which they were carried out. Teruel, which German technicians had helped to fortify, was thought to be almost impregnable. Yet the Republican Army carried through the whole operation with far fewer losses than in any previous large-scale attack. The secret of its success was that, with perhaps a single exception, none of the strongly

125

fortified rebel positions was attacked from the front. The Republican command singled out all the weak spots in the insurgent line of defense and drove wedges deep into the enemy's rear. The strongholds of the enemy were thus isolated and fell with little difficulty when attacked from behind. In this way, during the seven days of the offensive, position after position fell into the hands of the Republicans, while the circle of insurgent territory round the city itself grew smaller and smaller. Finally, there remained nothing but Teruel and two heights immediately to the east. The final operation consisted of driving a wedge between Teruel and these positions. Republicans entered the town simultaneously from the north, northwest, and south.

The capture of Teruel was of great strategic importance to the Republic; it placed in its hands a new, shorter road to Madrid, enabling the transfer of troops and materiel from the Aragon front to the Madrid front or vice versa much more rapidly. Insurgents who had been taken prisoner were conveyed by hundreds from Teruel to Republican towns and to the seacoast city of Valencia. So rapid was the operation of surrounding the city that barely a man escaped. And all the arms and munitions that the rebels had accumulated there fell into the hands of the Republicans.

Many of the International Brigades situated in reserve near Teruel rested but suffered the coldest winter ever recorded for these mountains in Spanish history. The Lincoln Brigade volunteers were among them.

6 February 1938, Barcelona
Sunday. A pleasant day—not too warm, not too cold. I phoned Eddie Rolfe last night in Madrid and he said he would phone this morning to tell me when he's coming to Barcelona so we can plan the next issue of the Volunteer *together. No call from him. Chances are he's unable to get through.*

At a gathering at headquarters I was introduced to Charlotte Haldane, wife of Professor J.B.S. Haldane, eminent British scientist. She is on tour of Spain as a representative of the Dependents Fund of England. I asked Alonzo Elliott to request an article from her for the Volunteer *detailing the work and function of the fund. She promised to do it, and if she does not finish it in Spain, she said she would send it from England. She is a small woman, intelligent and relaxed, but I don't know how she can stand her high-strung husband.*

Bill Rust, British correspondent, joined the gathering. He told me he sent a story to the London Daily Worker, *detailing the participation of the British in the fighting at Teruel. Later in the afternoon he gave me a copy of his story for possible use in the* Volunteer.

At 5:00 P.M. I left this group to join a meeting of the German section of the International Anti-Fascist Club in the building across the street. After Ernst Busch [a volunteer and songwriter] sang a moving antifascist song and Erich Weinert [another volunteer and a poet] recited a revolutionary poem, the chairman of the occasion introduced representatives of the Catalan Coordinating Committee for the Socialist and Communist parties. The Socialist spoke first. The remarks he made fell as flat as stale beer. He said that the members of the International Brigades were immigrants who had come to Spain to fight and find a refugio. *He referred to the brigaders as* extranjeros. *He was an old man and I don't believe he meant any harm, but the Communist representative of the Coordinating Committee took his friend very nicely to task for the way he put things. When Arndt, a German volunteer who had escaped from a Hitler concentration camp to come to Spain, spoke, he set the record straight: "The fighters of the International Brigades did not come to Spain to seek refugio. They left one front in the battle against fascism to fight in another. Today it is in Spain, tomorrow in Germany and Italy and France and England, and everywhere that fascism spreads its poisons."*

The air cleared after Ernst Busch sang more of his gripping martial tunes with antifascist words; everybody joined in. He has a knack for inducing audience participation. After more poetry recitation by Weinert, the affair broke up with the singing of the "Internationale" and with the old Socialist bear-hugging of everybody.

I am helping Busch straighten out his English pronunciation. He still has some trouble with a few words: he insists on singing "v-e-r-k-e-r" for worker. When he pronounces it slowly, he can say it right; when he sings it, he lapses into error.

Many fine songs came out of the Spanish Civil War. Ernst Busch recorded an album of six of the best and most popular songs of the Eleventh International Brigade, better known as the Thaelmann Brigade of antifascist Germans. The album, called *Six Songs for Democracy*, was made while Barcelona was being bombed day and night, when electricity was interrupted, and when people were buried under rubble from crashing bombs. The songs became popular among volunteers of all languages and among the Spanish people, as well. During the past forty-five years, these songs have been duplicated and rerecorded both in European countries and in the United States.

In February I also visited Dolores Ibarruri, La Pasionaria, to solicit a short contribution from her for the *Book of the XV Bridgade*. A coal miner's daughter who married a coal miner, Ibarruri was a leading Communist member of the Spanish parliament and committed her energies and eloquence to mobilizing her countrymen to resist the army revolt and fascist followers. In meeting halls and over the radio, she entreated her audiences: "It is better to die on your feet than to live on your knees." She also coined the phrase *No pasarán*, "they shall not pass." On hearing my request, she sat down and in longhand, in my presence, wrote the following and handed it to me. These remarks, in Spanish and translated into English, became the last page in the first *Book of the XV Brigade*.

TO YOU

You ask for a few words from me for the Book of the XV International Brigade.

You ask for a few words? It is a modest request. You, the nameless heroes of the XV International Brigade, together with those of the other Brigades, are deserving of more than that. Our people owe you a debt of eternal gratitude and love.

You have shed your blood generously on the soil of Spain, Spain that is being redeemed for us and for you, by winning it for freedom and democracy.

Many of your comrades sleep the eternal sleep beneath the earth of Spain. Over their graves shall wave the laurels of triumph and the unfading flowers of our remembrance. Comrades whom we so deeply love, be assured that your sacrifice will not be in vain.

And tomorrow . . . on that victorious morrow that is already dawning on the horizon over Spain, we shall be able to repay the debt of blood we owe you, by helping you to conquer for your respective peoples, the peace, the well-being and the liberty for which so many heroes are today fighting and dying in Spain.

February 1938

"*Pasionaria*"

"Pasionaria"

2 March, Tuesday, 10:00 A.M., Teruel
Left with Ernst Blanc for the 15th (English-speaking) and 11th (German-speaking) International Brigade Headquarters, which, we were told, were located close to, if not on, the Teruel sectors of the front. Ernst is editor of the German edition of the Volunteer for Liberty. *Vasco, for this trip, is our chofer. After a few minutes we had to return because I forgot my portable typewriter.*

When we arrived at Alcorisa, near Teruel, we reported to brigade estado mayor. *Harry Hakam, whom I spotted walking along the highway, gave us directions to brigade headquarters which, he said, was on kilometer 18 on the road to Teruel. He volunteered to ride with us most of the way and from him we got the scoop that there is talk our brigade is going to spearhead the capture of Saragossa, a city in Aragon that had been in enemy hands from the beginning of the generals' uprising. It was pitch black when we finally arrived at 9:00 P.M. and bumped into Shamrock, a runner. He introduced us to José Maria Sastre, acting brigade political commissar, who, when he learned of our mission, promptly led us to 15th Brigade Commissariat about 5 kilometers up the road. Ernst took off for the 11th Brigade. After a brief, warm exchange of greetings with various officers, we mutually agreed to postpone discussion of the English edition of the* Volunteer *and other matters until the morning. I welcomed the delay because of the long, tedious trip—I was dog tired. I slept on some smelly hay in a room with several others, among whom I recognized Miles Tomalin, a British volunteer, and Sandor Voros, who worked out of the political commissariats in Albacete and was now assigned to the brigade political commissariat staff. Voros I find hard to take: imperious, authoritarian, arrogant.*

3 March
After breakfast, José Maria and I visited with John Gates. When I explained that for the Volunteer *to continue publication we would have to have a subsidy from the brigade, Gates quickly agreed to contribute 1,000 pesetas per issue. Before he gave me an irrevocable commitment, however, he said he wanted to discuss it further at headquarters.*

At midafternoon I left for estado mayor to round up support for my projects. Lutz, with whom I had spent time earlier, sent his chofer to pick me up because Major Robert Merriman wanted to see me right away. I was guided into an underground shelter, which served as headquarters. When I got there, Merriman's big body was sprawled on an old chair, which looked on the verge of collapsing. With his head thrown back, thick white lather puffed around his face, and a towel across his chest, he was being shaved. As he talked, his Adam's apple bobbed up and down. I outlined our desperate financial situation and told him, as I had told Gates, that we might have to discontinue printing the Volunteer. *I also told him that the English-Spanish grammar he commissioned me to prepare was ready for printing. Like Gates, he said he wanted to further discuss these matters with additional officers and commissars of the brigade. Would I come back about six—dinnertime? What choice did I have?*

Following a good supper of eggs, boiled potato soup, oranges, and coffee, Merriman, José Maria Sastre, Gates, and I sat around an improvised table and talked. It was very friendly. Gates didn't say much; others leaned back and let Merriman talk. Once in a while a question was put to me. When I spoke about the grammar, Martinez [a brigade staff officer], standing beside Gates, joked: "Well, Johnny, are you now in the publishing business?" The brigade commander, Lieutenant Colonel Copic, who made a brief appearance, asked Merriman to handle the entire matter at his discretion. Decisions were to be final.

I showed Merriman the latest issue of the Volunteer, which carries a full-page letter by the brigade staff with their signatures. He studied the paper and was pleased. He agreed, after much hassle, to send us 1,500 pesetas per issue. About the grammar, I told him the printing costs would be a little over 4,000 pesetas for 2,000 copies; it would be paperback, simplified, and dedicated solely to help our men pick up Spanish rapidly. He gave the go-ahead and even suggested to the staff that it be sold for 5 pesetas to replenish the brigade treasury. Someone said that if we don't sell all 2,000, "We'll ship the rest back home after the war." José Maria Sastre expressed doubts about the value of the grammar. He said we'd probably end up eating the book. Gates: "At least we will have digested some Spanish." I was asked to return the next morning after ten and pick up the money.

A note about the estado mayor. It is a dugout and one gets to it only after walking through a long and winding underground tunnel. It looks bomb-proof. We talk, work, and eat under a dim carbon light. It is always full of people, mostly officers running in and out. We talk between phone calls, reports, commands, laughter, and persistent hum and chatter. I feel as if I am in the eye of a hurricane. Despite the cold and the many hardships that come with this subfreezing weather and the many gripes about shortages of materiel, food, and dependable news (this is a big item) about the outside world, morale is higher here than in the cities, especially Barcelona.

The division commissar, who is a bit hunched, walked in while we were having supper. He shook my hand so hard I could feel my knuckles crack. He asked how things were in Barcelona. Between mouthfuls, I assured him that thanks to the good job being done at the front, the rearguard was in good shape. I brought him greetings from Gallo and others. He beamed and asked me to return the compliments.

Vasco and I decided to sleep in an ambulance at 11th Brigade. It was a sleepless night, mercilessly cold and only two blankets between us. He complained all night and kept bothering me about when we were going back to Barcelona. He was a Madrileño and didn't like Barcelona, but then he said, "After this, I'll never complain about that city again." I came here on important missions, and I mean to stay until the questions I have in mind are resolved and am not about to go back empty-handed just because of someone's discomfort.

4 March

Vasco and I, helplessly cold, stepped out of the ambulance at the first rays of dawn. We looked for warmth and strayed into a dugout, where two Dutch volunteers were well wrapped in blankets. We lit a fire and hovered over it until we shared a *breakfast of coffee, crusty old bread, and marmalade. Then we drove to 15th Brigade HQ to wash, pick up the stories for the* Volunteer, *collect the funds promised us, and head back to work. When we arrived at the commissariat, we found instead of yesterday's hubbub of a typically busy frontline community a deserted, ghostly looking headquarters. All that was missing was the tumbling tumbleweed! Division estado mayor told us that the brigade had been moved toward Aliago, to the town of Hijar. What a surprise! I felt as if I'd been conned. Brigade must have known it was moving, yet Merriman hadn't uttered a word the previous night. All that talking and planning had been for nothing. If they didn't want to subsidize my proposals, they should have said so. [I found out later that they were just as surprised to be suddenly ordered to move as I was to find them gone.]*

When we returned to the 11th, Ernst Blanc was waiting impatiently. He had feared we had left for Barcelona without him. Then he went off with the chofer, *while I hung around all day doing nothing but sleep, think, and daydream. I fantasized that the end of the war had come, that the fascist armies had collapsed, and that England and France, with the United States falling into line, had called a halt to Hitler's and Hirohito's plans of world domination. Then I woke up to the cold and to reality.*

5 March, still Teruel

We slept in our car, where we were warmer and more comfortable than previous nights, though it was still ghastly cold and dreary. We feared we'd be buried in snow.

In the morning, as we prepared to leave for the town of Hijar to pick up the publication money from brigade HQ, I watched two Spanish soldiers—brigade motorcyclists—stretched out on a slope beside their dugout studying the alphabet. I sat beside them, listened, and forgot the cold. One, holding a Spanish primer, pointed to each letter as the other identified it. Both nodded happily when the student answered correctly. With printed letters the student didn't do badly, but with script letters he fumbled. The student would put his hands on his red bandanna, wrapped around his stomach in peasant fashion, frown, and struggle to call out the letters correctly. He was so determined to learn that anything that distracted his attention annoyed him, even a passing car or truck, or the distant sound of artillery. At one point the student was stumped by the letter O. The instructor pointed across to the slope of a distant hill, where a shepherd was leading a flock of about five hundred sheep away from the front lines, and asked him the name of the animals. He said, "oveja," and promptly identified the letter.

The peasant's face was as lined and weathered as the bark of a tree; many of his brown buck teeth were parted from each other. Like most peasants, he looked older than he really was. So husky and young. How was it possible for him not to know the alphabet? His eagerness to learn was clear; to him, this was what this war was all about. When I asked him why he was so anxious to learn so quickly, he said he wanted to be able to read letters from his novia *(girlfriend) and be able to write her himself, instead of depending on others to do so. When his companion tried to postpone the lesson, he urged, "Venga" (come on, let's continue). He read to me the following, I suspect from memory: "La Republica esta invadido del fascismo internacional. Nosotros luchamos para la cultura." (The Republic is being invaded by International Fascism. We are fighting for culture.)*

The lesson was interrupted by a military order calling his unit to formation.

Reluctantly, he folded his primer and carefully stuck it into his back pocket, then rushed to the road, where I watched him take his place with his motorcycle.

When I phoned Gallo to tell him what happened, he ordered us back to Barcelona headquarters immediately.

THIRTEEN

Barcelona

17 March, Barcelona, I.B. Headquarters, 3 Pasaje Mendez Vigo

Last night, immediately after the church bells struck ten beautiful chimes, the piercing screams of air raid sirens sounded, followed by the deadly drone of fascist planes. Eddie Rolfe and I put out the lights and leisurely walked from our second-floor offices, where we were working, to the courtyard to be near the refugio, just in case. We were commenting on the beautiful full moon and how bright and peaceful it looked when the sudden and familiar whistling of falling bombs, the surprise explosion, the trembling of the ground under our feet, the tumbling of buildings, the crackle of bursting rocks, and the spray of debris drove us in a mad rush to the courtyard trench that some dare call a refugio, a 25-meter-long open trench, dug by those of us at headquarters. A blind flash in the street (which we discovered later was nothing more than shrapnel) drove those standing in the doorway back into the house. The cook, with her infant in her arms, dashing away from the flash ran into a closed door. Both she and her baby fell to the floor. Things happened so fast and so unexpectedly that we all felt this time it was the end for sure.

It was a heavy bombardment. After it was over, Ed Rolfe and I walked across the street to the Anti-Fascist Club, where Jack Taylor, a Canadian correspondent, was scheduled to speak to a group of British and Americans. They had remained in the building, in the dark, listening to and watching the bombardment, because there was no shelter they could go to. Alonzo Elliott and Kathleen Cresswell continued their special executive meeting in a separate room in the dark during the bombardment. A nurse and Cresswell, also a nurse, invited us to walk the streets to see if we could help anyone injured.

The first building we got to was the one closest to us. Half the building was out on the street; the other half looked like it was hanging from a tightrope. A small crowd was already at the scene. Electric wires were strewn over the street and we were warned of live wires. Part of the wires lay in a bomb crater about four feet deep and about as wide. Windows in adjoining buildings were partially damaged; a few roofs had caved in. People who could still walk came out into the street; others were being carried out. Police would not let us near, nor would they let us help, even when one of our group identified herself as a nurse.

We left this area and soon approached a bakery shop in flames, which firefighters were working hard to bring under control. Antiaircraft batteries once again fired their guns while our searchlights scoured the sky for another wave of enemy bombers. Red tracer bullets hunted enemy planes, and sometimes the din was so confusing that bomb explosions were indistinguishable from sounds of our antiaircraft batteries.

When we saw that we could not be of help because local police and civilian officials didn't want any unauthorized people around, we headed back, dodging for cover every now and then into doorways or buildings when we heard the whistling of bombs. I had to stop to take a leak several times, as often happens when I'm under tension or scared. The last uncontrolled leak was when we were taking cover in the doorway of a hospital. Ed and I got back shortly after midnight and went to bed. But in a few minutes we were flying down to the refugio *again, under a thunder of bombs. Finally I said, "to hell with it," and went to bed and slept soundly the rest of the night; I found out later the bombardment continued to 1:30.*

This morning at 7:30 the bombardment began once again. I dressed hurriedly and went downstairs. I don't know why. If a bomb hits the building, you're just as bad off downstairs as upstairs. At such moments I find and feel more secure to be with others.

We could tell by the sound of falling rock that this group of daylight bombs was hitting close. When we investigated later, we found that the church, which breaks the monotony of the day with its doleful hourly chimes, had been hit, but because it is a heavy stone structure, it resisted serious damage. A tranvia *(street car) 50 feet from an explosion had all of its windows knocked out, and its conductor, standing beside it, fist raised to the sky, complained, "Look what they did to my* tranvia. *Cobardes!" At the same time a woman was being carried out of a building, her right leg drenched in blood, her face pale, covered with sweat, but though she writhed in pain, she did not whimper.*

Two blocks from the Paseo de Gracia, a house was leveled, and its white rock and brick barricaded the street; police by now had roped it off. Not far from here, a building behind the Catalonian Generalitat Propaganda Headquarters was in flames. Because they were hampered by the litter of rock, broken glass, household and office equipment, window frames, and doors that blocked movement, the bomberos *[firefighters] were having a hard time bringing the flames under control.*

Another short walk, and we came to the Treball *[name of a newspaper] building, with its iron doors and windows blasted out by concussions. A bomb had not hit the building but had exploded on the street near it. The same blast smashed in the front of a bookstore and set a parked automobile on fire, which was still smoldering when we got there. The telephone and electric wires seemed to be everywhere. A dead man, a blanket covering his body, lay in the middle of the* paseo *[path]. Part of his head was visible, and one open eye stared at us as blood trickled along the ground from his body.*

Later, on my way to the printer, I walked through the Plaza Universidad, and next to the university building, I saw another terrible wreckage. A bomb or bombs had struck the back yard of the Mutual General de Seguros, a life insurance company, and had damaged buildings and homes in one square block. In addition to the buildings with structural damages, there was not one building with a window or door intact. An American I bumped into told me that ambulances were busy for hours pulling away the injured, while military trucks hauled away piles of the dead. He said that he was in the movies last night when the bombardment began and that the audience panicked. When he went back to his room, he found that a bomb had hit the park near the building where his I.B. delegation was staying, crushed a large statue, and killed a number of young couples who were in the vicinity.

After taking care of my work at the printer, I joined Canapino (editor of the Italian edition of the Volunteer for Liberty*) on a trip to his printer. We had to drive through* Barrio Chino, *Barcelona's working-class district, the most punished part of the city. We were detoured a number of times because homes and buildings and their contents lay in ruins on the streets. The streets in this section are narrow, the buildings high, the population dense, so that one bomb here does more damage to people and property than in the more spacious parts of the city. Once we were detoured, not because of debris, but because three horses, soaked in blood, spread across our path.*

When we finally got to the printer, Canapino was greeted in the street by the shop workers, who showed him the damage a bomb had done to their print shop. By good fortune the workers were having dinner at their cooperative at the time, so no one was hurt. Some workers were subdued, others angry, a few disheartened, and a couple of women cried quietly. Canapino, to celebrate the fact that none of them was hurt, took them all for drinks at a nearby cafe, which strangely, despite all this holocaust, was still open.

With no work to be done at the printer, Canapino and I went to interview an Italian prisoner, captured recently in Aragon. I was shocked beyond comprehension. If this young man is typical of the present generation of Italian youth, then Mussolini and fascism have set back the Italian people by many generations. He knew nothing about what was going on politically in his own country, or anywhere else in the world. Canapino explained to him that he, too, was an Italian but fighting in the People's Army of Spain, under the banner of Garibaldi, for the liberty and independence of the Spanish and Italian peoples. The prisoner was at least 21 years of age, but he looked at us blankly, not understanding. We asked him why he came to Spain. He said to fight bolshevism. We asked him what bolshevism meant to him and he said it was the reds. And what were the reds? "The enemies of Italy." He said he had been a machine gunner and that when his crew ran out of ammunition he was captured. We asked him whether, if he had not run out of ammunition and we had had him surrounded, he would have surrendered or fired on us. He said he would have fired on us. He was short, brown-complexioned, black straight hair, round face with popped glazed eyes. I hate to say this, but he is a Sicilian and comes from a town close to where my parents were born. He said he was employed as a farm worker. I tried being friendly to him by talking to him in Sicilian, but I gave up and classed him as an idiot in mind and body.

* * * *

There were 16 bombardments in less than 16 hours. Casualties officially reported as 1,400 dead, so far. There's no effort to count the wounded and injured.

Canapino and I often met together, exchanged ideas and materials for our respective editions of the *Volunteer*, ate in the community kitchen, even slept in the same small bedroom on the top floor of our headquarters building. Because I was raised in a house where only Sicilian was spoken, my regular Italian was bad. Canapino spoke and wrote perfect and beautiful Italian, and I had no trouble understanding him. He took my bad Sicilian dialect in stride, never ridiculing me, nor showing openly any difficulty in understanding me. Sometimes I just dropped Italian and spoke Spanish. I often wished I could speak French because he was fluent in that also.

His sensitivity to approaching aircraft made him especially handy to have around. Whether it was day or night, awake or sound asleep, he noisily jumped or sat up, his body stiffened, his ears cocked, his face turned pale, and the sparse hair on his head literally stood on end. One look at him and I knew planes were about to appear. I learned to know what came next. He would make a fast beeline down the stairs to the air raid shelters. Sure enough, after Giacomo's unofficial warning, the ear-piercing sirens would sound, followed by the terrifying explosions of bombs. Sometimes I, too, went downstairs; at other times, especially if I was too sleepy and tired, I said "To hell with it" and just shook with the trembling buildings. Besides, I never liked the shelter. It was just a shallow trench we had dug in the courtyard, and I always had the feeling it could be a shallow grave.

Before I left for home in April 1939, I spent a day in Paris with Canapino; he toured me through the Louvre, where he recounted the history of each painting till my head burst with temporary knowledge. While a political refugee in Paris, and before he went to Spain, he had spent many idle days in the art galleries of that city.

Canapino was his adopted underground name. He was born Giacomo Calandrone in the seacoast town of Savona, in the Alpine province of Liguria, on 7 March 1909. By the time he was in his early teens, he was a steel worker in the ironworks of Ilva, a town in his province, and active in work stoppages, demands for better wages and working conditions, and other union-oriented programs. Before his twenty-first birthday, he joined the clandestine Communist party in his mill and community. Young, vigorous, outspoken, he soon came under the scrutiny of Mussolini's fascist police. In 1933, when warned that his arrest was imminent, he made his escape to France. This did not stop the black-shirted tribunal from trying him in absentia and finding him guilty of high crimes against the state.

In France, Calandrone immediately set himself to the task of organizing the Italian Socialist, Communist, and antifascist exiles into functioning anti-Mussolini groups. He directed organizational activities in several provinces. Despite a generally favorable political climate, the surge toward United Front political action by the parties on the left, and the subsequent election of Socialist Leon Blum as prime minister, Calandrone was considered too dangerous for France and was expelled unceremoniously from the country in 1935.

Facing jail in his mother country, expelled from France, he went to Spain. When in July 1936, Franco and his insurgent generals began their violent coup against the newly elected Republican government, Calandrone, together with other exiled antifascist Italians, formed a column and joined the Spanish people in their resistance to the military rebellion. It did not take long for this initial group to grow into a battalion and then into a brigade, becoming famous as the Garibaldi Brigade. Calandrone was an officer attached to headquarters and as raw and inexperienced militarily as the men he led. However, the Garibaldi volunteers served as an example of discipline, of efficient organization, and of fierce resistance to the advancing, heavily mechanized and better-equipped fascist troops.

After Calandrone was healed of the wounds inflicted by the bomb that made him fear the very sound of aircraft, he returned to the front but was assigned the duty of establishing a frontline newspaper for his news-hungry comrades. The newspaper (often only a single mimeographed sheet) was named the *Garibaldini*. Later, when the *Volunteer for Liberty* was initiated by the Political Commissariat of the International Brigades, Calandrone was made its Italian editor, both in Madrid and in Barcelona. In April 1938 Calandrone returned to his Garibaldi Brigade to take part in the actions and retreats in Aragon and in the recrossing of the Ebro.

Calandrone was among the group of about forty of us from International Brigade Headquarters who in February 1939 walked over the Pyrenees into France, avoiding at all costs any encounter with the French border police, whose instructions were to seize and intern all refugees from Spain. In Paris, Giacomo completed his work on the history of the Garibaldi Brigade in the Spanish Civil War, then left for Saint-Étienne to continue his antifascist political activities among his emigré countrymen. He was soon arrested by police and jailed for six months for violating his 1935 expulsion order from France. When he was released from prison, war with Germany had started, and he continued his militant political work among Italians in France. However, he now concentrated on introducing antifascist propaganda among Italian troops wherever he could induce them to lay down their arms and desert to the side of democracy. In spite of his excellent work in behalf of the Allies, he was once again arrested by the French on the technical charge that he had violated his expulsion decree and was imprisoned for six more months.

After the liberation of Paris, Calandrone agitated openly among Italians in France and Belgium for a Free Italy. While in Belgium, he was arrested and expelled from that country. By the end of the war, he was back in his own country, where he took on the editorship of the Milan edition of the Communist party organ, *L'Unita*. Once the regularity of the paper was established, he accepted his party's assignment to go to Sicily to become secretary of the Communist Federation of Emma, Siracusa, and Catania. He subsequently also became secretary of the Sicilian Peace Movement, a movement he helped launch. He remained in Sicily for twelve years. Though he was not a Sicilian, his popularity and prestige were so great that he was elected to represent Sicily in the House of Deputies in 1948 in Italy's First Republic and later in its Second Republic, serving to 1958.

The next time our paths crossed was after World War II, in Rome in 1950. Gallo (now Longo) wired Calandrone in Sicily, and on the same day we had a spirited reunion with hastily assembled mutual friends, some of whom had played a leading role in the Italian resistance and in the antifascist partisan movement.

Calandrone was still tall, broad-shouldered, athletic in appearance, and his battered face still looked as if it belonged to that of a prizefighter. We maintained occasional correspondence thereafter. When his book, *La Spagna Brucia* (*Spain in Flames*), appeared, he made sure I got a copy. However, on my last visit with him, in 1971, this time with my wife, May, we found that he had lost much weight and though he was still tall, his shoulders were slightly stooped, his walk was slower—almost a shuffle—his former vigor and exuberance painfully diminished. But his mind and memory were still sharp and clear. He was active in the movement for world peace, I was told later, till the day he died. He was survived by his wife and adult daughter, a student of English, who used to translate my letters to him.

18 March
    Press Association correspondents report from Insurgent Spain that two Italian divisions, the Littorio and the 23rd of March, with not less than 12,000 each and auxiliary units, are participating in the Aragon offensive together with German and Franco falangistas.

23 April
    Salamanca official communiqué, as reported in Italian press, states that Italian casualties from March to April in Ebro battles number 530 officers and 2,482 men. Our estimates are much higher. Italian press does not mention the prisoners captured by our forces.

I sent a brief letter to my family to assure them, among other things, that I was still alive and that there was no need to memorialize me.

Barcelona, 4 May 1938

Dear Dom,
    . . . I wrote to Gladys Stringer and thanked her for the two boxes of Hershey bars she sent me. Also, I received your round tin containers full of good chocolates. Everyone around here has shared in eating from these boxes and everyone has asked me to thank you for satisfying their sweet tooth.
    I am still editing the Volunteer for Liberty *and am working on the May issue that will have 16 pages. As soon as it's off the press, I'll send you a copy, as I have done with past issues. I hope you're safeguarding them for me.*
    I'm also sending you a copy of the English edition of the XV Brigade Book, which we finally got printed and transported from Madrid before the road to Barcelona was cut off by the fascists. Show mom and pop my picture on page 113 so that they can see I'm still alive.
    I don't know who's passing those rumors about me being wounded or dead. As far as I know I have never been killed.
    And for God's sake, no more memorials to me—I'm coming back—ALIVE!

Another urgent letter to my brother to ease my family's concern and to explain that the war was not lost:

9 May 1938

Dear Brother,

Yesterday, Sunday, I received another letter from you expressing concern about my health. There is nothing really to be worried about.

You also say that the U.S. newspapers give the impression that because the fascists have cut to the sea and have divided Catalonia from the southern part of Spain the war is over and we have lost. This is what the fascists would like the world to think and thereby head off further growing support for the Spanish Republic. Don't you and others allow yourselves to be taken in by such reports. The fascists are not going to have an easy victory; the resistance of the Spanish people is getting stiffer.

Yes, Barcelona is in Catalonia, and until recently the population did not face the war as keenly as the rest of Spain. Remember Madrid. The people stopped Franco's mercenaries and legionnaires only when they got to the city's doorsteps, then the fascists were hurled back and they did not pass—even to this day.

The same thing is happening in Catalonia. It took this recent fascist drive to arouse the population to the cry They Shall Not Pass. Barcelona is now a war city. Last month's big aerial bombardment, which killed 1,500 people in 18 bomb attacks within 40 hours, did a lot to arouse the anger and determination of the Catalans. All peoples, all organizations—political and trade union—are banding together in a common front against the enemy. The bombardments did not cause demoralization and disorder—the effect Franco must have hoped for. A fifth column revolt did not open the way for him to march into Barcelona with ease. He has failed in Barcelona as he failed in Madrid when in November 1936 he said that before the end of the month he would have coffee in the Puerta del Sol. The Catalonians are as jealous of their independence and freedom as are the people of the rest of Spain.

The other day a fleet of 40 enemy planes dropped 450 bombs on a small fishing village on the coast not far from Barcelona. The damage to the people and their homes of course was great because they had no defenses against air attacks. In their desperation to break the morale and will of the people, the fascists instead are unwittingly helping to firm up all our forces in steel-like bond against the approaching enemy.

I spent May Day at the front with our Brigade and with a delegation of UGT and CNT trade unionists who were visiting the men at the front to assure the fighters that the rearguard was secure and that all trade unionists were working together for final victory. This is important because these unions, until recently, were bitter rivals. The UGT [Unión General de Trabajadores—General Union of Workers] is made up of workers who are influenced by the socialist and communist points of view, while the CNT [Confederación Nacional de Trabajo—National Labor Federation] is led by the anarchists. They have buried the hatchet, so to speak, and have come together as brothers and sisters in a joint effort to win the war. . . .

14 May

Saturday. Spent the afternoon at the Barcelona Exposition with Maria A. Vazquez [the oldest of four beautiful sisters whose brother worked for our head-quarters]. To get there we had to climb a series of hills that run along the southern shores of the city and from these heights we could look down on all of Barcelona. After leaving the exposition, we sat on one of the highest points of the hill just below the big jail house and had our merienda—*snack*—*of bread and sardines and American gum. This was our picnic. We ate and talked till the sun went down and the sky became gray; when it got chilly, we headed home. By the time I got back, I was tired and slept hard.*

15 May

Sunday. It was a warm day and nothing special happened except that in the morning Sandor Voros, now battalion staff member, phoned, but Luis, who didn't know I was working in the shed sorting documents and books, shouted for me and when I didn't respond told Sandor that I was out. When Voros called later, we made an appointment to meet at the Gran Via Hotel after lunch, in his room, number 16. In the meantime, Mietek, a Polish officer, who had arrived from the 13th (the Dąbrowski) Brigade, asked to borrow my portable radio, which I reluctantly surrendered, knowing full well I was kissing it goodbye. Money seems to be the only thing our comrades return.

As I paced the hallway of the Gran Via looking for No. 16, Al, a member of the Mac-Paps [his last name escapes me now], stepped out of a nearby room. With him was Bill Rust, the Englishman, who joshingly reproved me for having sent A. Elliott to him for a man to work at headquarters sorting books. This I denied.

Al and I barged into Sandor's room. By doing so we surprised him before he had a chance to hide the chocolates we suspected he was hoarding. We were right. He was lying on his bed, with a mouthful of chocolates, reading. After shamefacedly passing some of the sweets around, he handed me some pictures and copy to be used in the Volunteer for Liberty. *He suggested that I do the town with him. When I declined, he asked Al. Sandor wanted bread. I told him to come to headquarters, where I would requisition some for him. Then he peeled off a fairy tale about a number of American deserters in Paris waiting to be repatriated; when I challenged the source of his information, he quickly retracted and admitted it was only a rumor.*

25 May

It is not strange there were no bombardments today, for the sky was clear, except for beautiful patches of fleecy wads of cotton balls that would have made it difficult for enemy planes to hide for long among them from our effective antiaircraft batteries.

Two Italian pilots were captured when 18 enemy planes were shot down on the Aragon front. Planes: Junkers, Dorniers, Fiats, Heinkels, and Messerschmidts.

26 May

I'm having quite a bit of trouble getting out the Volunteer for Liberty *now because of shortages of electric power in the print shops. We are faced with all kinds of obstacles, not only in electricity, but manpower as well. Young men have been drafted for the front. The printers work at night when there is electricity, and if there's a bombardment, work is held up. Right now I am working on the* Volunteer *alone.*

It is beginning to get warm, though the Spaniards say it is still cool. On a day like today, people at home would be swarming at seashore points or at nearby lakes.

The papers carry an account of a speech made recently by the fascist General Yagüe to a large audience in the rebel zone, denouncing the German and Italian troop movements in Spain. In the speech he accuses Franco of having sold out Spain to the Axis powers. The reports also refer to rebellions among the Falangistas and state that a

*thousand, recently jailed in Pamplona, broke out and were being chased by the Italians.
[The Falange was founded in 1933 by José Antonio Primo de Rivera, who
advocated fascism, the Mussolini Blackshirt brand. It adopted the symbol of the yoke
and arrows, the same as that of the Italian Fascists.] In Motril, on the southern coast,
rebellions against Franco have also taken place, according to these same newspaper
reports. If these reports are true and conspiracies to commit rebellion are being
discovered, Franco and his insurgent generals are due for a hotfoot from their own
people and from the Loyalist troops at the front.*

*The reports of rivalry and hate between the German and Italian troops are
common knowledge. We get plenty of that dope from refugees from the other side. The
Italians complain that the Germans get preferred treatment and that they (the Italians)
are the foot soldiers and do the dirty work while the Germans get to be officers and get
the best food, the best accommodations, and the best hotels. This preferred treatment is
creating antagonism and jealousy on the part of the Italian mercenaries. They are
quoted as saying, "We do all the fighting and they get the best of everything."
According to a Spanish prisoner, even the question of houses of prostitution becomes a
point of contention leading to arguments among the fascist forces. According to this
prisoner (information confirmed by our own sources), the Germans get the best
whorehouses, the Italians the next best, and the Spaniards and Moors share the worst.
It is said to be that way with food, equipment, transportation, leaves of absence, sleeping
quarters, and who goes to the front lines. This probably explains why the Spaniards are
the easiest to convince to come over to our side. The Italian soldier, when urged to
desert by leaflets dropped from our planes or by our sound truck, often responds readily.*

*Unquestionably, the longer the war lasts, the more difficulties Franco will have
with his unhappy soldiers at the front and with the disgruntled civilian population in
his rear.*

1 June

*Today, while I was sitting in a barber chair getting a haircut, the air raid alert
sounded. All talk in the crowded shop suddenly halted. Ears cocked, like those of a
bird dog, tuned to the terrifying hum of approaching planes. No bombs. The hum
faded into the distance, then disappeared. Tensions relaxed. Eyes and ears dropped and
conversations resumed where they left off.*

*The thought occurred to me while the barber continued working: "What would I
do if he suddenly dashed to the refugio, leaving me with half a haircut and a towel as
large as a bed sheet pinned around my neck? Would I also run? Would I stay?" Or
suppose he was bold and defiant or fatalistic like a lot of Spaniards and continued
working on my head with scissors and razor? Do I tear the sheet off and run, or do I,
a nervous customer, trust to an improbably steady hand?*

*Passersby looked at me oddly when, walking back to headquarters, I burst out
laughing at the picture of myself, half a haircut and sheet full of hair, running to the
Metro, following the barber, his tools in his hands.*

17 June

*Feeling ill today, I visited a doctor, who tells me I have intense albumin in the
kidneys, whatever that means.*

*Ben Gardner dropped in with a friend, who borrowed a book but who hesitated
in giving me his name, until Ben gave him the nod. They contributed, unsolicited, 230*

pesetas for the Volunteer. *Both must be on special assignment because they travel in civvies and act secretively. Ben is from Philadelphia, so we exchanged information about mutual friends.* [Ben Gardner was killed in World War II while storming the Normandy beachhead with the U.S. Infantry on the opening day of the great Allied Second Front invasion of northern France.]

Number 21 issue of the Volunteer, *with its tricolor full-front-page photomontage, is received by our brigade with raves. We are all pleased.*

José Bello visited with two other Cubans: the president of the Antonio Julio Mella Club, Jacinto Aguilo, and another whose name I didn't catch. They requested transportation to visit our brigade at the Ebro, which I was happy to arrange. When they also asked that I accompany them, I readily agreed, since I was planning to go to brigade anyway in a few days. I dared not tell them about my health problem for fear they might insist I remain behind, so I went to bed early with hopes of recuperating fast.

18 June

Though I had planned to travel to the Ebro on Sunday, I changed my mind when I found out that John Gates [brigade political commissar] was in town. To see him about brigade matters was one of the reasons I consented to accompany the Cuban delegation to the front. Now I had to chase around to Cuban headquarters, several homes, and offices, to locate those I committed myself to go with and call off my going.

In addition, Ed Rolfe arrived on 24-hour leave with copy for the Volunteer; *it was important I remain with him. After laying out the next issue, we discussed the war, politics, home, and family, and visited with friends on the Plaza de Cataluña and at the Majestic Hotel.*

On our way we bumped into Zofia Szleyen, assistant editor of the Dąbrowszczak, the Polish equivalent of our Volunteer, *who was with her landsman, Józef, just in from the front, grimy and broke. Zofia asked me to lend him 300 pesetas, a request I couldn't refuse because of the many things she has done for me; besides, I count her and her husband, [Captain] Mietek, among my closest friends, but the loan cleaned me out.*

When, for any reason I was not able to get to the printer's, Zofia graciously went in my place with layout and copy and spent the necessary time in making sure they put the *Volunteer* together in accordance with my instructions. Because we had no difficulty in communicating in Spanish, each time her husband, Mietek, returned from the front lines, it was an event for getting together and discussing the military happenings. He reviewed for the language editors of the *Volunteer* and their staff the actions of the Dąbrowski Brigade while those of us present revealed what we knew of other battalions and brigades, as well as information each of us may have been privy to. By doing so, we found we got a broader and clearer view of the events that were taking place. Sharing information and consulting with each other frequently resulted in more accurate reports for our respective news sheets. Now it is not unusual for students, writers, authors, and instructors in the history of the Spanish Civil War to quote extensively from the pages of the *Volunteer for Liberty*, especially in the language editions they can read most easily.

On 19 June, from 3:00 to 5:00 A.M., a heavy bombardment hit the city, but I slept through it, except that drones of planes sounded like the buzzing of bees, and I imagined myself brushing the pests away from around my ears. I heard neither antiaircraft nor bomb explosions nearby.

19 June

 Sunday. Warm and sunny. A massive and paralyzing air raid started at 5 A.M. When bombs dropped so close that our building began to swing and sway, shake and quake, I tumbled out of bed and almost rolled down the steps to the outdoor shelter, a trench we built in the courtyard about 25 meters long and 6 meters high. I moved even faster when I heard a crash behind me. Later we found that drawers containing knives, forks, dishes, pots, and pans had vibrated open and come crashing down.

 The Cuban delegation, due to leave at 6 A.M. for the trip to the Ebro front, where our brigade was waiting for them, started out late because of this bombardment. There were not enough seats in the jam-packed autobus, so several rode on the rooftop luggage rack.

 Rolfe and I visited the Cuban club, in the hope of meeting and talking with Cubans recently arrived from the U.S., but an afternoon dance was in progress. We were in no mood for dancing, but Maria Vazquez prevailed on us, so Ed danced twice and I left. I did not have to feign illness. I'm still weak, my legs feel like buckling, which accounts for my being in the dumps all day, and after supper while resting I fell asleep listening to the news.

 Victor [real name: Seweryn Ajzner], editor of the Polish edition of the Volunteer, *returned from the front. Said he had a lot to tell me.*

 For the first time in all the months I've known and worked with Ed Rolfe, I've really felt relaxed with him. He did most of the talking and, listening, I realized how wrong I had been in looking at him as another stuffed-shirt intellectual. His sallow, intense, serious-looking face, his quiet, impatient, and nervous manners hid a gentle, dedicated revolutionary poet. His chain-smoking left yellow-stained the first two fingers of his right hand, which I hadn't noticed before because the color matched his previous jaundiced look. Ed had come from the States directly to the staff of International Brigade Headquarters, without first having served in combat. There was some mild lifting of brows about this because everyone had been part of a combat unit at one time or another, including the women cooks and even the old man, a refugee from Santander, who is now maintenance chief, janitor, security guard, and occasional chofer.

 However, when staff had to be trimmed because of manpower needs at the Ebro front, Ed volunteered. His drawn face did not hide the fear he admitted. When he left to join the Lincoln Brigade, he looked weak, frail, and tired. I felt sorry for him and feared the pressures of combat would make him a physical and mental wreck and that he would be sent back to his native New York a shambles, if he came back at all. Instead, this soft-spoken, talented poet, withstood the rigors of combat—advances as well as humiliating retreats—at the Ebro with greater fortitude than some physically stronger men. He is now happier and healthier. No longer nervous and restless, he talks, walks, eats without being picky about the pea, the lentil, or the garbanzo as in the past, and works with confidence and composure, with the presence of a seasoned soldier of a People's Army. He is still skinny, though.

20 June
    For breakfast: coffee, bread with butter—a first for butter in Barcelona.
    *I was getting copy ready for the printer when Rolfe and Mike Hill came in. Ed
promptly pitched in to help with this issue of the* Volunteer. *Hill was still sporting a
neat-looking beard. We got more compliments on the No. 21—the tricolor—issue of
the* Volunteer. *Abe Lewis phoned. He wanted me to plan a trip to the town of Sagaró
when Oscar Hunter became commissar. (Lewis and Hunter are both black Americans.)*
    Ed and Hill treated me to a sumptuous dinner of bean and potato soup,
alcalchofa *(artichoke), egg and potato omelette, lettuce with cherries, and for dessert,
wine followed by coffee. The dessert wine was a little different than the table wine we
had during the meal. [A reference to the quantity and quality of food indicates an
extraordinary event, worth noting because it was a departure from regular meager
rations that left one perpetually hungry.]*
    *We all had plenty of pesetas but no way to spend them. So I ordered a pair of
high military boots, custom made. The leather was as soft and pliable as a beaverskin
hat.*
    *Victor returned the 300 pesetas I loaned his Polish friend who had had his
wallet stolen.*
    It was a long and active day; I went to bed early.

21 June
    *Surprise! There were no bombardments all night. Last night we were friendly-
betting on the time the enemy planes would appear. It was my contention that they
showed up only during nights of bright moon or around 5:00 A.M. I argued that it
seemed to be their practice, and by then a habit, to arrive at either or both times.*
    *I was feeling much better; I was anxious to get well. The warm Barcelona sun
was magnificent. I went to the waterfront with Maria and her sisters, where we viewed
the considerable damage caused by fascist planes. After a brief swim and sunning
ourselves alongside a wrecked pier, we took some pictures and then went home, where
their mother had prepared a well-cooked, tasty meal of rice with tomato sauce,
artichoke, salad, and coffee. I ate lightly because I knew this was cutting into their slim
rations. Their mother is a widow, who, before the war, worked aboard ships traveling
to and from New York. Her command of English is so poor that I wish she'd stop
struggling with it.*
    Corrected proofs.
    *In analyzing the recent speeches of Prime Minister Negrin and General Miaja
[who was in charge of the defense of Madrid], Victor seems to think that two very
distinct and important current national problems are surfacing: one, a growing Catalan
separatism, which claims that since Catalonia is cut off from the rest of Spain, she
should not be under national government rule; and two, Miaja warns that the fascists
and the fifth column in Valencia are maneuvering to provoke a national crisis in order
to seize power. This element, Miaja said, had failed to destroy the people's will by
military means and so wants to seize the reins of government through chaos, disruption,
and confusion. Then, of course, would come the wholesale slaughter and imprisonment
of those who so valiantly resisted the enemy. Victor may be right, since he reads
carefully and completely all speeches, reports, and the local and foreign press and spends
much time discussing events with many people who make it their business to know what
is going on.*

Dan Kramen, American photographer attached to our headquarters, and two of his Czech friends on 48-hour leave, went to see a Spanish movie filmed in Madrid, En Busca de Una Canción (In Search of a Song). The admission was 16 pesetas and they said it was not bad at all. Dan, like me, finds it hard to turn down invitations of one kind or another from friendly guys who just drop in for a while during their 24- or 48-hour well-earned leaves. Once in a while he locks himself in his studio, works without interruption, and answers to no one. He advises me of this in advance, though, in case of an emergency or if he is wanted by those upstairs. I am to give a prearranged knock on his door and at the same time slip a piece of blank paper under it for him to know it is me.

22 June

I am awakened by aerial bombardments at 4:50 A.M., and I scan the dark, starless sky for what sounds like low-flying bombers, but see none. Antiaircraft spotlights do not seek them out. I can hear our chasers buzzing past, which accounts for the absence of our antiaircraft fire. Each bombardment means loss of work time; continuous interruptions are enemy tactics planned to delay and cripple smooth production and cause terror and weariness from lack of sleep.

Newspapers report good resistance on the Levante and coastal fronts.

Between interruptions, I read Frank Jellinek's The Civil War in Spain. *I find it excellent, informative, a textbook of historical facts treated objectively, the kind of book I'd like always having with me.*

When I went to the Cuban club to get a report on their group's trip to the Ebro front and to our brigade, I was told that because the autobus broke down they never got there and that they were stuck in a narrow, mountainous dirt road with nothing to eat all day. They did not get back to Barcelona until 4:00 A.M. the next day, drained of enthusiasm and disappointed.

By the time I went to bed at 10:00 P.M., there had been no bombardment today.

23 June

I picked up Jim Bourne, adjutant brigade commissar, at party headquarters with the house car. He looked sick.

A Britisher brought me a note from Mark Rauschwald, a post-office worker, who says he'd like to do artwork for the Volunteer. *[In 1984, as I was finishing this book, Mark was still an active artist living and painting in San Diego.]*

Gallo, at a 4:00 P.M. meeting, was sharply critical of the Volunteer. *He said I must cut it down to eight pages and have it appear more frequently; the quality of paper was too expensive, the cost was too high. A paper shortage was imminent and "we must make every effort to conserve." He pointed to the May First edition of the* Volunteer *and praised it highly; then he complained about the last issue because it did not, he said, have enough stories of the personal activities of the men at the front. He said there was a treasury of stories out there and that I should go and dig them out. Because of a policy decision, I had changed the masthead to* El Voluntario de la Libertad, *the Spanish equivalent of the* Volunteer for Liberty. *Now he wanted it changed back. I was glad of that. I can't say his criticisms were unfair. But the manner of the discussion left a bad taste in my mouth. Gallo, though quiet and soft-spoken, often cut through like a knife. Coming from him, the incision hurt!*

Bill Rust introduced me to Corrigan of the political bureau of the British Communist party.

24 June
  I got a surprise visit from José Maria Varela, who is presently with divisional school but remains commissar of the 59th (Spanish) Battalion of our brigade. Jim Bourne, representing the commissariat of the 15th Brigade, also came and said that $5,000 from the States was handed over to André Marty and Gallo for use in the International Brigades. Our guys were to receive new issues of clothes, alpargatas (sandals, usually of canvas, with hemp soles), canteens, and other needed supplies but have gotten none. He also complained that packages from home were not getting through to our men. He wanted to know what gives and wanted answers from the International Brigade Commissariat. In a session with Gallo, I translated for Jim. He then went to visit Constancia de la Mora and was to return for more powwows.
  I went to a party meeting for high-level political discussions on current events in Spain. The discussion was held in Spanish, with everyone having his own brand of accent. Because I didn't understand the young French editor's chopped-up Spanish, I got confused by what he was trying to say and I asked a question, which I knew immediately was foolish, but it was too late for me to retract it. Gallo promptly expressed amazement at my ignorance. He took me to task for not having read Negrín's latest declarations. Had I done so, he said, I would not have asked that question. He said I had better do my homework.
  Rauschwald, from the post office, came to offer his services as makeup expert to the Volunteer. *If he's any good, I can use the help. He's coming back tomorrow evening after work for our first session.*
  In the meantime, Jim Bourne got satisfactory answers to his two main questions: one, distribution of equipment already purchased will take place during the next two weeks; and two, packages from home were held up because of shortages of trucks and because of snafus in the postal organization, which misdirected a shipment to Valencia.

25 June
  It was uncomfortably hot practically all day. I have been reading proofs for the Volunteer *special supplement containing Negrín's speech. Above normal number of copies were ordered from the same printer who did the English-Spanish grammar for us.*

Dr. Juan Negrín, the prime minister of the Spanish Republic, had delivered the speech over the radio on Saturday evening, 18 June 1938. After translating it into English, we printed it as a five-thousand-word supplement to the *Volunteer for Liberty.* The French, German, Italian, and Polish editions published similar supplements with translations of the speech into their respective languages. We headlined the speech "To Resist Was and Is the Path to Victory."
  Its first part dealt with the need to resist in order to give the Spanish workers more time to build a war industry. Negrín placed the issue sharply in focus when he said: "Owing to the criminal policy of nonintervention, which favored our enemies and apeared to have no other end than to strangle Spain, we were faced with a terrible crisis in war material." He added that Spain had no war industry to meet the present needs but was building one as rapidly as possible.

Then he traced the beginnings of the war and summarized the fascist scheming in this way:

An atmosphere was created in which the uprising might appear a defense and the revolt a preventive measure; and both, defense and revolt, might aspire to appear redeeming revolution. It was hoped to establish a military, political, and economic hegemony by the triumph of a faction. It was a well-meditated plan, but the Spanish people defeated it. The attempt was frustrated. What was to be an insurrection became a civil war and very soon a war of invasion.

In the last part of his speech, he stressed the reasons that made the Spanish people fight so loyally and with such tenacity:

The harvest is not yet ripe, for not all nations are awakened as ours. . . . We are fighting to guarantee the absolute independence of Spain without hindrance or limits—other than those imposed by a common right to establish bonds and relationships between peoples.

Independence means liberation from invaders, means rejecting guardians, means giving the worker the right to enjoy the fruits of his own hands instead of being the victim of foreign plunder, means a political life and economy directed, regulated and exploited by and for Spaniards.

We are fighting for the integrity of Spain. . . . We are fighting so that Spain, without ever interfering in the domestic life of any other country, shall be able to consider as her own the interests of nations whose ancestry and language are common to her own.

We are fighting for a people's Republic of a democratic nature; for the monarch had lost all connection with national sentiment and was responsible, in a decadent Spain, for its own overthrow.

We are fighting for a strong government, for a firm executive, depending on the will of the nation expressed in the ballot, for a government which would place the State above all political parties.

We are fighting so that, without weakening the national unity, there will be respect for the peoples which form Spain. Unity on the outside, diversity within. . . .

We are fighting because we want the State to guarantee the enjoyment of full rights to every citizen, complete respect for conscience and creed. We cannot tolerate the intervention of the church as an institution in the life of the State, nor can we admit interference by its leaders in the disputes of citizens. But at the same time we are fighting to guarantee freedom of worship. We owe this to the principle which we profess. We owe this to the countless thousands . . . of Catholics who are fighting at our side.

We are fighting so that the fruits of the land may be for the man who works it. We are fighting to suppress the shameful exploitation of the individual by a wealthy class which in turn converts itself into the ruler of the State and loses sight of and almost always goes against all collective interest.

He reminded his radio audience that though the country was in civil war the Spanish people were pacifists by nature. Calling for reconciliation after the war, he urged Spaniards at the front to "wage war with courage and bravery" and closed with this sentence: "We are fighting—heed my words—so that Spain may belong to the Spaniards, and this we shall achieve."

As I was checking the proofs of the speech on 25 June, Constancia de la Mora came to discuss ideas about how to deal with U.S. newspapers and reporters. Head of the propaganda department for the Spanish government in Barcelona, she was married to Republican air force chief Hidalgo de Cisneros, and her uncle, Miguel Maura, had served as minister of the interior at the beginning of the Second Republic in 1931. Because I was under such pressure to get the issue of the *Volunteer* with the supplement out as quickly as possible, we agreed to meet at a later date for a fuller discussion.

Zofia Szleyen, of the Polish edition of the *Volunteer*, asked me to go with her to a concert the next day, but I was reluctant to do so. Music, especially classical music, relaxes me, and I would have a hard time fighting sleep.

Abe Lewis, a black American volunteer from Philadelphia and a close friend of Fred Lutz's, phoned and we made arrangements to walk the Ramblas—a broad, tree-lined boulevard, where thousands walk day and night—after supper, but he didn't show. Just as I was leaving for the printer's at 9:15 P.M., Mark Rauschwald, who had been assigned to the postal section and censors, and Dave Thompson, of motor transport, appeared in the doorway. After discussing the *Volunteer* with them, I agreed to phone Mark when I had enough material to make up the next issue. He volunteered to do layout work on the paper during his off-duty hours.

I went to the printer's at midnight and stayed until 2:30 A.M. correcting proofs. We worked in the dimly lit basement, where we could be buried alive if a bomb hit the building. Located in the heart of the industrial and waterfront section of the city, which was getting hit the hardest, the print shop was already partly damaged from an almost direct hit earlier. There was no bombardment while I was in the shop, but one did start while I was walking back to headquarters through pitch-dark, and by then lonely, streets. No one asked me the password, so I figured the guards were dodging in and out of doorways as I was.

26 June

I slept until ten this morning, then took a cold shower because there was no hot water. The new plan proposed by the discredited Non-Intervention Committee was explained in detail in the newspaper La Vanguardia. *More rationalizations, more words, more delays, more deliberate hypocrisy from the great European powers designed to appease Berlin and Rome with a calculated sellout of the Spanish Republic. The Spanish government's continued participation in these discussions with France and England merely meant Spain was prostrating herself for continued goring. Others, in headquarters, said, "Well, what else can the Republic do?"*

In the afternoon (5:45) Maria Vazquez and I went to the Julio Mella Club, where another dance was being held. The city is set on fire from the sky, yet people still dance. We stopped for a glass of orangeade—water with coloring, very light coloring—which Maria compared to the taste of water at the club's swimming pool. Then we walked through the Barrio Chino and the Paralelo in search of ice cream. When we found none, we had coffee near Café Español. Continuing my tour under Maria's supervision, I noted that the area looked like red-light district with thriving cafes every few minutes. She said, "So!" She also pointed to an electric power plant a block away and said it had been a special target of fascist bombs, so much so that one day a fluke bomb dropped into the plant's chimney and exploded. No electricity for that part of the city for days.

She rejected all advances from me unless I promised to marry her. She chided me about the picture I received from my Madrid teenage teasing friend, Teresa, the daughter of one of the women who worked in our Madrid headquarters. Teresa had sent me a photograph of herself, and across the bottom she had neatly written: "Esta foto para tus ojos, el original para tu corazón." (This picture for your eyes, the original for your heart.)

Sid Kurtz, veteran of the Jarama campaign and radio announcer in Madrid, arrived at night from the southern zone of Republican Spain. I got him a bowl of soup and sleeping quarters. He said Madrid is still a rock of hope. Defeat is not in their vocabulary.

28 June

Tuesday. When I went to brigade today, I sat in the back of a commissariat mail truck, and my kidneys were sore as hell from the bouncing over bad roads. For the German chofer, who survived a back wound on the Madrid front in November 1936, it was even worse. Though he stopped several times because his back hurt him, he never complained. These Germans are as tough as nails, both physically and politically. He once said the hardships of the war were nothing compared to the miseries of the concentration camps back home.

I spent the afternoon visiting with the Mac-Paps and Lincolns. When I walked into Mac-Paps Company Two, a heated discussion was taking place as to what to do with the American deserter who claimed at his trial that he had fled because he was demoralized by the rumors of collapse of the army, the capture of the brigade leadership, and talk by the men in Company No. 2 themselves, who had planned desertion. He said that these same men had sung songs of wanting to go home.

Ed Rolfe gave me his red sweater, which he treasured because it was a gift from his wife, Mary, who had knitted it for him and sent it to Spain. He asked me to take care of it for him.

I slept overnight at Fred Lutz's pagaduria (paymaster's headquarters) with Abe Lewis in a narrow and short bed. Needless to say, we were both uncomfortable and neither of us slept well.

For lunch I was hosted at 11th Brigade (German) by Ernst Blanc, editor of the German edition of the Volunteer, *with several others. Hernandez, former commander of the 59th Battalion (Spanish) of the 15th Brigade, now with the 11th, joined us. The two kilos of pears I had bought on my way here from a roadside farmhouse for 14 pesetas was our dessert.*

There was very little shelling, much cooperation, and I got a lot done. After spending a little time with Joe North (reporter for the New York Daily Worker*), who was making the rounds of all International Brigades, I visited with as many of our guys as I could find up and down the line. Morale is very high; their optimism is contagious.*

30 June

Back to Barcelona with an armful of stories, poems, letters, and accounts written by men in battle during their occasional leisure, much of it extracted by Ed Rolfe, who did some arm twisting. Earmarked for him was some material he wanted me to safeguard for his use for a book he planned to write when he returned home.

Jack Taylor of the Toronto Daily Clarion *came to complain that he did not get the story about the International Brigades being withdrawn from the war. He said Toronto had to scalp it from one of Herb Mathews'* New York Times *stories, dateline 26 May. Why such a fuss, I don't know. Taylor, who is also Canadian political commissar, may have been on one of his many political trips.*

Air raid sirens were sounding again. Ten trimotors were bombing Barcelona. The waterfront was being hit hard.

Rauschwald came to admit futility in his efforts to get anything done for the Volunteer *because of his other responsibilities.*

At 11 P.M., there were sirens again, but no bombs.

Today I picked up my custom-made boots; they were excellently constructed and fitted my feet to perfection. Cost: 310 pesetas.

3 July

Got a long-distance phone call from Colonel Copic, who was headed for Barcelona and wanted to see me about the Volunteer, *the grammar, the book, and other brigade problems, but he didn't show. [At the time of the phone call from Copic, I thought it strange that he, the military commander of the brigade, would want to talk to me about political matters, subjects essentially of the brigade political commissariat. But then strange things were always happening in that strange war. I found out later what may have kept him from coming to Barcelona, for the next day Colonel Vladimir Copic, who had been with the Lincoln Brigade from the very beginning, was given a well-deserved rest. In a ceremony honoring him, he was replaced by Spanish Major José Antonio Valledor, one of the leaders of the revolt in Asturias in 1934. He fought in the Republican armed forces in Asturias in 1936 and 1937, until he was made prisoner. When he escaped from a fascist prison, he made his way to Republican Spain, where he was well received by the battalions of the Fifteenth International Brigade, which by now was largely Spanish.]*

Fred Lutz arrived from the Ebro. Since he has become Brigade paymaster we see each other more often. This time we headed for a tour of the waterfront area to examine the damages from enemy aircraft and to walk on the beach. We didn't get that far because the air-raid alarm sounded and we hustled back. We stopped at a cafe for shelter and had vermouth and Tissiana. We talked about plans for after the war. He suggested we bicycle throughout Europe. I told him I had an unfinished job: the unionization of the Campbell Soup plant. I left him at the Grand Via Hotel and went back to the commissariat; still no message from Copic. Later, Fred and I went to dinner, then to see Mr. Deeds Goes to Town. For 205 pesetas we had a supper of vegetable soup—with only strains of vegetables—breaded veal cutlet, one mouthful of strawberry dessert, wine, and undrinkable coffee. One thing is for sure, with the quantity of food we get, there is no danger of getting fat. My stomach has shrunk so badly that I can put my hands around my waist and have them almost meet.

Headline in today's local newspapers: ''Fascist Countries Are Trying to Chain the Continent.''

July Fourth, our Day of Independence, is special to Americans. To draw attention to this fact, I encircled the day in red on a calendar in the pressroom of

International Brigade Headquarters. Present were two German officers of the 11th (German) Brigade who, to get to Spain, escaped from a Nazi concentration camp, two from the Polish Dąbrowski Battalion, who had served prison terms in their native land for antifascist activities, a British visitor and his two local Spanish friends, and Canapino of the Italian edition of the *Volunteer*. I started to explain the importance of this day when slowly I realized that they not only had a scholarly comprehension of our unique American Revolution, but also perceived its significance as clearly as the average American, if not more so. To this small cross-section of contemporary Europeans, the American Revolution and the United States Constitution were beacons in their lives; the Russian Revolution of 1917 was another. There was consensus in the statement by the Spaniard when he observed that it was no accident that the present constitution of the Spanish Republic was patterned after that of the United States and that the Spanish people were spilling blood in defense of that kind of constitution 160 years later.

After this enlightening exchange, I devoted the remainder of the day to preparing material for the *Volunteer* and translating articles from Spanish into English until 8:30 in the evening, when Lutz unexpectedly popped in with a Spanish lieutenant paymaster of the 59th Battalion. For hours they briefed me about activities at brigade: the hardships, the successes and failures, the shortages of weapons, trucks, fuel and cigarettes, the promotions, the often poor quality of food, the high morale despite the weariness of some of our forces, and scores of other details I failed to jot down.

Almost immediately after they left at 11:30, the ear-piercing sirens once again screeched through the hot night, then earth quivering bombs. Though the raid didn't last long, it was devastating to property, lives, and nerves.

5 July
   I spend the morning with Major Allan Johnson, who is arranging to leave Spain and for whom I prepare two cartons of 15th Brigade Books to carry back to the States. If he gets the books into the U.S., it will be the first batch of books of the history of our brigade to cross the ocean. It is not certain we can get bulk shipment.
   When Lutz arrives, the three of us commission a camioneta *[a small truck] and tour the city. Fred drives and I direct him. I'm beginning to feel like a guide for every American on pass or leave. It does, however, afford me a break from the tediousness of work, and at the same time it gives our comrades relief from the tensions of the front. A number never get to the city. Others who do, after they're here, are glad to return to the front lines, where aerial attacks are less frequent and where they are less likely to lose sleep due to night raids. On the front lines, air raids usually take place during daylight hours; in the city the opposite is generally the case.*
   After dropping Johnson off at the Gran Via Hotel with his two cartons, Fred comes with me to the print shop to check over the proofs before this issue goes to press, and I am to go with him to the bank to pick up payroll for our men at the front, but plans are changed because of frequent air raid alarms.
   At 11 P.M. on the button, enemy planes drop their load.

6 July
   I accompanied Fred Lutz to the bank, where he carefully counted and meticulously packed 1,336,940 pesetas in one suitcase. He carried no pistol, nor was he

concerned about being robbed—no armed guards or armored truck. It would have been unthinkable back home to saunter through the streets with a suitcase full of money and even stop leisurely for a cup of coffee. Yet that was what we did.

Fred is perfect for this job. He's a stickler for details, has a scientific mind, is learned and brilliant, methodical and accurate. I wonder if he ever makes a mistake. He's probably only in his late twenties, but his thick hair is snow white. Back home we had been political acquaintances; here we have become close friends. Sometimes, however, I feel as if I'm in one of his test tubes, the way, in his soft-spoken incisive manner, he examines and dissects every word I say. He's also that way with others.

We shared carrying the heavy suitcase and limped back tired and hungry. After a scanty supper, which left us still hungry, we went to Dan's (Kramen) Den across the street from headquarters and had our pictures taken. Dan let us watch him work in his darkroom.

Oscar Hunter visited today and seemed awfully sulky. I must find out what's bugging him.

I got another injection today, but I don't feel stronger. Maybe there was nothing in the needle but water. Besides, this doctor drove the needle in my arm as if he were handling a jackhammer.

I worked till midnight editing material that Fred had brought from the front. Then I went to the printer's for more proofreading until an air raid alarm caused the lights to go out.

17 July

Again I went to brigade, this time with the mail truck. While in a little town asking for directions to the American units, I ran into Hans Goepel, a German refugee, whom I knew as a student at Brookwood Labor College. He was overjoyed at running into us. He said he had lost the brigade at Caspe, had joined a Spanish unit, and had been hanging around Lerida ever since. At his request, we dropped him off at brigade estado mayor.

I had a work session with Rolfe, who is now brigade correspondent for the Volunteer. *His interest in the paper is still strong. He was unbelievably generous with his food and clothes, as well as with his time and efforts for the* Volunteer. *In the evening we were joined by Joe North, of the New York Daily Worker; Menendez, one of my traveling companions from the U.S.; Peter Kerrigan, from Glasgow, Scotland, commissar of all the British; and Captain Leonard Lamb, commanding officer, First Company. I was troubled to learn of the desperate shortage of cigarettes and of the infrequency of mail delivery. What little mail we brought today was eagerly received, and even that may not have been here had I not insisted on coming with the truck to make sure there were no detours.*

A dull gray fascist plane passed over us low and at high speed, the first of its kind I've seen; a new type I was told, probably a reconnaissance.

In the meantime, UGT and CNT union delegations from Barcelona are being hosted by our 59th Spanish Battalion. After the dinner honoring the delegations, John Gates, 15th Brigade political commissar, Major José Antonio Valledor, the new brigade commander, and representatives of the trade unions made short, enthusiastic speeches, everybody saying the right things and nice things about all present and calling for unity of the forces at the front with unity of workers in the rear until final victory.

Johnny Gates enjoys confidence, respect, and affection of everyone, including the

Spanish and other non-English speaking. I know that his prestige at Barcelona International Brigade Headquarters is high, almost as high as that of Merriman. Lamb and Milton Wolff are placed in number one categories also.

Spaniards of the 59th greeted the delegates with a dance starting down the road. They entered the dining hall singing and dancing around what looked like lighted pumpkins. I wondered why the candles in them did not extinguish. Enraptured, we watched as their bodies flung to and fro in time with their flamenco—strains of Andalusian and Moorish influence—sometimes slowly and at other times vigorously. They did not slow down even when perspiration poured like rivulets of rainwater from their bodies. To me their dances resemble those of the American Indians—proud, dignified, defiant.

I returned to Barcelona with the union delegations, arriving at about 5 A.M. to a city dark, peaceful and quiet, and, perhaps, a little tired of the discomforts of war, yet a city that dares not succumb, for the fear of fascism is greater than the fear of food shortages, the lack of electricity, the restrictions of war, and even the inevitable hazards of bombardment.

At headquarters I was briefed on what happened while I was away, especially the various meetings analyzing the events at the Ebro, the government's concern at France's continuing refusal to permit tanks, artillery, and other war material we badly need and purchased from the Soviet Union from crossing the border into Spain. This like denying a glass of water to one dying of thirst.

On the light side, a story several delighted in repeating was the one about Lucia, head chef, who slept through a heavy bombardment, but when the air raid off-signal siren sounded, she jumped out of bed and ran down the stairs to the shelter, passing others who were returning. She exhorted them to follow her to safety, but those returning from the shelter tried to explain to her that the raid was over, that she should turn around and go back to bed. It took her mind a while to clear and for her to realize that she was the one out of step; then she, together with everyone else, burst in hilarious laughter. Lucia was about five feet, six inches and very heavy; when she laughed, which was often, her body and her rolls of fat bobbed up and down.

FOURTEEN

The Ebro Battles

23 July
   *At a staff meeting of all language editors with Luigi Gallo and André Marty,
we were ordered to promptly put out a two- to four-page special edition of the
Volunteer to accompany the Republic's impending offensive due to start all along the
Catalonian front. This surprise announcement created great excitement and raised
morale. I've never seen so many work so hard, so enthusiastically, and so selflessly.
Everyone is helping everyone. There is no time for strolls, dances, movies, or idle
chatter. Even when we take a break for coffee in Dan's Hole [Dan Kramen's small
photography room], we talk about plans to facilitate foreign press coverage and to
improve supplies, mail delivery, literature, communications, and hospital contacts.*

26 July
   *Stories are filtering back, newspapers verify and gloat: our forces have crossed the
Ebro River and taken Amposta, the town south of Tortosa, and captured the town of
Mequinenza, north of Mora de Ebro at the junction of the rivers Ebro and Segre.
Thrusts have been successful so far. We got out a four-page Volunteer in record
time—attack number, no. 26.*
   *The mail truck returned without making delivery. The driver claimed he couldn't
find the brigades. He was replaced on the spot, and the new driver was told not to
return until the mail was delivered, regardless of how fluid the front lines were. The
first driver said he was afraid he'd drive into enemy territory. Nobody believed him.*

27 July

Wednesday. In a one-hour meeting, Gallo gave us a blow by blow description of the fighting. He had just returned from the zigzag lines and spoke to us while still covered with grime and dust, unkempt and unshaven, and, as usual, unsmiling. His driver told us of having been encircled and almost captured; their khaki-colored staff car was pitted with bullet holes.

From my excitedly scribbled notes of his account: Our forces captured a number of towns, including Corbera, Mora de Ebro, and Fatarella, and more than 3,000 prisoners. The offensive started at exactly midnight last Sunday, 24 July, with the crossing of the river by boats. The 35th Division crossed north of Mora de Ebro and was to take positions north of Gandesa. The 46th Division started farther south and was to meet the 35th in the heights surrounding Gandesa. This was effected properly. However, the 3rd Division, which was to come down from Mequinenza and meet the troops around Villaba, did not execute its operations well.

The 14th Brigade of the 45th Division crossed at Amposta, but only one complete battalion, Commune de Paris, and a few scattered units were successful in the crossing. Maneuvers were screwed up, communications lost, orders became confused, and leadership almost nonexistent. Consequently, the rest of the brigade was wounded, killed, or drowned.

The 13th Brigade performed best. It was the most united and the most disciplined, with the fewest casualties. The 15th Brigade did well the first day by penetrating at least 20 kilometers into enemy territory.

Further chaos and confusion caused by fascist opening of dams, destroying our makeshift bridges and so preventing our artillery and tanks from crossing in support of troops already on the west bank of the river. Unless new bridges are built soon, machine-gun crews and riflemen will run out of ammunition. The situation is desperate, at least not hopeful, unless communications can be re-established soon.

28 July

I am at the 35th Division Commissariat HQ.

There is no change in the situation at the front.

The enemy has been reinforced with men and materiel and is successfully resisting the vigorous attacks by our troops. Their artillery is very actively bombarding Corbera and the road at Alcalá del Pinar, key to Tarragona and other positions important to us. Their mortars are persistent singsong to our ears. Enemy aviation is constantly in the air, bombing, strafing, harassing.

The following are a few of the serious difficulties facing us:

1. Ammunition. Our troops are not getting enough replacement of ammunition and arms. Our Anna Pauker artillery unit is across the river, but has no ammunition, nor means to get closer to the enemy.

2. Transportation. The 35th Division is down to three transport trucks on the combat side of the river This makes for the most serious problems of delivery of materials and weapons.

3. Our primary objectives are not fulfilled. Gandesa is still in enemy hands. Superiority of enemy planes, artillery, mortars, and machine guns, and their better equipped troops have stalled our offensive.

4. Sanidad (Medics). Evacuation of wounded is a monumental task. We have only two ambulances for two brigades. Bajas (war casualties): the 57th Battalion, 170

wounded and dead; and 120 for the 58th. Casualties almost all American.

5. Troops haven't eaten all day.

30 July

The 58th Battalion of the 15th I.B. attacked one enemy position as often as nine times, to no avail.

The food kitchen finally arrived on the combat side of the river, and food supplies are now closer to normal. Welcome, hot coffee!

Bajas [casualties]: The 58th lost three company commissars and three company commanders. One of the commissars died. Services now functioning better, almost well under the circumstances. Commissars are working feverishly and heroically with military commanders, in some cases acting as military commanders in place of a command casualty.

The fascist 74th Division arrived the night before last from Extremadura. It is composed mainly of Falangistas and Requetes, Basque religious nationalists recognized by their red berets. Its commanding general and commander of the sector is Juliquet, whom the Spaniards refer to as the notorious rabid fascist butcher.

An enemy group staged a surprise night attack and captured a machine gun from our Spanish Battalion. The gun crew, furious, counterattacked and not only recouped the gun, but captured a key position dominating an area of enemy approaches.

Because the enemy is so well fortified at Gandesa, with greater quantities of automatic weapons in operational use and adequate artillery and aviation support, our stubborn drives against them ended up in high casualties for our side.

There was violent and bloody fighting all day. The 16th Division was unable to achieve its preplanned objectives, which, had it been successful, would have permitted our forces to advance faster and step up the offensive.

That day I took time out to write my sister-in-law, Antoinette ("Toni"), a long-overdue letter. Her last letter stated that she had read in the U.S. papers that I had been wounded, so I asked her to send me the clipping because I wanted to see if I could trace these false reports. I had been one of the lucky ones—never to a hospital, except to visit the wounded.

I also related to her an encounter that I had had in Madrid.

One day, when I had ventured to the outskirts of the city and to barricades of cobblestones, brick, and rock (raised hurriedly, mainly by women and children in early November 1936, when the fascists almost took Madrid), I was challenged by a Spanish guard. After I identified myself, he escorted me to the main guard post located on the first floor of a much bombed-out house. While discussing with the guards permission to walk farther through our trenches toward the enemy lines, I saw a soldier stretched out on a cot engrossed in an English-Spanish grammar. I addressed him in English and you should have should have seen his face light up. He told me that he had been studying English for some months and that this was the first time he had heard it spoken; he had never had the chance to practice it. Would I help him?

This was the beginning of our friendship. He was from Barcelona—a proud Catalan. His English pronunciation at first was as bad as an American's pronunciation of Spanish. Since our print shop was close to where he stood guard, I would visit him and help him with his pronunciation. We would take long walks through the trenches and in the bombed-out areas of the city and we would speak to each other in English. This pleased him, as it did me, and he would always insist on my correcting him. When our headquarters moved from Madrid to Barcelona, I wrote to him. His reply, in blue ink, was carefully and clearly written. Knowing the heroic effort he must have put into it, I guessed that it must have taken him many painful days of writing and rewriting.

I sent Toni a copy of my student's letter with his exact punctuation and spelling.

15 of May of the year 1938

My dear firend John.

To-day I shall be, obliged to answer your attent letter of the month second of present year. All, it what you tell me, is very interesting, and I am very satisfied, becouse all your activity, looks the end of war and naturally with the people's victory.

We, the Speniards shall be very pleased by your important assistance.

Always, we will to remind your valious sacrifice. I would like, what the bombs has been falled very far of your department.

If you wants something, you may go ontu my sweet-home and my parents will be very pleased by your kind-goodness to vissiting theys. My father, mother and sista will be at your disposition.

The address of my home into Barcelona, is the following:

..

Actually my health is very strong and I feel myself o-kay. My wish is, you are as well as I.

You shall pardón me, because I have a lot of work to do. I come obliged to study very much.

Salud, your most sincere and affectionate friend, Emili

This letter was Emili's epitaph, for not long after receiving it, I was informed by his family that his English studies were ended forever by a sniper's bullet. He was taken away from the battlefield with his English-Spanish grammar still under his buttoned shirt, next to his bare chest, where he always carried it. It was our brigade's recently published English-Spanish grammar, which I had sent him.

31 July

A group of us went to Bonanova Hospital to visit wounded comrades. We brought armfuls of cigarettes and literature. Wade Ellis [later killed at Sierra Caballs] was there with a wound in the left arm. Louis Secundy, commander of auto-park transport, with a wound in the ass, said that five trench mortars in succession exploded near him before the last one got him.

Fred Lutz came after 9:00 P.M. with a happy story about "Minuto" and Stepanovitch, who were captured by thirty young fascists. While they were being led back to the enemy base, the sergeant in charge ordered everyone to the side of the road for a rest. "Minuto," a Spaniard with our brigade, talked fast and convinced the young recruits into surrendering. The thirty became the prisoners of the two.

1 August

A conference with Gallo. He said some materiel was now getting across the Ebro; enough, he thought, to accomplish the objectives of the offensive. However, bridges were being bombed hourly by squadrons of 20 or more fascist planes and much of our materiel was being destroyed. The 35th Division was located north of enemy-held Gandesa, and a strong effort would be made today to take it in a coordinated drive all along the front. He said that more rebel troops were arriving from Extremadura, reinforcing their weakened lines. The 15th Brigade, he added, was closest to Gandesa, about 800 meters. Our casualties, however, were high, about 1,500 for the division.

Parts of a battalion of the 11th Brigade, Gallo told us, had broken and run. But he attributed this to a few unenthusiastic officers who were tired of the war. Steps were being taken to replace them.

Tensions were high this week, so I welcomed an invitation from Fred Lutz and William Beeching, a Canadian, to have dinner together and to walk the Ramblas to the waterfront to view the damage done by enemy bombers before continuing my work.

3 August

Bombing began at 11 P.M. sharp. It sounded as if there were a couple of squadrons in the air as we watched our spotlights center five enemy planes. We cheered when one of them came down in flames. The rest disappeared into the darkness and did not come back. The Barcelona antiaircraft searchlights are now more powerful than ever, with their bright beams scouring the sky like long, menacing fingers. They penetrate the night clouds for miles and are capable of exposing a locust if it dared cross their path. I marveled at this excellent antiaircraft equipment, which must have gotten through the Non-Intervention blockade.

There is plenty of talk still about the Non-Intervention Committee, mostly condemnatory. It is unanimous at HQ that the Non-Intervention restrictions are aimed primarily at the Republic, while Franco and his rebels, without restrictions and with impunity, receive not only all necessary small arms, heavy equipment, and planes, but also thousands of organized German and Italian ground and air troops, overpowering our forces with material superiority.

Our side is strong in morale, determination, dedication, and aspiration. The fascists have more and better weapons.

8 August

I became sick again. My stomach can't hold food. I spoke to Gallo about sending me to France until I get better. He said OK, but I know it won't happen because there's too much to be done. Besides, my conscience is already bothering me. I think about the Spaniards who are suffering great hardships and tragedies with great patience and endurance, in the face of continual bombardments, shortages and rationing of food and of other simple everyday necessities. Yet there are very few Americans who have been here as long as I have—one and a half years. I do need a couple of weeks' rest and recuperation.

Marcel [a French photographer who visited frequently] and Dan Kramen urged me to go to the movies with them. They said it would help me out of the dumps. We saw Marineros del Baltico [Sailors of the Baltic, a Russian movie]. It didn't help much, but I did nap right through it.

Another letter to my family:

26 August 1938, Friday morning

. . . This note, with enclosed pictures and things, is being delivered to you by Juan Peinado, Consul for the Spanish government in Philadelphia. My meeting with him was purely by lucky chance. When recently I was mistakenly paged to answer a phone call intended for someone else, I discovered who I was talking to and that he was leaving soon for Philadelphia. Of course, I promptly made an appointment to see him. Mr. Peinado has graciously agreed to deliver these few personal things to you and to assure you in person that my health and spirits are both holding up.

The government's People's Army recently recrossed the river Ebro (a feat few people believed could be done) and drove the fascists back many miles. Mussolini has been sending more thousands of young Italians to die on the battlefields of Spain. Do what you can to convince the Italians in our neighborhood to protest directly to Italy its shameful intervention in the affairs of Spain. If you do your share, it can help us win the war—and maybe help also arouse the Italian people to free themselves from the monstrosities of fascism. . . .

27 August

Ed Rolfe came before lunch, stayed, and arranged the center spread of pictures for the Volunteer. When he left I gave him a stack of pictures to give to Joe North.

For lunch: watery lentil soup, an invisible piece of meat, a peach, a couple of grapes, tea, and a slice of bread. There has been less food than usual for the past week and the quality has been inferior. No wine, no seconds—and no gripes or complaints. We all know we are eating more than the civilian population.

At 3:00 P.M. Mickey Mickenberg came again. When he was here a couple of days before, he had his right hand bandaged, claiming that it was injured during an artillery barrage. After shaving, I joined him for a walk to the Majestic Hotel because he wanted to locate Rolfe and I wanted to find Lutz, who, when he was in town last, promised to be here today to liquidate some printing bills.

Two of us took time off to visit John Murra, who had a bullet in his lung and was in No. 9 military hospital. Calle Tallers, sala 7, cama 8. He looked good but was anxious to go home. He told me how pleased he was that so many comrades came to visit him and helped him celebrate his birthday three days ago. The Spaniard in the next bed to him had spent 14 years in the U.S.A. and was good company for John.

Left Mickey on a corner at about 6:15 P.M. and headed back to HQ in a messy drizzle—cloudy and damp all day. Passing the Emporium I heard jazz music. My curiosity was aroused, and because I wanted an excuse to get out of the rain, I bought a ticket for two and one half pesetas. I found myself in a commercial dance hall being solicited by a young woman on each arm. I pretended a need for the men's room and slipped out the rear stairway.

On entering HQ, I was set upon by Favetto, the Italian who lost his left arm at Guadalajara and who is Gallo's all-around representative. In addition to orders, he handed me four salvos conductos (safe-conduct passes) for each of the following: Harry Pollitt, general secretary of the Communist party of Great Britain; Peter Kerrigan, political commissar for British volunteers; Lieutenant Gregori, trade union representative of Catalonia; and the last pass for me. Orders are that I am to lead the group *to the Ebro River front, locate division and brigade headquarters, guide these men to wherever they choose to go and be their troubleshooter and translator.*

Am I glad that Puns, the Catalan who knows his way around Catalonia blindfolded, is to be our chofer. *Departure time: 3:00 A.M. No use going to bed; I have scheduled proofreading at the printer's at midnight.*

Before the war Puns had belonged to the Anarchist youth organizations. Since then, however, he had joined the Communist party because, in his words, "It was the major party which had advocated and forged unity out of all the political parties, with the winning of the war and the defeat of fascism as its main goal." He was proud of and had praise for the Communist Fifth Regiment and the role of the Communists in initiating the organization of military units that entered the toughest battles after the uprising took place in July 1936. His heroes were La Pasionaria, Lister, Modesto, El Campesino, and the many volunteers he got to know in the International Brigades.

Enrique Lister and Juan Modesto were two principal organizers of the Fifth Regiment. Lister had been a quarryman, and Modesto an exwoodcutter. Both were Communists. When the government began developing a unified command, the Fifth Regiment, the most effective fighting unit to emerge in the new People's Army, was integrated into the divisions and corps of the Army of the Republic.

28 August

Sunday. At 3:00 A.M. sharp, we were off to the Ebro front with British guests Harry Pollitt and Peter Kerrigan. Lieutenant Gregori canceled out at the last minute. On the enemy side of the Ebro—ground which our forces had recently reconquered— our car got stuck in a narrow, sandy road, and I had to use our treasured cigarettes to bribe enough Spaniards to help us lift and shove the car out of the rut. They were bearded, tired, and unenthusiastic.

When we finally located the 35th Division HQ, after getting lost and on the wrong road several times, we had hot coffee. But in the evening we were treated to a delicious meal of a veal cutlet and eggs with plenty of wine and fruits. Lieutenant Eli Biegelman cornered me and made me promise to write letters to Madrid for him. His Spanish girlfriend can't read English.

As I wrote notes of this trip for a story for the Volunteer, *I learned that thirty of our men were being given leaves of absence to foreign countries, beginning the day after tomorrow. There's plenty of muttering about so few leaves.*

Pollitt, through my translation, bluntly told Major Merino, 35th Division commander, that all the British and American volunteers should be sent home immediately, not in dribs and drabs. He said the men were exhausted, they have done very heavy fighting, and they should be sent home for a rest. Besides, he said, the political effect of the returning veterans would be electric, making it possible to mobilize further support more easily for the Loyalist cause and facilitate the raising of additional funds so badly needed to purchase food, medical supplies, and arms and equipment for Republican Spain.

Major Merino looked bored and unimpressed. However, for more than an hour he patiently and in great detail explained the current military activities and why Pollitt's demands were unthinkable. I wish I had been able to take shorthand because his long and uninterrupted recitation of events was not only fascinating, but convincing as well. He said that to pull our men out now would lead to great demoralization among the Spanish forces.

Merino also said that our meager air force appeared eight days after the Ebro offensive started while the enemy covered the skies for one month, haunting our advancing troops with three to four hundred planes. Yet our troops advanced, fought so well with professional tactics that the enemy became demoralized. In spite of our handicaps, the first phase of the operation was realized with ridiculously few machine guns, rifles, or ammunition, and above all, with hardly any artillery. It was our brains against their overpowering arms, yet we outmaneuvered them with courage and skill. The enemy's air superiority, the continuous bombing of the bridges over the Ebro, the heavy artillery firing on our positions without letup, the sixty to seventy tanks battering our lines, the heavy machine guns and mortars could not stop our comrades from pushing doggedly into enemy territory. In spite of all this firepower, the fascists failed to dislodge our troops.

Moreover, Merino continued, all was not so rosy: our troops were perched on the rocky mountains of Hill 666, where it was difficult and often impossible to dig and fortify positions. But the enemy didn't have enough reserves, at that point anyway, to knock us off our present posts; they couldn't do it with just artillery or aviones. It had to be done by ground troops. Franco, for reasons of his own, was not using foreign troops for these hard mountains; maybe because the foreigners refused. So the enemy troops facing us consisted of Banderos del Tercio of the 16th, 17th, and 18th brigades, made up of Moors and Navarros.

Merino, well versed in what was going on in the fascist zone because of his talks with prisoners, told us that recruiting by the enemy was done in rebel detention camps. A fascist officer would come along and ask for "volunteers" to fight the rojos (reds), and one either volunteered or else. These men usually ended up on our side as eager prisoners who then fought with our forces with great enthusiasm.

To win the war, he said, it was necessary that our Internationals remain until the Loyalist army has trained skilled commanders for the battlefield (they are presently being trained at a feverish pace at government officers' training school) and that Loyalist Spain acquire arms and equipment to meet the enemy at least half way. The fascist morale is a fake; when they are defeated in battle, they are at a complete loss. Enemy deserters say that their chiefs figure that it isn't possible to attack government troops frontally, so they try encircling movements. Fascists are not able to face difficult battles and win them. Their morale is built on easy victories. Merino admitted that the 15th Brigde had had a hard time in the fighting, that it had faced the brunt of three heavy enemy counterattacks, but that our brigade had held fast and kept the enemy at the barbed wire. Merino said he was proud of his division and told of the many stories about its capturing 3,500 prisoners.

About Major Merino: he is 25 years old and a former university student who majored in mathematics and rose to his present command position as one of Campesino's battalion commanders. Valentin Gonzalez, who was known as El Campesino (The Peasant), was military commander of the respected 46th Division, and it was considered a unique honor for one to have served in it and to have been promoted through its ranks. Merino said that he was now much more of a university student than before. He said also that the majority of the exact science students had joined the Republican cause, even sons of the wealthy, while many of the social studies students did not. Mathematics, he jested, does not lie. He qualified his remarks by admitting that the division chief of staff was a former lawyer.

3 September
  Major Allan Johnson arrived while I was at the port area. He left a note for me advising that he'd be back by 3:00 A.M. The day had been cloudy, with occasional bursts of rain and violent showers. I got back from the printer's shortly after midnight and waited up for Johnson, who arrived with Eddie Rolfe about 3:00. I translated for Johnson in his conversation with Gallo, who ended up giving a safe-conduct to Johnson, which guaranteed him clear passage to France and home within ten days. Johnson and I spent the day together. I helped him make final preparations for his departure. At the end of the day he gave me a wonderfully knitted sweater and his pistol.
  Mickey Mickenberg visited while we were having supper. The conversation dwelt mainly on Jarama and Johnson's difficulties with division and brigade leadership. Johnson detailed the attack of 5 April 1937 at Jarama, which I remember very well. What I didn't know was that this attack was the one that got Johnson in hot water, first with the 35th Division commander, General Gal, then with Copic, brigade commander.

However, Johnson who had been in command of the American training base at Tarazona de la Mancha, was not returning to the United States because of past difficulties with leadership but because he had been badly wounded when his staff car was riddled with bullets and he was now well enough to travel. That September day, he sketched for me a map of the troop positions during the controversial events at Jarama on 5 April 1937. I have used the map with material of that date.

4 September
  When the air raid alarms shrieked at 10:15 A.M., we waited for the roar of planes, but none came. I noticed that the building across the street, Casa delgi Italiani—House of the Italians—has been occupied by a small army of women. No one on our side of the street knows why, but I suspect it's a party school because I saw La Pasionaria with them yesterday.
  In the evening I walked to the Cuban club where, with Maria, we sat around and talked with some of the members about the course of the war, world developments, and the bold and tireless activities of many Cubans in various units of the army. Those we spoke to believe that the Cubans who are able to do so will filter back into their own country after the war to carry on the struggle against Batista.
  Of course, there was the usual music for anyone who cared to dance. With the uncertain way the war is going, I don't know how anyone can enjoy dancing and because of this I left for headquarters in bad humor.

7 September
  In a morning discussion with me, Sandor Voros said that he was undecided whether he would accept my job as editor of the Volunteer, *but when he returned in the evening he said it was decided he should accept. With whom he discussed it I don't know, nor did I ask. I presume it was with the politicos of the brigade. I can't do the*

historical work Gallo assigned to me while under the pressures of editing the
Volunteer. *Unfortunately, Voros is the worst possible choice for the cooperative atmosphere in these headquarters. He is authoritarian—knows it all, has all the answers—and insensitive to other people's ideas, attempts to dominate any discussion, and is often abusive in his remarks. I don't expect him to last long. Comrades around here have gone through plenty and they won't take to his constant bragging about how much he has done and how brilliant he is.*

11 September

Today was a big holiday in Catalonia. On this day in 1714, Rafael Casanova, symbolic national figure, inspired the people of Catalonia to take a last stand against the foreign invaders, so the story goes. The local press devoted much space to this important day and to its history.

Before noon, as I walked to the Gran Via Hotel to look up Fred Lutz, I ran into Lou Secundy. When we found that Fred was not in, we left him a message and then went to Lou's room at the Bristol Hotel. Over some wine, Lou told me of his frustrating affair with an anarchist girlfriend the night before. Instead of an evening of love, as he had hoped, it developed into a discussion of the politics of the many Spanish parties and of the various trade unions.

After lunch Fred, Lou, Bill Beeching, and I visited the Casanova statue, which, by the time we got there, was decorated with scores of Catalonian and Republican flags, and some flags from other friendly nations. While uniformed guards stood at attention, soldiers, men and women, some with children, and others passing by pinned little Catalonian flags on a large red pillow nestled at the base of the statue.

After leaving Casanova behind, we picked our way through the crowds to the Plaza Catalunya, the main square, where we sat in a cafe watching people go by. For supper at Bergamin's we had what was called a Jewish meal of small portions of soup, meat and potatoes, salad, and melon, costing 35 pesetas per person. This restaurant is reputed to be the hangout of Catalonian fifth columnists and speculators. To have been able to finger any such disreputable individual among all those people would have required more skill and knowledge than was in all four of us.

18 September

Sunday. Four of us went to the National Exposition, which started at the Plaza de España. While we took pictures of the exposition, chidlren followed and dogged us until we agreed to snap theirs also. Since I had by then run out of film, I was overly generous with my empty camera in the number of pictures I took, which made everybody happy. By acting nice and by accepting their flowers, we finally freed ourselves from these youngsters and ended our tour at Maria's, where we had lunch of bread, burnt beans, and fish with tomato sauce. When I returned to headquarters, I read and worked throughout most of the night.

19 September

Fred Lutz told me of some harrowing experiences he had during the days and weeks of the Ebro offensive at Quinto and Belchite. One took place the night he heard I was either at brigade or division headquarters. He and Abe Lewis decided to take a long walk and ferret me out. The battles were winding down, with as many as a 1,000 prisoners in our hands, and despite heavy losses, morale was high and they were in a proud mood. From Spaniards in our outfit (though the 15th International Brigade is English-speaking, we have one battalion of Spaniards), they got directions to head-quarters, and they were either deliberately misled or there was a language foul-up. The latter is the more likely. For instance, a Spaniard will say, a la derecha, *which means "to the right." He may also add* derecho, *which is intended to mean "straight ahead." It's all easy if you get the* a *and the* o. *But if you catch a Spaniard who throws both words at you while simultaneously pointing to the left, then your best bet is to sit down and cry.*

Anyway, Fred and Abe got lost. They didn't know whether they were walking into enemy territory or away from it. The Johnny Parks truck that drove into enemy lines death trap at Jarama was still unforgotten. Their pace slowed, then froze at the sound of feet shuffling and stone falling against stone. Too dark to see anything clearly, but they had good ears, and their ears got better when they sensed big trouble. The clanking of a chain, a muffled nervous cough, suddenly aroused the sweat glands of their bodies. Abe felt a sudden urge for a bowel movement, but their experiences and training of the past year and a half permitted them to remain calm. Fred described it this way:

"We drew our revolvers and sank to our elbows. Behind some mounds and against the sky two heads slid closer, cautiously closer, and at about thirty feet from us they halted, taking stock of us; we were just as suspiciously scrutinizing them. For five minutes the four of us stood frozen, but it seemed awfully much longer. Slowly they withdrew and vanished."

Next, Fred and Abe heard footsteps from the direction they had come. Two men appeared with drawn pistols. It was time to act. When the glistening pistols got within twenty feet from them, the point of no return, the point of deadly confrontation, Fred made one last effort to avoid a firefight. He shouted: "Camaradas, camaradas!" Halting, but still pointing their guns toward Abe and Fred, the Spaniards asked: "Internacionales?" With joy and relief both Fred and Abe answered, "Si." Still shaky about them, Fred asked for directions back to the American lines, but when he heard the safety of one of their pistols snap, he was uncertain if the safety was put on or put off. To play it safe against being shot in the back, he urged the two Spaniards to accompany Abe and him part way; unhesitatingly, they did so.

Fred let out a deep breath and said: "In a short while, we came out on a road and smack into a big, beautiful, monstrous Russian tank that we almost kissed." The Spaniards went on to join their battalion.

Fred also told me of an incident he experienced the night the Lincolns stormed and took Belchite during our recent Ebro offensive. He entered the city while it was still full of fascist troops and while our men were still bombing and hand-grenading enemy strongholds, and with some street fighting in progress. His instructions were to immediately set up headquarters for the collection of enemy provisions, livestock, equipment, and anything else that could weaken their will to hang on. For this purpose he selected a large house, especially because it had a refugio, *or air raid shelter. He was mindful of the previous day's fifty-two enemy planes that made innumerable sorties on our lines. He felt certain more raids were in the offing.*

With three armed Spanish guards, rifles at the ready and grenades handy, Fred began his policing of the refugio. *He quickly found a load of mattresses and canned foodstuffs. "Holy mackerel!" he exclaimed to the Spaniards, who probably thought he was talking about religious fish. The tunnel was long and narrow and they had to walk squatting in pitch-dark, with an electric torch. The shelter's path bent to the left. Suddenly a head peeked from under one of the mattresses, and the guards shouted for the head to surrender. Out popped not one head but two scared heads, pale and trembling. Fred and the guards, with cocked weapons alert for betrayal, backed out of the tunnel with the prisoners following closely. Outside, the prisoners protested that they were civilians, not fascists. They said also that there were women and children hiding in the* refugio. *Fred, still on guard, ordered one of them back into the shelter to lead the way to others and to call to them to come out. A woman's voice answered. At another turn of the trench a very fat, trembling woman with a crutch unveiled her face, then a slight woman with a child on her back appeared with an old woman using a broom for support and leading another child.*

Fred related: "We make them advance one by one because fascists have often played the trick of forcing women and children to walk ahead of them until they get close to us, then surprise us by suddenly opening fire. We've lost many good comrades that way, especially at Brunete. We weren't taking chances. We back out once more. The poor cripple on her hands and knees was crying in terror. They were fed such terrible tales about the rojos *that they expected the worst. Instead we gave them water, for which they thirsted, food, and assurances of their safety. We go back again with the same man. He calls through the tunnel until we come out from underneath another house. No fascisti aqui [No fascists here]."*

Next, Fred recounted an episode that happened on the morning of the same day as the above. While he was exploring a section of the city already in our hands, an officer from another brigade requested help for some wounded fascists. With a Spanish guide, Fred found them huddled in a spacious dark room of a bombed-out house. When he entered, the overpowering foul odor almost hurled him back out. The divisional doctor, who later took care of them, said all of the wounded were gangrened. They had been under the care of two nuns dressed in white with black veils and two first-aid men wearing fascist emblems. Since none had had water all day, Fred put together a detail of able prisoners and led them to a nearby factory with a clean well, now in our hands.

"The nuns were apparently taking it quite calmly. They appeared to be efficient and I wondered what they were thinking, since they, too, must have been bombarded with horror stories about us."

20 September

Number 32, my last number as editor of the Volunteer for Liberty, *appeared today. Sandor Voros has taken over as editor. Now I can begin the work of gathering material for the book* Two Years of the International Brigades, *Gallo's project. The German and Italian comrades are already weeks ahead of me. This will mean many weeks of intensive work at long hours. The doctor, on my regular visit today, advised me to take it easy. I couldn't, even if I wanted to. But I did take it easy today by going to a free movie, where I met Mario, Spanish representative at I.B. Headquarters, and José Maria Varela, 59th (Spanish) Battalion commissar, who had been to I.B. Headquarters for a meeting with Gallo. We were treated to a Russian film of the Paris Commune, which featured the leadership role of the Polish-Frenchman Dąbrowski in whose honor the Polish International Brigade was named.*

23 September

There was a great deal of excitement at headquarters all day. Negrin made a speech on the twenty-first at the League of Nations in Geneva, in which he declared that the Republic would withdraw all International volunteers, including those combatants who had taken out Spanish citizenship after 5 July 1936. We had expected Alvarez del Vayo, the foreign minister, to make this announcement. Willy, the German comrade, did not seem pleased. I recalled that Ernst Toller had remarked to Valledor (as told to me by Ed Rolfe) that the German volunteers had hoped for a home base in Spain while they worked toward the final defeat of Hitlerism.

Everybody appeared jubilant, except the Spaniards on our Headquarters staff and Willy.

24 September

Saturday. Yesterday, several of us were summoned to a meeting with Gallo, who, in a brief session, assigned us the task of writing assorted articles for the Ejercito Popular *(Popular Army), the Spanish army journal. I accepted the subject "The Fraternization of the International Brigade Volunteers with the Spanish People." I worked on it promptly and submitted it before the day was over, to everyone's surprise and Gallo's satisfaction.*

Today's newspapers and newscasts featured Czechoslovakia's call for mobilization of her reserve armed forces and of all able-bodied citizens. Whether this represents the first real challenge to Hitler or is to be another case of public shadowboxing while sellouts are being negotiated behind steel doors, only time will tell.

When I called on Eddie Rolfe, who had just returned from the front, I saw that he was exhausted and shaken. Our brigade was badly cut up in the last couple of days, he said. When the 14th Brigade broke ranks, our men jumped into the breach and got decimated. His friend, Jim Lardner, a journalist and son of Ring Lardner, was either captured or killed. The Lincolns, he believed, were left with fewer than a hundred men. The British were also shattered. Enemy artillery and air craft were active without interruption and were deadly accurate. Our men went into action without the definite knowledge, except for rumors, of Prime Minister Negrin's announcement of the demobilization of the International Volunteers at Geneva. Strangely, no newspapers, Spanish or English, which carried Negrin's speech, had been delivered to the men at the front in the last couple days.

I received my first letter from home in weeks, a long one from Ed Thompson, pipe fitter and staunch unionist in the maintenance department at the Campbell Soup plant, who detailed trade union organizational efforts there and told of the many frustrations of these efforts.

Homage to the International Brigades

Part Five

WITHDRAWAL OF THE INTERNATIONAL BRIGADES

September 1938–April 1939 and Beyond

FIFTEEN

The Order to Withdraw

26 September
    Tension, as heavy as fog, hovered over the family-style dinner tables. There was little eating but much talking. War was expected! Hitler was to speak this evening. Would a war in Europe hurt or help the Spanish cause? Would not the diversion of German and Italian armed forces, now committed in Spain, to the battlefronts of Europe give the Spanish Republic the breather needed to smash the Franco rebellion? Would not the defeat of Franco contribute decisively to the cause of world peace? These were some of the questions batted around. Each person at the tables could have said justifiably to England and France: "We told you so. You pampered Hitler, then yielded to him, now pay the consequences." None did. No one hoped for the devastation and tragedy of war to descend on other lands. They did desire, however, that the democracies should at last realize, in their self-interest if nothing else, that they must unequivocally sell to the Spanish Republic the arms and weapons needed to finish the job on its own brand of fascism. If the democracies fail once again to do so, they will face their retribution in the not too distant future.
    At a hurriedly called headquarters staff meeting, Gallo spoke at length. He threw a few shockers. The International Volunteers, he said, had served their usefulness. It would now be better for them to go back to their homelands and carry on the struggle for Spain from there. They had fought in most of the major battles of the war, and fought well. In 1936, they battled in the streets of Madrid; in 1937, at Jarama, where Madrid was saved from encirclement and the fascist armies stopped dead in their

171

tracks, which bought time for the Republic to build a Popular Army primarily of workers, peasants, and students; in 1937, at Guadalajara, where the Garibaldini— the Italian antifascist volunteers—routed Mussolini's crack regulars and captured thousands; also in 1937, at Brunete, where the Republic proved it could mount an offensive and hold onto ground won; in early 1938, at Teruel, where our men withstood the coldest winter in Spain's recorded history; and later in 1938, at the Ebro, where the Internationals acquitted themselves valiantly in the face of enemy superiority in small arms, tanks, artillery, and aircraft, albeit at great cost in precious lives. We have no apologies. We fought well and gave thousands of our best comrades to the soil of Spain. But after two years many of our men were tired and exhausted. Because some volunteers have been away from their homes for so long, their families have suffered. Unless the volunteers are sent home now, demoralization may set in.

Besides, Gallo continued, the Spanish cadres are seasoned soldiers, much better now than ever. The officers and men have had two years of experience in building a People's Army with practically no help from the regular army, which had, on the whole, enrolled itself with Franco from the outset. The People's Army developed and matured under enemy fire. Lessons were quickly learned and new techniques advanced. However, the army's greatest handicap is its shortage of the war materials that would enable it to deal a final, crushing blow to the enemy's demoralized troops. The Army of the Republic has well-trained and experienced artillery men, but no artillery. They have trained and experienced tank crews, but no tanks for them to fight with. Infantrymen are in reserves by the thousands, for there are not enough rifles. The same holds true for machine gunners and mortar men. Trained pilots by the score are sitting watching the enemy fly, but there are no planes for them to make the chase. The Spanish medical corps are now well organized, with adequate numbers of doctors and first aid men, but there are shortages of ambulances and medical supplies. What the Spanish troops mainly need is to be supplied with the means with which to continue their struggle till victory. Furthermore, by returning home now, Gallo said, the volunteers would be giving the Loyalist government an additional political advantage before the world: the volunteers on the side of the legitimate Spanish government would be going back to their homelands while the German and Italian mercenary troops remained with the Franco fascist side. Perhaps then the democracies would demand of Hitler and Mussolini that they withdraw their troops. Of course, this would lead to the collapse of Franco and his generals and ensure victory for the Republic.

Before Gallo unveiled the plan for repatriation of the International Brigades, he reiterated that the right time for the volunteers to go home was now. Our men must go back to their countries and make vigorous propaganda for the Loyalist cause. Their prestige would be high and they would be listened to. They must organize mass support for the people of Spain, and raise money to insure the purchase and delivery of medical supplies, food and, if possible, weapons for the Loyalist troops.

The procedure for demobilization, Gallo said, would be as follows: (1) the immediate pulling out of our volunteers from the front lines into rear positions for a two-day rest; (2) then the big job of transporting them to Barcelona for two more days of cleaning up and making ready for receiving awards, certificates, and medals from the Spanish government, followed by parades and festivities prior to departure; (3) the move to Camp Olot, near the French border, where plans were being finalized for the last step toward repatriation. He stated that the services and headquarters staff (that is

*us) would be the last to leave Spain. However, Gallo warned, if war among the
European powers broke out in the interim, we would face unforeseen problems,
difficulties and obstacles. The greatest of these would be for those who did not come
from democratic countries and for those who had not become French citizens while they
were refugees from their home country. The Italians might be able to squeeze into
France and somehow assimilate themselves into existing Italian communities. This
would be more difficult for the German refugees, the Poles, Hungarians, Czechs,
Rumanians, and Yugoslavs. Every effort would be made, however, to insure the safety
of every individual.*

*Gallo did not look well. The burdens of political leadership over the International
Brigades and their multinationals for the last two years have taken their toll of his
health. On his freshly shaved head, in place of hair were many small and large scabby
sores, starting from the forehead and traveling across the top and down to the back of
his neck. It looked to me like a bad case of nerves. During the big retreat from the
Ebro, his head was always bandaged to keep the dust from further infecting the sores.
His dark-set eyes socketed under droopy, black bushy eyebrows with strands of gray, and
his dark, unshaven beard gave his pale complexion a sick look. The crushing obligations
of his position of leadership seem to have caused a heavy crease down each side of his
face, from his nose almost to his chin, accentuating that melancholy look. During one of
his infrequent smiles or laughs, a gold tooth shows among teeth that look as if they
could stand a lot of repairs.*

*Generally calm, pleasant, and self-possessed, Gallo is never talkative, but at the
dinner table he is alert to conversation and does not hesitate to give his analysis or
opinions on the topic under discussion. His worst trait is his bad jokes, which always
fall flat. His greatest trait is his concern for the men at the front, to whom he gives his
prompt personal attention. This concern and the pressures from the front caused, I
believe, the sores on his body. He is soft-spoken, and when he speaks informally, he is
almost inaudible. Once, during a staff meeting, after returning from the Ebro weary
and exhausted, I slept through his monotone and though I had to be poked to be
awakened, he never rebuked me for it. However, when he shouts or speaks in public, his
voice often breaks at high pitch. He is not a good public speaker. Sometimes when he is
abrupt and impatient, he tries to be democratic, but is caught between his military need
to act arbitrarily and his political Marxist training to discuss reasons for decisions. For
instance, when the POUMists (Partido Obrero de Unificación Marxista—Workers
Party of Marxist Unification) threatened counterrevolution in the city of Barcelona, he
ordered us to the rooftops with rifles. When we questioned the reason for this order, he
became irritated and told us to do what we were told. Later he relented and told us of
the potential stab in the back by the Trotskyite POUMists.*

*Gallo is slight of build and not tall, perhaps five feet seven inches at most, but he
commands the affection, respect, and loyalty of all those at headquarters, the political
commissars from the brigades, whose superior he is, and the military officers and men
he associates with. Although he encountered some men who fell apart during the heat
of battle, he did not demand of anyone the abstractions of courage. Instead he inspired
everyone with his own coolness and efficiency under the most adverse conditions. He
inspires warmth and comradeship because he himself is warm and comradely. He is no
military giant, nor is he ostentatious about his political and organizational abilities. He
gets things done quietly, quickly, and effectively. He is unlike André Marty, that tall,*

heavily built, boisterous Frenchman with a booming, arrogant, domineering voice, whose path I strive to avoid—especially after the day I got a dressing-down from him for watching an aerial dog fight from our Headquarters second-floor window instead of flying down to the shelter as we are supposed to. Gallo would not have done that, at least not in front of others. In private he might have said, "I know I don't always go to the shelter myself, but I think you and everyone else in this building should, don't you think so?" He might also have added wryly, "But then, I'm expendable." Flamboyant Marty belongs on the battlefield leading the charge. Gallo, on the other hand, is at his best in what he is doing—being a political leader in a political war.

As an unswerving and dedicated Communist, convinced that the world would sooner or later move toward socialism, he devotes his life to that cause. He often repeats that the world must be aroused to unite in common struggle to stem and destroy fascism. Marty and Gallo are as different from each other as night from day, yet they seem to get along well. Marty dresses spotlessly and wears an oversized, flapping beret, spread on his big head like a giant mushroom. Gallo, informal in dress, wears his ill-fitting, unmatched uniform loosely. Except for formal events, he never dons his officer's hat and never carries side arms unless he is headed for the front. He is clearly uncomfortable in military uniform. On one occasion, when I told him I needed money to buy a new pair of khaki trousers, he said, "What! New trousers! Why don't you get a used pair somewhere. Look at mine. I got these from a comrade at the front."

1 October

Saturday. AT 3:00 A.M. I left by bus with a delegation of trade unionists from the local UGT Federation Headquarters on Paseo de Gracia. We headed for the Ebro front, where we were expected by the officers and men of the 15th Brigade, already out of the front lines and preparing their first stage homeward. The Barcelona trade unionists planned to honor our men before they left the battlefields. Our driver, who brought the bus from the Ebro for this occasion, was Al Hawke, former Brookwood Labor College student; his assistant was Silverman. We arrived at our destination, near the Ebro, at 6:00 A.M. But a larger bus, which had started out a half hour earlier with a full load of additional unionists did not arrive until 7:30 at night because of a flat tire, its occupants hungry, tired, and irritated.

Brigade put on a hospitable reception for the earlier arrivals. The handshaking, embracing, and fist saluting began at estado mayor *(a new location from the last time I was here), a house on the road from Marsa. While the unionists were being hosted by headquarters, I slipped away to visit with Fred Lutz at his improvised office in a barn.*

For a delightful lunch, headquarters delivered us to the town of Guiamets, two kilometers from the River Ebro. All seemed to be quiet, as if the enemy were lying low and knowingly allowing these festivities to take place so as not to slow down the departure of the dreaded International Brigades. Chatting with and entertaining the Barcelona guests were Alvah Bessie, Sandor Voros, and Saul Wellman, and Jim Bourne. They all got along fine without a translator. Women danced to music from a sound truck, and to the enthusiastic chants of "olé" from a receptive audience, until late in the afternoon, when guests were transported to the Marsa football field, where the main body of brigade soldiers had been waiting since 2:00 P.M. in field formation under the open skies and were by then getting restless. The schedule was thrown out of whack because the larger bus failed to show up on time.

The speaking began: Valledor, the brigade commander, spoke; John Gates spoke; the UGT delegates spoke. All were good, but all talked too long. Even when Valledor was presented with a gold watch from the men of the brigade, the flowery remarks were too lengthy. When all speaking had ended, there were loud cheerful sighs of relief. For dinner we returned to Guiamets for more food and more speeches. This time the officers of the estado mayor *and the brigade were presented with Activist Awards by the Spaniards, who honored the recipients in eloquent terms. (Gates was annoyed that he got this award while Valledor did not.) By far, the best and shortest speech was made by a young man from the Association of Socialist Youth, who, with great emotion, said, "Though the bodies of the Internationals may be leaving Spain, their spirit will remain permanently carved in the hearts and minds of all Spaniards, whether they may be in the frontline trenches, in the rearguard, in the factories, or in the fields tilling their land."*

The band played on, followed by singing and dancing until our bus left for Barcelona at 1:00 A.M.

2 October

Sunday. I woke up at 11 A.M. just as Hawke and Silverman, who had slept with us, were about to leave. I caught them just in time to give them mail, literature, clothes, and several boxes of cigarettes, chocolates, and candies to take back to our guys.

After a meeting with Gallo on the book, I moved from the present offices to the greater privacy of the offices across the street, occupied formerly by the Children's Committee.

* * * *

After a short nap in the afternoon, I went to the Cuban club to meet with Melvin Anderson, Jack Goldstein, and English Johnny and his two girlfriends; one looked like the mother of the younger. Cueria, a Cuban, who is now a major, also sat in on part of the session.

The first enemy bombardment began at 9:30 P.M. Their planes came five times during the night. One was caught dead center in our spotlights and the red chaser bullets streaming from our antiaircraft machine guns made a fireworks in the black sky. It looked like that mother of a fascist got away.

Sandor Voros arrived late at night with very little to say except that the day was dull at the brigade and that I had not missed anything by not staying an extra day.

4 October

Tuesday. Another bombardment at 10:30 A.M. Second bombardment around noon. We had been awakened by air raid alerts. The first night raid had started at about 9:15, just as Mario, from HQ, Enrique Barea (a Cuban), and I entered a movie at the Plaza Urgiñona. Police stopped all cars, and as one crawled without headlights trying to slip past, it was detained. The shrill sound of police whistles was too much like home. We returned without having seen the whole show, walking rapidly under an unusually bright moon, disturbed only by an occasional burst of antiaircraft fire. The planes repeated their visits about six times until daybreak. Our sleep was interrupted also by Giandante, the Italian artist, who kept jumping in and out of bed at the slightest sound from the outside. During one of the enemy's visits, we watched, fascinated, as one of their planes, cornered by spotlights, was stalked by our antiaircraft and red chaser bullets, which turned the sky into an unreal July Fourth spectacle.

To me Giandante seems an unusual person, and his artist's black pencil strokes always look stronger than he does. Not more than five feet tall and skinny, he appears to be under a hundred pounds. He has a drawn, esthetic face with a long Roman nose and practically no lips. If one looks at him frontally, one may see a perpendiclar line from the brow to the nose to the chin, with very little flesh on either side of this imaginary line, except for the eyes, which are shifty and nervous. Usually quiet, he keeps pretty much to himself and rarely gets drawn into a discussion. But when he does, he holds everyone's attention. He's supersensitive and can't take a joke. On one or two occasions he showed a fiery temper. He admits that he can hold a grudge against a person for years. He never goes to the movies, theater, dances, or any festivities. He is a talented artist and considers these diversions a waste of time. Though he's supposed to be thirty-nine years old, he looks much younger. Never without his blue beret, even in the dining room, he wears it carelessly over his half-bald head. On one occasion at dinner, when I playfully took his beret off his head and told him I would give it back after dinner, he almost threw a plate of food at me. The plate didn't stop him; what did was his look at the food in it.

Subdued and pensive, perhaps because of the years of hardship suffered in and out of Italy's prisons for revolutionary activities, he is really a fine comrade to have around. His big ears detect the least little sound, and like Canapino, he senses the approach of planes long before anyone else, often minutes before the air raid alert sounds. Lately, he has not been running down to the refugio *as often, but then others have not been doing so either.*

Canapino has also changed since he has been visiting the front lines more frequently. The sound of planes no longer sends him scurrying to the refugio; *his face still turns pale, but his hair doesn't become as disordered as before and it no loner stands on end.*

* * * *

At the invitation of Maria Claremont, whom I had met last Saturday at the Ebro with her delegation of Barcelona trade unionists, I visited the headquarters of Mujeres Libres (Women's Liberation), affiliated with the Anarchists. Although I had an appointment with her, Maria was not in.

5 October

At Mujeres Libres, Maria Claremont introduced me to a group of her companions. One of them said she had met me before, but I couldn't remember. A discussion for more than an hour ensued. They explained the efforts of their organization to free the Spanish women from the trappings of the capitalist system and the church. When I asked what they meant by saying that their organization was "based on ideological revolutionary principles," they were not clear. They must have sensed my confusion and offered to introduce me to more advanced members because they themselves, they said, were not intellectuals. I assured them I was not one either. "Who are your leaders?" I asked. They went into a long explanation about their organization and why they had no leaders—only orientators. I promised to return in the afternoon for more orientation and for a trip with Maria Clarement to the Juventudes

Libertarias (Libertarian Youth) for an introduction to Anarchist youth work. I phoned later and postponed this arrangement because I had to finish an article on the defense of Madrid, assigned to me by Gallo for possible use in the book to be called Two Years of the International Brigades in Spain.

While I was out Macdonald—an Englishman—came. When he started going through my papers, he was stopped by Voros, who told him no one was allowed to go through my things in my absence. Normally, this would have been correct for Voros to do, but with Macdonald it created hard feelings, for we had worked intimately in the past and I trusted him completely.

6 October

Newspapers carry stories commemorating the events of this day in 1934, when Catalonia and especially Asturias rebelled against their oppressors.

The Spaniards I spoke with today were not so pleased about our leaving their country and returning to our homes. They expressed strong feelings that they were being abandoned: first by the world powers and now by their friends, the International Volunteers. As one said, "Now we're being left on our own." I was rather surprised since I had expected a reaction to the contrary.

At Victor's and Zofia's invitation, I accompanied them to a funeral for a Polish volunteer at the hospital in Calle Talleres. In spite of several operations, he could not be saved from the wounds suffered at the Ebro. He had been in all the battles of the war, a longtime activist, then got hit on the last day, just before his unit was finally and permanently pulled out of the front lines. Speakers at the funeral included Poles, Spaniards, a representative of the Spanish Communist party, one from the Catalonian Socialist Unity party (PSUC—Pantido Socialista Unificado de Cataluña), and one from youth organizations. I am told the dead volunteer was a member of the underground Central Committee of the Polish Communist party. It was a sad but impressive affair. I left before the final speeches to look up Fred Lutz.

When I found Fred, I also found William Beeching, John Simon, Paul Osborn, and Harry Lichter who had chofered them. For supper at their hotel we had soup, meat, rolls, and cooked greens. The amount of food served may have satisfied a child in kindergarten. One of the guys ran up to his room and brought back two cans of salmon and a loaf of bread, which we shared.

7 October

Starting from the Gran Via Hotel at 9 A.M., Fred, Beeching, and I made a shopping tour. At a tailor shop, Fred ordered two custom-made suits. We located a store selling civilian shirts and picked up some nice buys. At Jorbe department store, Fred bought a blue beret; I bought gloves for 105 pesetas. Our eyes caught quality beaver hats of the Stetson type for 400 pesetas. Each of us bought one, but I had to borrow 300 pesetas from Fred before I could pay for mine.

At 6 P.M. I kept my appointment with Maria Claremont at the Mujeres Libres, CNT headquarters, Calle Durrutti. She led me to the foreign propaganda department of the organization and proudly introduced me to Emma Goldman, whom I knew by reputation only. She said she had heard some nice things about me and wondered if we might have a talk. When I agreed, she set the date for tomorrow at 6 P.M.

[Emma Goldman was a leading advocate of anarchism in the United States, with the reputation of being an excellent speaker, writer, pamphleteer, organizer, and activist.

She was also well known in Europe. She had come to the United States from Tsarist Russia when she was a child and quickly rebelled against the sweatshop conditions in clothing and corset factories, where she worked. She founded and edited a monthly magazine called Mother Earth. *When I met her, she did not appear to be what I had visualized a well-known Anarchist would look like. I found she could be anyone's mother, sister, or friend. She sat in a armchair behind a desk too big for this smallish and a little too heavy, matronly lady. She was friendly and soft-spoken, with the kindest of eyes.]*

Because there wasn't any electric power in their building, Maria and I had to feel our way through the hall and steps until we got to offices with lighted candles, where she introduced me formally, with flourish, as if I were a dignitary. Of her friends she said, "This is comrade _____, old-time Anarchist; comrade _____, youth Anarchist activist," and so forth.

* * * *

At a late staff meeting called to discuss the Popular Front in France and the Czechoslovakian developments, Giandante abruptly and in a demanding voice wanted to know why some of us believed that a world war was inevitable if Spain was defeated. He pointed to Ravera, who made no answer but who passed the buck to me. The smoothness with which Ravera ducked the question and put me on the spot caused some laughter. Fortunately, the artist was satisfied with my answers. I was afraid that since he is so supersensitive he might have misunderstood the levity and felt hurt. When I finished, he said shyly that he was just testing to see if we really knew what we were talking about.

8 October

Harry Lichter, short, blond, talkative but companionable, is returning to Brigade with the mail truck.

On my way to the subsecretariat of propaganda, I ran into effervescent Irving Weissman. As we were comparing notes, Juan Godoy happened along and insisted we join him for coffee at his home. The relative living with him had lost her husband and three sons at the front; her home in Barceloneta—the waterfront section of Barcelona—had been destroyed by bombs; now, she cried, her youngest child is without a father or brothers.

On my way back from the subsecretariat at 10:50 A.M., I was caught in an air raid, bombs dropping so close to the building entrance in which I was taking refuge, shaking it so vigorously that I thought the walls were caving in.

Near the Majestic Hotel, while hurrying back, I was surprised by a slap on the back; it was Captain Radumir Smercka, a Czech, who served with the 15th Brigade as chief of information. Tall, thin, and soldierly, with a well-groomed mustache, he is as warm a person as one would ever want to meet. Though he lost an eye earlier in the war, his hobby was taking pictures, even under the most intensive combat conditions. He confided that our forces had evacuated the Caball mountains.

In the afternoon Major Cueria, the indomitable Cuban with a herculean body, arrived with a request that I arrange a meeting for him with Gallo. No problem in doing so, for Gallo holds him in high esteem. I hit up Cueria for his biography for the next book on the International Brigades; he promised a get-together for that purpose.

* * * *

My 6 P.M. *appointment at CNT Anarchist headquarters for the scheduled interview with Emma Goldman fell through. One of her assistants apologized, saying that she had been unexpectedly called away and would I come back on Monday. I must have looked disappointed because he consoled me by filling my arms with pamphlets and books—all on anarchism, of course. [I learned later that Emma Goldman had left Spain unexpectedly and in a hurry. To me it was ominous, for it meant that the fascists were closing in on Barcelona faster than I had realized. I never saw her again.]*

Bill Gandall, ambulance driver, dropped in.

* * * *

A few minutes before midnight we were subjected to a fierce incendiary air raid, bombs dropping so close that Giandante, who was looking at the sky through an open window, was blown backward by a blast, his body covered with smoke. The moon was so bright that our chasers needed no spotlights in their pursuit of the enemy bombers.

9 October

Sunday. Another morning air raid. No damage.

Mario and I, in the afternoon, went to see Jimmy Cagney in Ciudad Siniestra *at the Ascaro. Admission, 3.75 pesetas. From there we went to the Metallurgico Union on Calle Deputación 277, where a festival was being conducted in honor of departing Internationals. Dancing to a lively band was going on in the courtyard. Ben Gardner and his group of mystery guys, probably connected with SIM (the military intelligence service, Servicio de Inteligencia Militar), were having a noticeably good time. Wine was plentiful.*

Harry Schindler, in a letter I got from him today with cigarettes (Luckies), said he was going home on a U.S. relief ship.

While I was in a cafe, smoking Harry's Luckies, a boy not more than ten years of age hung around my shoulders and, as I was about to choke the smoke, leaned over: "Dame la colilla, hombre." (How about giving me the butt, Mister?) He explained that when he accumulates enough tobacco he exchanges it for a chusco *of bread. Naturally, I parted with some unsmoked cigs. The waiters, I discovered, envious of competition, drive the kids out of the cafe because they want all the butts for themselves.*

President of the Republic Manuel Azaña made a speech, as reported in the press, advocating closer economic ties with the United States. It was an obvious invitation to Roosevelt, who has kept the U.S. neutral on the side of Hitler and Mussolini, to look at Spain as a potential market for his economic royalists. Roosevelt occasionally referred to American "economic royalists" with derision, but these businessmen, as suggested by Azaña, stood to profit more handsomely by doing business with a Republican Spain than with a Franco fascist Spain tied to Germany and Italy.

10 October

Visited the doctor for a checkup, then to bed after supper. He said that all my organs seem to be functioning well and that my persistent tiredness may be from too much work and, as is true of many people these days, not enough nourishment. For this

*reason, he said, he had been advising me to slow down, work fewer hours, burn less
energy.*

Air raid, 10:10 P.M. *Startled, I woke up as bombs dropped before the air raid
alert sounded.*

11 October

Air raid at 12:30 A.M. *Giandante shook me violently to wake me up. But I was
so tired of alerts that I pretended to be sound asleep. After a while he let me alone.*

Lutz and Bill Beeching came at 8:30 A.M. *to get me to accompany them to the
sastre (tailor) for Fred's suit fitting, then to the Tailor House Collective to order an
overcoat. The three of us tried to buy raincoats, but prices were 667 pesetas at Jorbe
and 1,200 at Ernest (a gyp joint). We didn't buy. Because it started to shower, we
darted into the Catalunya Cine and were treated to Paul Muni in* El Mundo
Cambio *and to* Doctor X.

*In the evening, while I worked, Dan took pictures of Lutz and Beeching and
others for the brigade history.*

12 October

Sunny and mild today. Finished reading Frank Pitcairn's book Reporter in
Spain. *It interested me because I had had several discussions with him in Madrid and
he struck me as being genuine. The last time we talked was while strolling through some
narrow streets and alleyways in Madrid, with that chatterbox Robert Gladnick on our
tail with his nonsensical interruptions. Pitcairn appeared at that time slender, emaci-
ated, and in ill health.*

*Hundreds of Internationals are in town window shopping, buying up the stores,
splurging on underclothing, outer garments, and suitcases, for undoubtedly their pesetas
will be worthless outside of Spain. I was awakened from an afternoon siesta to help
comrades in their shopping.*

*While downtown, I had a horrible glass of fruited ice, which didn't sit well with
me. Cost, 4.50 pesetas.*

Enemy planes overhead all afternoon.

I read myself to sleep with the short story The Reaping Race, *by Liam
O'Flaherty. It was great! During the night I heard the siren air alert, but slept right
on; then I heard the off-signal siren. No bombs.*

13 October

*Up early. After 10:45 air raid tumult that occurred in the middle of a meeting
on the second brigade book, I hurried to the government subsecretariat of propaganda to
sort out pictures for possible use in our work.*

* * * *

*Cigarette paper no longer available—for free, love, or money. "No hay" [There
is none; out of them].*

* * * *

Thought I saw General Miaja riding in a staff car but wasn't positive because I saw only the back of his head, until I checked with Macdonald, who assured me the general was in town. If true, his visit may be portentous, for the famous general rarely leaves Madrid, the city under his command from its earliest days in the war.

* * * *

This afternoon I was witness to a bizarre incident in the Plaza Catalunya. A woman, returning from shopping, had spilled her ration of cooking oil on the paved ground. Distressed, she got on her hands and knees, and with cupped hands gathered the oil and replaced it in a bottle. A child was helping her by soaking a cloth in the oil, then wringing it into a tin can—dirt and oil. When the woman was reprimanded by one of the many onlookers, she said: "Either we do this or go hungry." When she stood up, as if she were finished, a young man pulled a chunk of hard bread from his pocket, carefully and shamelessly soaked it in the remaining oil on the ground, then placed the softened part to his mouth, biting easily while simultaneously spitting out the dirt.

In front of a nearby restaurant I saw a little girl of about five or six years of age staring through its windows. I asked her if there was something inside she wanted. She mumbled shyly, "Yes, una perra," pointing to a dog.

"Why?" I asked

"To give it to my mother."

"And where is your mother?"

"In the Metro, where we live."

"What town are you from, Pequeñita?"

"We are from Provincia Santander," she looked up wih big, brown, melancholy eyes and added matter of factly, "but the fascists are now there."

I handed her some pesetas, a stamp, penknife, and some other items. I emptied my pockets. Before I finished fishing for more, she grabbed the items and ran happily toward the mouth of the Metro.

* * * *

A small U.S. tabloid called Fact *interested me (we get it regularly at our commissariat headquarters). In it were several short stories. The one called* Sweat *told about a young woman whose armpits sweated badly and continuously. She was so ashamed of this that she overperfumed herself until reproached by her boyfriend, who assured her that her odors were not only not obnoxious but stimulated him sexually.*

The second story, named On the Road, *related the problems of an unemployed worker looking for a job. While tramping along a lonely road, he was caught in a sudden rainstorm. When he darted into an abandoned hut, he encountered a young woman who, after listening to his woeful tales, gave him sympathy and a pound note.*

The last story was about an immigrant Jew in Canada who had left his suitcase with an unemployed friend. Give Me Back My Suitcase *tells the sad story of this man, shot inadvertently by police, who mistook him for a burglar when he returned for his suitcase.*

For relaxation in between meetings, bombardments, visitors, and writing, am reading Seven Red Sundays, *by Ramon Sender.*

14 October
    During a meeting on the progress of the International Brigades' withdrawal, Gallo spoke the entire time by candlelight because an air raid was in progress and electric power had been cut off. The first air raid started at exactly 8 P.M., the very minute Premier Negrin began his speech to the nation over the radio.

15 October
    Today was the warmest of the past few weeks. Before lunch I visited Angel at union headquarters for a detailed briefing on how his union functions. He said the Catalan government was bourgeois-controlled through the Esquerra and Rabassaire PSUC (middle class farmers and owners of small plots of land). These groups have large influence because they form a sort of tightly controlled trade union among small business farmers. Forced collectivization by the CNT of small businesses, such as barbershops, bakeries, restaurants, two- and three-man shops, etc., had been opposed by the Communist party of Catalonia because the little businessman rarely got a square deal, and collectivization would, moreover, create unnecessary discontent and division in the common struggle against the main enemies, Franco and his cohorts.

A letter to Toni Tisa:

> Pasaje Mendez Vigo, 5
> Barcelona
> 16 October 1938

    . . . I wrote you and the family recently to tell you that I'd be home soon because the Spanish government had decided to withdraw the Volunteers of the International Brigades.
    The withdrawal is proceeding more slowly than we had expected. An international commission made up of generals and colonels representing ten different nations has been appointed by the League of Nations to supervise the withdrawal. . . . Of course, the Spanish government is anxious for all non-Spanish combatants to be withdrawn from Spanish soil; if the Italian and German armed forces are likewise withdrawn, then the estimate is that Franco and his insurgent generals would face the insurmountable growing might of the Republic and the organized discontent of the people he's already conquered. Victory for the Republic would be assured. Unfortunately, for this very reason, though, the International Volunteers will be withdrawn while the German, Italian, and Portuguese troops will, I believe, remain—the balance of power and military might again to favor the fascists. It will be non-intervention double-dealing all over again. . . .
    Don't be surprised if I don't arrive home at the same time as other repatriated Americans. I shall be among the last to leave Spain because it is absolutely necessary that I remain to finish my work on the book Two Years of the International Brigades. *IF I CAN HELP IT, I'LL BE HOME BY CHRISTMAS.*
    . . . I'm in good health but bombs drop too often for comfort. I'll try not to earn the dubious distinction of being the last American wounded or killed in Spain. Food is scarcer than usual. American chocolates would help. The cold weather is setting in; shoes can't be bought; clothing is expensive when available; morale is high despite the hardships. The Spanish people's hope in ultimate victory is unquenchable. They are grim in the face of all difficulties but resolute in their determination to win.

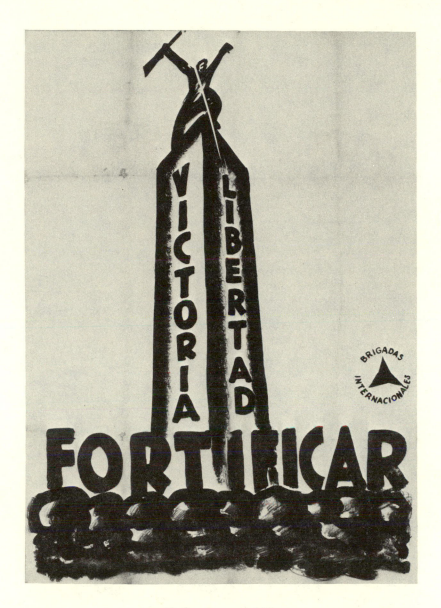

Fortify for victory and liberty

SIXTEEN

Farewells

18 October

    Left at 8 A.M. on Sunday for division headquarters near the Ebro to take part in holidays and farewells to the departing International Brigades. After returning on Monday morning at 7:30 and before going to sleep, I wrote the story of this fiesta for the Volunteer. At the festivities I met a nice girl named Magdalena from the town of Rens, who invited me to visit her. She described her house as being next to the town's cemetery and near the dress factory where she works on tejidos *(textiles). She works only on Saturdays and Sundays because there is no electricity during the week, but gets paid for a full week anyway. She is small—the top of her head reaches the bottom of my nose—brown eyes and brown hair curled on an iron. An enthusiastic and skillful dancer, she turned down no one who asked her.*

    Dinner at division: more than one could eat of rice, meat, bread, apples, pears, sardines, coffee, red wine, vermouth—and plenty of champagne. Champagne corks were popping all over the place. One was aimed at Major Smith, missed him, and splattered and soaked a blonde, non-Spanish woman (I think the wife of one of the German officers), who not only did not get angry, but joined in the horseplay. Americans were playful and prankish, throwing at each other small wads of bread, olive pits, and bones from meat, arguing and scrapping with each other like any friendly group around at a penny-ante poker game. Milt Wolff, Abe Lincoln incarnate, filled one guy's pipe with rice and wine, handed it back to him, then sat back and waited for him to light it. But the smoker sensed this play through the corner of his eye and casually, and without reproof, emptied the pipe, cleaned it, refilled it with fresh tobacco, looked around with a twinkle at the disappointed kibitzers, lit it, and puffed the smoke into Milt's face.

The Polish comrades, on the other hand, remained serene, serious, and attentive and called for quiet by hissing at the noisy Americans, embarrassed, it seems, by the display of drinking and horseplay.

Eddie Rolfe, who is beginning to look frail again, appeared for a short time with his new military khaki beret and leather jacket.

When I spoke with Gates and Dave Gordon about material for the second brigade book, they informed me that they had given Sandor Voros a pile of stuff for me about a couple of weeks ago. Sandor, to this day, hasn't said a word about it. I'll wait a while longer before confronting him.

19 October

After I picked up pictures from Major Smercka at the Majestic Hotel, he and I visited Eddie Rolfe. Ed took us to the room of sculptor Jo Davidson, who was working on a bust of Milt Wolff. Photographer Robert Capa, who was also there, showed me his photo album of Spanish war pictures, allowed me to select a few I was interested in, and will have copies made for me in a few days.

*   *   *   *

Air raid at about 11:00 A.M.

*   *   *   *

When I returned to headquarters from these visits, including one with Fred at the Gran Via, Canapino greeted me with an introduction to two of his latest girlfriends. The first one, whose brother was killed in an aerial bombardment, is attractively named Marija. The other, Aurora, has a brother and brother-in-law with the artillery at the Ebro, comes from Cartagena, and works in a war factory making bullets.

25 October, Espluga

Tuesday. As one of the delegation representing the I.B. Political Commissariat Headquarters, I attended another government fiesta send-off for the Internationals, this time at Espluga (near Montblanch), southwest of Barcelona. Chairman for this occasion was Delage, political commissar of the Ebro Army. Packed shoulder to shoulder in the town's square, the volunteers, now veterans, listened to speeches. André Marty spoke first, and he was absolutely eloquent. Juan Modesto, who spoke next, brought unabashed tears to the eyes of many—tough guys, men who had fought and survived the worst battles and retreats and saw their comrades die, but who had no time to cry. The last speaker was Premier Negrin, who, upon arriving by car, did not get out even though the band played the national anthem over and over. We remained at attention with arm raised in the clenched fist salute waiting for him to step out. When he failed to do so, one by one, arms drained of blood dropped down, mine included. Finally, he stepped to the platform and made his speech. He looked unhappy, talking like a man begrudgingly granting an unwanted and untimely divorce. The most colorful contingent was the Garibaldi, ostentatiously wearing their new bright red neckerchiefs with the Spanish purple and gold flag colors sewn on the tips.

Our fighter planes flew protective cover during the ceremonies. After all, one bomb could have wiped out much of the International Brigades and a good part of the government. The weather accommodated us by waiting until after the speech making and festivities were over to begin drizzling.

After having dinner with the Polish comrades at their estado mayor, *I returned to Barcelona in the back of the mail truck. Hitchhiking with me were Giandante, two Czechs, two Spanish guards, and two* chofers.

27 October

Niedler (a German), Ravera [staff officer of the International Brigades], Canapino, and I left in the early evening by the mail camioneta *for Casino de la Rabassada in Tibidabo, where an official banquet was to be held in honor of another group of exiting Internationals. We were among the first to arrive. Venerable General Pozas, commander of the Catalonian front during the March retreats at the Ebro, spoke to Ravera, then handed him a letter to pass on to Hans (German commander). Why he himself didn't go directly to Hans, who was standing not too far away, I couldn't figure. General Ascensio, often referred to as "the traitor of Malaga" (for his alleged lack of vigorous resistance to fascist forces) who was undersecretary of war and military adviser to Largo Caballero, the previous prime minister, stood in front of me in the hall. I recognized him only after he was greeted by name by a passerby.*

Canapino asked me to sit with him and his Garibaldi friends. After a meal of salami, liverwurst, wine, champagne, and bread, we were treated to short speeches. Hans spoke in German. Translated into Spanish, the speech lost its impact. Negrin gave a short, emotional talk, which was well received—by now I can almost anticipate the things he's going to say.

By 10:00 P.M. the main events were over, and our group headed back to Barcelona for the Colon Hotel, where the Cubans were having their own departing festivities.

28 October

Friday. A great day for the Internationals.* All Spanish newspapers pay lavish tribute to the volunteers of the International Brigades. Hundreds of thousands of people lined the streets of Barcelona to cheer and many to cry as they watched our troops parade down the broad and stately Gran Via Diagonal, the main avenue of the city. Marching at the head of the parade was Gallo, flanked by Hans to his left and Morandi [an Italian exile and commander of the Eighty-sixth Brigade, Southern Cordoba Front] to his right, followed by the men of the International Brigades in numerical order: the 11th, 12th, 13th, 14th, and last, our brigade, the 15th. Negrin and other government officials waved from their platform while people on the

---

*My dairy gives the date of the farewell parade as Friday, 28 October 1938, and another eyewitness, Zofia Szleyen, confirms this date in her book, *Wiatraki i Messerschmitty* (Warsaw: "Iskry," 1965). Some writers on the Spanish Civil War, however, place the parade on Saturday, 29 October. See Hugh Thomas, *The Spanish Civil War* (New York: Harper and Row, 1963) or Arthur H. Landis, *The Abraham Lincoln Brigade* (New York: Citadel, 1968).

pavement broke ranks and embraced and kissed the marching soldiers. The International Volunteer Nurses were especially embraced by women, girls, men, everybody. Flowers were thrown at us like rice at a wedding. Friendly planes soared over the city and buzzed the parade. Tanks, artillery, trucks, and medical teams were part of the march. I couldn't help wonder why the equipment was not at the front instead of on the streets of Barcelona.

The displays of warmth by the Barcelona population, their wild expressions of gratitude, their endless shouts of approval, their raised clenched fist of international solidarity stirred equal responses of affection from our veteran Internationals, even from the most sophisticated. It was a great day!

30 October
Sunday. The Pioneer Children of Barcelona held a morning stage festival in honor of the volunteers in a theater on the Ramblas. It lasted until 1:00 P.M. Marty and Gallo were present. Marty made a short thank-you speech. The performance was not only technically excellent but so obviously genuine that it softened up even a couple of guys I know who are hard-boiled and cynical.

In the afternoon, Fred, Beeching, and I went to a concert at the Palacio de la Música for more tributes. However, there was a power failure, so that the recitals had to be given in the dark. I enjoyed the poetry recitals, especially the one on Seville.

In the evening we went to the Julio Mella Club, by now a busy center for visiting North and South Americans, for those on temporary leave and looking for something to do, and for those passing through on their way to the States. When here, too, we were hit with a power failure, we trotted back to headquarters, where we faced the same situation.

4 November
Friday. The UGT (General Union of Workers) held an elaborate dinner in honor of the Internationals at the Palacio Nacional. Three to four thousand were present. Brigaders were split up to sit with trade unionists. Abe Lewis and I sat with a group of women from the Dressmakers Union, who, while accepting our American cigarettes, would not smoke. They said they would take them home to their fathers and brothers. More probably the cigarettes will be used in exchange for food.

Speakers included Gallo, Osario Tafall, and La Pasionaria. Each was brief and effective. La Pasionaria's mere presence electrified the audience. After dinner they adjourned us to a concert at the Palacio de la Música for more than two hours of Spanish music, Aragon dances, poetry recitations, and superb guitar playing. The house was packed, the atmosphere enthusiastic, and there was no electric power failure.

On assignment from headquarters, I had made several trips between Barcelona and Ripoll, a town near the French border, where volunteers of our brigade were waiting for clearance to enter France for their return to the United States. I was going there again.

5 November, Ripoll
Saturday. With Favetto and his wife, and Cabello as the chofer, we left for Ripoll, where we delivered boxes of brigade documents, books, and other material

destined for France. While there, I had a long talk with John Gates about more biographies and the material he said he gave to Voros for me, which Sandor has not yet turned over because he claims he can't find it.

After lunch, Fred and I took a long walk in the mountains under a warm, pleasant sun. The town sits in a valley flanked by distant, snow-capped mountains, which cast shadows, preventing the sun from hanging around too long. Fred checked me in at the Estrella, the hotel in which the International Commission of the Non-Intervention Committee is staying. I am told the members of this commission are a queer group of generals asking odd questions and seem to be more interested in probing each individual volunteer about his or her background than in speeding up repatriation. Not only do they ask the volunteer his age and citizenship, but also want to know if he is going to live illegally when he leaves Spain, and if so, where. Members of the commission are reported to be inviting Internationals to secret sessions. Of all the volunteers in town, only two accepted. These two, I learned, did so after being prompted by the Servicio Inteligencia Militar.

6 November

Sunday. With Harry Randall, I went through photo albums to select pictures for possible use in the brigade book. None appealed to us. The pictures of Jarama, the biographies, stories, and material that I want are in Voros's possession.

In the afternoon, a group of us sat at a sidewalk cafe watching the parading Sunday crowd—the boys and girls flirting as any place else.

[I bumped into Ernest Hemingway and other newsmen, as has happened from time to tim for the past year and a half.]

Hemingway asked me if I wanted a ride back to Barcelona with his group. I accepted. The other passengers included Herb Matthews of the New York Times, Robert Capa, photographer, and Charles Mowrer, Daily News correspondent. Hemingway drove; it was Matthews' car and it behaved badly. Just outside of Granollers, Matthews spotted antiaircraft batteries, and it wasn't long before they let loose deafening explosions in pursuit of enemy planes. We drove through darkened Granollers at a snail's pace, without headlights, under a fiery umbrella of red chaser bullets streaking across the inky sky in search of their illusive targets. By the time we limped into Barcelona, the heavens were tranquil again, and we had a late, peaceful supper. Hemingway drank whiskey, sharing some with us.

8 November, Barcelona

A day for radio programs. Voros spoke in English over the Barcelona radio and I spoke in Spanish. After the many tributes to the International Brigades by the Spanish government, its army, and people, we reciprocated with our salutations and expressions of gratitude to them for the opportunity afforded the Internationals to serve the Spanish people and their antifascist cause.

International Brigade Headquarters had its own farewell dinner for officers, staff members, and employees. I left right after dinner and missed the goodies, speeches, and champagne, so as to be on time at the theater show presented by the Women's Club across the street, where I was to meet Maria Velen Vazquez and her sister.

I find it increasingly difficult to take part in these farewell parties; the realization that we are really to leave these people I've grown to love depressed me all evening.

*   *   *   *

Orders from Gallo: All personnel of every language group working on the Volunteer *must pack and be ready to leave in the morning. I am ordered to take over the English edition of the* Volunteer *once again and arrange for its continued publication, which means I must stay in Barcelona longer.*

*   *   *   *

Am reading An American Testament, *by Joe Freeman.*

*   *   *   *

9 November
    Many have already left headquarters for the northern camps and towns closer to the French frontier. Now that the unbelievable departure day approaches, a weighty sadness has gripped me. I am feeling very emotional. There was a time I wanted badly to go home. Now I am repelled by the thought.

What are you doing to stop this?

SEVENTEEN

The Final Weeks in Barcelona

11 November
   Finished reading Agent of Japan, *by Amleto Vespa. It's the story of how the author was forced to be an agent of the Japanese Secret Service after he and his family were threatened with death. Serving the Japanese from 1932 to 1936, he made his escape when he was suspected of having helped the Chinese irregulars in guerrilla raids and acts of sabotage against the very Japanese he was supposed to be aiding. He recounts the horrors the Japanese committed against other human beings and the brutalities he was often compelled to take part in. One story that moved me was that of a young Jewish student, a talented pianist and son of a wealthy hotel owner, held hostage for ransom by the Japanese agents, then butchered by first having his ears chopped off before he was finally killed.*

* * * *

   Often, when I offer a cigarette to a Spanish coworker he accepts it graciously, breaks it in half, saves one part for future smoking, re-rolls the other half into a cigarette paper, looks up with a grin and says, "This way I get two cigarettes out of one."

12 November
   Air raid at 10:45 A.M. *while I was on my way to the Mexican Embassy. From*

193

where I was walking on the Paseo de Gracia, I could see smoke rise from the port area where the bombs must have scored. The smoke cleared quickly, however.

* * * *

Oscar [a German] said that while he was in a hospital located just outside Barcelona he recognized my voice over the radio on the day I spoke.

* * * *

At 5:30 P.M. I attended a meeting—on the subject of children—sponsored by the Mujeres Libres in their building across the street. Before the discussion period, we heard a short speech by Antonio Ruiz Villaplana, author of Doy Fe, *on children and mothers in the fascist zone. Slight of build, wearing tortoise-rimmed glasses and a leather jacket, he was a quiet but effective speaker, and thoroughly informed on his subject.*

The inimitable Dolores Ibarruri, La Pasionaria, was present. A striking woman of about thirty-five years of age [she was actually 41], she parts her hair on the right side, black hair mixed with thick threads of gray, and pulls it back and neatly knots it on the back of her well-shaped head. With her fine aquiline nose, and smooth skin and features, she is a strong and handsome woman.

* * * *

Food is getting less and worse. For supper: plate of rice, salad, and bread. No seconds.

I am told that fifteen hundred French volunteers crossed the border into their home country.

13 November

At 8:55 this morning our antiaircraft fired loudly, frequently, and furiously at roving bands of enemy bombers, dotting the sky with giant powder puffs.

An American Testament *by Freeman is giving me a good insight into the history of the American left of the early 1900s. It details the early efforts of party organizers and the positive role of the magazine* New Masses. *It also shows how struggling writers lived and wrote in Greenwich Village. The account of the Stelton Anarchist Colony is interesting.*

14 November

After lunch, Ben Gardner, Dan Kramen, and I went to a cafe near the Plaza Cataluña, where we sat, talked, and flirted with the girls. When one responded, I joined her at her table, but she was only interested in complaining about the uselessness of the war and the shortages of food, and in expressing her hatred and bitterness toward the government. In this she was boundless. After a while I discovered why. She said her name was Margarita and that her father had had a business and had been rich; now the business was closed due to shortages of material, but he was still compelled to pay the same amount of taxes. Though she was twenty-one years old, she had never worked until recently. Now she was employed by a children's welfare organization, a job she hated but continued to hold because that was the only way she could get food. She was studying French because someday she was going to leave Spain for France and join her rich friends who had gone there at the outbreak of the civil war. She lived along the port area, which was a daily target for enemy planes, but while homes around her had been hit and some demolished, hers was still intact. Though there was no refugio near her home, she was no longer afraid and refused to go to the cellar during bombardments for fear of being buried alive, as some of her neighbors had been. She said she simply snuggled closer to her mother and prayed. Fascists, she added, signal warnings of impending bombardments to their friends with short bursts of machine-gun fire into the air before the air raid alarms sound. Bombs of 50 to 100 kilos, which dropped in the port area and in her neighborhood yesterday, did not explode. When I did not sympathize with her many beefs about the war, the government, the plight of the rich, the shortages of good, and the poor quality of ice cream, she changed the subject and told me how much she enjoyed reading the book No Pasaran *by Upton Sinclair, which she praised highly.*

"Gee, it must be wonderful," she sighed, "to go to America away from this war. America must be so beautiful." On the one hand, she sounded like a fifth columnist, and on the other, like a misguided, hungry young woman. At the sound of an air raid alert we parted.

* * * *

In the evening a group including Dave Gordon, Dan Kramen, Ben Gardner, G. Murray, and me went to the Capitol movie theater to see Guerrilleros, *the exciting account of Soviet guerrilla fighters around Vladivostock at the time of the White Guard and the Japanese counterrevolutionary invasion of Soviet soil.*

A Catalan member of our headquarters staff, Pujo, borrowed fifty pesetas from me. Because I couldn't say no, I now have less in my pockets than he has in his.

16 *November*

The Anglo-Italian Pact, which recognizes Italy's conquest of Ethiopia and gives Franco belligerent rights, was put into effect.

Today was a quiet uneventful day. Harry Richter and I completed the day with an inadequate meal at Bergamin's and suffered indigestion at the movies, where we saw Dede, *a French film.*

17 *November*

Children are having a fiesta across the street. La Pasionaria is again present, talking, joking, and playing with them. She is about five feet seven inches tall. Today her black and steel-gray hair is pushed to the back of her head in a roll and held together by a coffee-colored comb. Her eyes are deep-set under black eyebrows and a smooth, high forehead. Though heavy in body, with high, full breasts, she looks well proportioned. Her beautifully chiseled face exposes an unconquerable personality; she radiates warmth and confidence; there is nothing artificial about her. Her voice is deep and of full resonance, almost masculine. When she applauds, which is frequently, her clap is loud and her long-fingered hands come togther continuously and smoothly like well-oiled pistons. I am told that she is annoyed because someone who is supposed to be here with gifts for the children has not yet arrived. What innate quality does she possess that makes a roomful of people suddenly halt what they're doing and stare at her with awe, admiration, and affection?

* * * *

Finished reading American Testament.

20 November
    My plans to attend the sports festival held in honor of the International Brigades fell apart when I went to pick up Maria V. and she wasn't home. In the evening we went to the sports festival party and dance, but I didn't enjoy myself because there were too many farewells.
    I slept for the first time in my new room away from brigade headquarters at No. 1, Calle Caspe and Claris. The room is pleasant, and the landlords, a middle-aged couple, are very accommodating. Their daughter lost her husband at the Ebro and is now a widow with infant twins.
    By now most headquarters staff members had moved to separate parts of the city for security reasons. Gallo felt that concentration of leading cadre posed too much a temptation for the fifth column to try a strike while we were asleep. After all, he reminded us, the enemy was moving closer to Barcelona.
    Gallo came to supper for the first time in civilian clothes. In the past he'd always frowned on nonmilitary dress. Victor Ajzner [editor of the Polish edition of the Volunteer], *who had been in civilian clothes during the day, changed into uniform to avoid being reprimanded by Gallo. When he walked into the dining room, he was startled to see Gallo out of uniform. Of course, it became a big joke with the rest of us because we knew of the switch.*
    I spent the evening writing a long letter to Harry Schindler, who is now back home. Today I started reading The Evolution of Man and His Culture, *by Bibby.*

21 November
    Food getting bad, smaller quantities, poorer in quality. Noon: small portion of rice, lettuce, bread, and wine. Supper: watery lentil soup, lettuce, bread, and wine. Good butter for breakfast.
    Very little to do, so I went to the movie alone in the afternon, but after about an hour the electric current was cut off, preventing the full showing of Jane Eyre *and* All Is Rhyme.
    Soap in the city is scarce. Shoes can't be bought or even repaired. People nail rubber or tire strips to replace worn soles. Kids give me their addresses with pleadings that I send them chocolates after I get back home. Barcelona is becoming barren; not even the cafes are as crowded as they used to be. Poor quality sodas are sold at gouging prices; imitation ice cream costs 3.75 pesetas at the Turia. Suitcases are now impossible to buy. Trains and trolleys are crowded; trolleys run only at certain hours.
    Dave Gordon, Dan Kramen and I went to an operetta at the Tivoli. I slept through a good part of it.

22 November
    Gallo called us in and told us that now that the work on the book is completed

we must start a compilation of facts on the role of the International Volunteers at the request of the Central Committee of the Communist party of Spain. He said it would take a couple of additional months of work, but the final decision as to whether to accept or reject this extra work was left to each of us.

Eddie Rolfe visited and told me that in response to his request that he be relieved of his assignment as correspondent in Spain for the Daily Worker, *Clarence Hathaway wired his suggestion for one of the following three to replace him: Alvah Bessie, Dave Gordon, or me. Ed was anxious that Dave take over. For me to do so would mean a stay of several more months, and I am now eager to get home as soon as possible, though I'd surely like the job.*

I went to a lively and pleasant affair given by the Juventud Socialista Unificada (United Young Socialists) at the Hotel Colon.

23 November

Chamberlain and Daladier meet in Paris today. The Spanish press, reminding them that Spain is not Czechoslovakia, warned these dudes not to try selling out Spain. We were subjected to an air raid at 11:00 A.M. with plenty of bombs dropped—as a special greeting to the Chamberlain-Daladier talk fest, no doubt.

The press carries stories that Hitler continues to persecute Jews.

At this very moment (12:39 P.M.) as I am writing, another air raid siren alert is shrieking. About ten bombardments took place throughout the city today. One bomb found its mark inside the Bank of Spain, killing fifty people.

Eric Reed left for the U.S. Pictures borrowed by Voros were finally returned by Harry Randall.

24 November

At a 6:00 P.M. meeting called by Gallo, the commissars of all the International Brigades were present. After the many problems were batted around, including those of repatriation, finances, food and comforts at the base, and political problems confronting some of our volunteers who can't return to their native country, Gallo informed those present of the completion of our latest book, Two Years of the International Brigades *and of the initiation of a new project, the military and political documentary history of the International Brigades. The commissars manifested keen interest and responded enthusiastically to Gallo's proposal, pledging immediate cooperation at all levels. Johnny Gates suggested that I promptly go to Ripoll while the remaining Americans waiting for passage home are still available to help. Parenthetically, he informed me that Voros was severely reprimanded for holding back photos and materials designated for my use. Gates did not like the last issue of the* Volunteer— *not enough items about the men and women of the Lincoln Brigade.*

Just a couple of light bombardments today.

26 November, Ripoll

By 8:30 A.M. I was on the back of a mail camion, heading for Ripoll and vomiting all the way. When we arrived at 12:30 P.M., I was hungry, frozen, and so sick I could do little work until evening. But by then I was talking to many, gathering much information, and making copious notes; and I felt much better. Fred and others treated me to a local movie. But in the middle of the show a notice was flashed on the screen directing the Americans in the audience to return immediately to their barracks. On the outside we discovered that the message was intended only for those Americans scheduled to leave for France in the next few days.

Fred and I talked the whole night—almost. This trip was undoubtedly the last time that I would be seeing many of my comrades in Spain.

27 November, Ripoll to Barcelona

All stores closed, so I loafed around waiting for my appointment with Smercka, who didn't show up until late afternoon. The wait was worth it since he was very helpful by providing me with photographs he himself had taken during the war. Never far from his camera or binoculars, his command of English excellent, he had served with Slavic-speaking battalions, but by personal preference he remained with the Lincolns and was our brigade's chief information officer. We spoke of the many battle actions he was part of and of the many times he was wounded, including his loss of an eye. He also drew for me maps with detailed information about troops and plans, advances and retreats, almost to scale, which I placed among materials to be used in the book Two Years of the International Brigades, *if it was ever to be published. At the end of our session he presented me with a picture of the two of us together, arm in arm, which he nicely inscribed and signed.*

The train I boarded for Barcelona left almost one hour later than scheduled due to enemy air activity. As the train rumbled on, I had a long and interesting conversation with a group of Catalonian women and one Madrileño, the gist of which revealed a consuming faith in the final successful outcome of the war. To them the departure of the International Volunteers signaled supreme confidence on the part of the government in its ability to stem the fascist tide. The Republic, they held, now had well-organized military forces developed from the ranks of the workers and peasants. Never would the Spanish people permit big industries to be returned to private owners for their continued merciless exploitation of their workers, who before the war were paid starvation wages. Never, they seemed to think, would the Spanish people allow big landowners and the church to control the land as before, while the peasants hungered for a piece of it.

29 November

Because José Díaz [general secretary of the Communist party of Spain] was to speak, I went to the Iberio-Americano affair, where for one and a half fascinating hours he expounded on the subject "Lo que España Enseña a Europa y América" (What Europe and America can learn from Spain). He had been ill, which accounted for his weak voice and lack of forcefulness. He wore a gray suit, which fitted him loosely. Speaking calmly and in a scholarly manner, only occasionally gesturing by pointing a finger in lawyerlike fashion, he held everyone's attention from the beginning to the end. The only exception was La Pasionaria, who shifted in her seat frequently and looked around often as if searching for someone.

Premier Juan Negrín was present, but when he entered there was, strangely, not a ripple of applause. I thought of President Roosevelt, who, had he entered any hall back home under similar circumstances, would have been acclaimed loudly.

On the platform, in addition to Díaz, Negrín, and La Pasionaria, were Juan Modesto, André Marty, Luigi Gallo, and several others I didn't recognize.

El Campesino (Valentín González, commander of the 46th Division) was in the audience dressed in a light-tan civilian suit. I got a good look at him: piercing black eyes, short, stocky but muscular, fearless and fiery looking, black beard and dark parched skin. He looked every bit the bounding, blustering peasant he was reputed to be.

30 November

At Gallo's invitation, I attended a meeting of the Spanish Communist party's Central Committee, where André Marty gave a factual, interesting, and detailed analysis of the current situation in France, including the general strike commencing there today. This old warrior can be brilliant, patient, gentle, and considerate in his dealings with people, as well as abrupt and rude. Today he was at his best.

1 December

Today I begin the arduous task of compiling the history of the International Brigades (English-language part), using official documents, dispatches, orders of the day, maps, field reports, and military and political reports, just to name a few sources; and perhaps, we'll have the use of some copies of government materials pertinent to our needs.

2 December

When I arrived for breakfast, I was told that planes had roamed the city throughout the night, dropping their bombs indiscriminately. I had slept through it all.

At this moment (11:00 A.M.), eleven of our planes are patroling overhead. They are now referred to derisively as aereos de Osiris, Egyptian god of the dead, because of late they have been appearing only after the storm has done its damage.

Today the first organized group of Americans left Spain for the United States.

3 December

It is exactly 10:40 A.M. Five enemy planes are bombarding Barcelona, dropping bombs everywhere. Terrorizing the population seems to be the sole objective.

Mañana I am to go to Calella to seek out first hand the facts on the sinking of the Ciudad de Barcelona.

6 December

At lunch today I sat at the same table with Ignacio, the hardworking house cleaner for the I.B. Headquarters. She is small in stature but wiry; her black hair is bundled at the back of her neck as is the way of so many Spanish women; her eyes are large and seem to want to pop out of her head; her tanned, wrinkled face makes her look older than her fifty-nine years. She has four children, one of whom is also named Ignacio. Of her three sons, one is presently home from the front with an elbow wound, the second has not been heard from since the government's offensive at Teruel, and the third is enlisted in one of the Spanish battalions of the International Brigades. Her husband died of a heart attack during a recent enemy aerial bombardment.

Before the war, she said, she had worked for twenty-eight years as a cleaning woman in a soldiers' barracks near Toledo. On 7 November 1936, at about 4:00 A.M., when one of her sons had rushed home and shouted for them to run for their lives, she and her daughter dashed toward the Toledo Bridge, stumbling and falling all the way. Behind her, not more than three hundred yards, she could see Franco's dreaded North African Moors approaching. At the bridge she was succored by the *militiamen. Besides her modest home, she left behind all her personal belongings, her life savings of 10,000 pesetas, two pigs, and some sheep. She said she had little more to lose and wanted the war against fascism continued until victory was won.*

7 December

At a party cell meeting, we decided to participate in the recruiting of men from the camps to help build refugios *in the many Catalonian towns. An enemy offensive and increased aerial and artillery bombardments are expected; the* refugios *will afford the local population some protection and also make it easier for the army to "defend every inch of ground."*

We also voted to contribute two pesetas per meal per person for the purchase of better and more food, if possible. We are now short of fruit, vegetables, meat, dairy products, and wine. If we run out of garbanzos and lentils, we starve.

We also voted to subscribe to the Campaña de Invierno—Winter Campaign—*by having each of us contribute one day's pay per week. Purpose: to raise money for food, clothing, and other needed things for the civilian population.*

8 December

Still sin novedad en los frentes—*nothing new on the fronts. It looks ominous. The fascists must be preparing something big.* Frente Rojo, *a local newspaper, warns of a possible big final push.*

12 December

E. Rolfe visited briefly. He said that the fascists will attempt to break through between Tremp and Balaguer to Cervera, but that the forces of the Republic are ready to meet them head on.

Colonel Modesto, and Generals Rojo, and Sarabia also visited. They told Gallo that Miaja had plans already prepared to launch a diversionary offensive if the enemy attacked Catalonia first. However, if the enemy does not launch its offensive in the next ten days, the armies of Catalonia will be prepared to start another Teruel-type offensive.

24 December

Christmas Eve dinner with Dave Gordon, Abe Lewis, two French newspaperwomen, and two Spaniards at a private home in the southern outskirts of Barcelona. Along with a well-prepared and delicious meal of lentil soup, arroz con pollo, *and garbanzos, we shared the carton of chocolates, cheeses, salami, and coffee sent to me by my family and delivered by Juan Peinado, Spanish consul in Philadelphia, who so thoughtfully carried it all the way from the States.*

There was no enemy bombardment to take the kick out of the wine and cognac; but because the house was equipped with an electric stove, we could not cook supper until ten, when the power finally came on. We had neither candles nor lamps, but there was an open fireplace that kept us occupied keeping it lit. It was pleasant, huddled around a warm wood fire, engaged in friendly, though sometimes heated, conversation about the events currently of concern to us all: the war, the explosive political atmosphere in Europe, the Soviet trials, the revolutionary conflicts in China, and a dozen other subjects, including girls, sex, and some off-color jokes.

*   *   *   *

Electricity has been a nagging problem. The main Catalonian power stations are in fascist hands, and what improvised and limited power exists is turned off at eight o'clock in the morning. If you oversleep, there is no hot coffee or breakfast for that day. The power is turned on again for a couple of hours during the day to allow trolleys and subways to transport workers to and from their jobs. During these hours, the vehicles are packed shoulder to shoulder with government and industrial workers. Children riding with their parents (during working hours they are cared for in the factory's nursery) often find it safer to wedge themselves between the legs of adults. If you are unlucky enough to stand face to face with someone who has had a meal with garlic, you cut your ride short. After the rush hour has ended, the power goes off until late at night, when it is turned on again for the night-shift production worker—that is, if there are no enemy interruptions from the air.

* * * *

The Daily Worker, *dated 15 December, which we just received, announced that the ship convoying the last large group of American volunteers to the U.S. was due to arrive on the 16th. Fred Lutz was in this group, which means he has already seen my family.*

The middle-aged couple I had been staying with moved with their daughter and her twins toward the French border, so I took advantage of the calm of Christmas Day to move in with Amparo and Soledad Niembo at their apartment at Salmeron 201. I was introduced to them by one of the Spaniards at our headquarters, and they were presented to me as anarchists but loyal to the Republic.

I've discarded much accumulated excess baggage. Now I have only one suitcase, which remains packed for rapid mobility—just in case.

31 December

At a New Year's party in a private home, away from the bombardment area, eighteen were present, including some Englishmen, two English nurses, Americans, Cubans, and Spaniards, one of whom had an accordion, which he played skillfully, enthusiastically, and endlessly. At times he sang or hummed beautiful flamenco tunes as he played. The party was a success, if you can call it that in view of the dark prospects facing the government, the armies, and the Spanish people at the birth of this New Year 1939.

Precisely at midnight, as church bells loudly chimed, fascist planes roaring over Barcelona skies released through open bomb bays twelve deadly bombs. The bombs were spaced so that they could be easily counted. The city shook, and residents trembled. The bombers then turned full circle and fled the coast of Spain before they could be tracked and fired upon.

There was immediate speculation in our gathering on the meaning of the brevity of their visit and on the fewness of bombs dropped. The accordion player gave us an explanation by mentioning a tradition that some of us had never heard of before. In Spain, he said, it is customary for people to eat twelve grapes, one for each month of the year, while toasting and welcoming the advent of the New Year. In that case, were the bombs telling the Spanish people that they soon would be choking on their grapes with the tightening of the Franco noose? There was a long silence.

EIGHTEEN

The Loss of Catalonia

11 January 1939

Angelita (from the I.B. secretarial staff) and I went to the meeting held by el Partido Socialista Unificada de Cataluña (Unified Socialist party of Catalonia) on the Paseo de Gracia, 92, where Giorla, a member of the party's political bureau, spoke for one hour on the necessity of mobilizing every able-bodied man for the front. As soon as he finished, a sixty-year-old man, with three sons at the front, volunteered to join the proposed "Battalion of Volunteers." He was promptly turned down, but just as promptly made president of honor of the meeting, in spite of his protests.

The discussion that followed Giorla's speech was lively. When one man commented that the women must forget their femininity and join the life and death struggle alongside the men at the front and in the rearguard and when he added that women were too slow and incompetent in performing their duties, he was bitterly criticized by Ruth, the wife a German officer of the 11th (Thaelmann) Brigade, who was sitting next to me.

The current fascist offensive is placing all Catalonia in peril. Indeed, the situation is most grave. Frente Rojo is making daily appeals for additional volunteers both for the front and for the building of more fortifications in every town and village. The fascists are nearing Montblanch. Espluga is lost. The Extremadura offensive seems to be slowing down.

* * * *

When Spaniards want to say so-and-so, it is "fulano y tal"; for silly, they say "jili;" for lousy, "piojosa."

13 January

Fascists take Montblanch; fierce fighting around Falset. Newspapers clamor for greater mobilization. Five more quintas *(drafts) are called up.*

Fascists troops are approaching Valls. This is largely an offensive by Mussolini's Italian troops. It looks as if the enemy is determined to take Tarragona first before moving on to Barcelona.

The military situation is becoming even more grave.

In Extremadura the Republican troops take positions south of Peñarroya.

21 January

A day of furious aerial combats. More than a dozen enemy bombers, accompanied by their fighter planes for protection, roam freely over Barcelona. We saw one plane brought down and a pilot bail out, but we didn't know whether he was one of ours or one of theirs. In spite of being met by heavy antiaircraft fire and by our chaser planes, the enemy made repeated visits.

We saw a Red Cross ambulance with victims of the bombardments.

Fascists are near Vendrell, about seventy kilometers south of Barcelona and south of Igualada.

Police, stationed on street corners, stop suspicious-looking young men to examine their documents. I have been stopped several times already. Fewer and fewer draft-age men are seen on the streets. Either they are in hiding or have already been mobilized.

I visited Federico, a badly wounded novio [boyfriend] of one of the Vazquez sisters, in the morning, and then the Vazquez family. All are nervous, especially the Vazquezes, who are harboring a refugee from Valls, originally a refugee from Santander. Loose talk is going on about the impending entrance of fascist troops and the expected ensuing slaughter.

Living with Amparo and Soledad Niembo is not as pleasant as it used to be. Both quarrel frequently. Soledad has stopped going to the Military Academy because, she says, the discipline is too strict. I have reason to believe it is a dread of being found there when and if the fascists enter Barcelona.

The happy, friendly, confident faces of the local people are fewer and farther apart; nothing but long, sad, worried looks. Nervousness and anxiety have gripped many.

22 January

Air raid alerts all night long. Another bombardment at 11:00 A.M.

Fascist troops have gotten as far as Villafranca and Villanueva y Geltrú. Now they've occupied Igualada. One thousand women from the Military Academy parade through Barcelona in support of the government's resistance to the enemy. They pledge to fortify the front lines.

The atmosphere in Barcelona is tense; nerves are wound like a coil and can spring at any moment. Fear and uncertainty prevail among many. The fifth column is hard at work with defeatist rumors. I overheard one well-dressed little old man tell another loudly, referring to the government, "Quieren acabar con la juventud" (They want to kill off the youth). People seem to lack the same spirit of resistance as that possessed by the Madrileños. But this is not *1936* or *1937*. There are long colas *(lines) for the little food that is rationed out; no heat, no electricity, and shortages of cooking oil. Frequent bombardments night and day make rest and work almost an impossibility. The political parties of Catalonia, except the Communist party and the Partido Socialista Unificada de Cataluña, are not at all energetic in calling for mobilization and resistance. The Independent Republican party is no longer heard from. Even the Anarchists seem to be strangely silent.*

Our commissariat is ordered to be prepared to move—direction north, naturally. We are warned to beware of a fifth-column stab in the back. Everyone is armed and on the alert. We man the building from the rooftops and from every window, changing guards every two hours. The gravity of the situation is depressing. When I told the Spanish women working with us that the I.B. Headquarters was pulling out, they became almost hysterical. They are packing their things and are planning to evacuate also.

I went to Figueras with a camion *loaded with headquarters archives, returned, and am getting ready for another trip. Roads are getting crowded.*

23 January

The bombardments, the nervousness, and the fear of being cut off and trapped in the enemy noose kept most of us awake all night.

We make frantic preparations for leaving. We are packed and ready to go. Enemy planes come again and again. Our antiaircraft artillery is firing badly. To add to our worries, we hear enemy artillery swish over the city. A state of war has been declared over the radio by General Hernandez Sarabia. What has it been so far!

By 5:44 P.M. *we are on the road to Figueras. Victor Ajzner, Polish editor of the* Volunteer, *and I ride atop the truck. Angelita Palacio and the other Pole ride in the cab. The roads are congested with trucks fleeing Barcelona. After snaking our way through the darkness, not daring to use our headlights, we arrive in Figueras at 11:15* P.M.

24 January, Figueras

Victor and I slept with our clothes on, huddled on a narrow mattress, without any blankets. Bitterly cold. Morning took a long time to come.

The military situation is so critical that many International volunteers not yet repatriated have asked to join Spanish troops at the fighting fronts. Requests were granted. Many have already rejoined the battlefronts.

Angelita and I spent a good part of the day looking for rooms for the remaining staff and for working quarters. We had very little luck, except for finding some rooms at Garcia Hernandez, 3.

As we walked through the streets in search of quarters, an air alert sounded. When we dashed to a refugio, it was so crowded with people pushing and shoving, some in panic, that we decided to stay out. Fortunately, no bombs.

Hundreds, thousands, are pouring in from Barcelona. They bring the message that the city is under continuous bombardment; air raid alarms sound every fifteen or twenty minutes.

25 January

Since we arrived, the weather has been cold and windy. The room I slept in had broken windows, and with only one light blanket for cover, I could not sleep well. Air raid alarm at 8:45 A.M.; no bombs.

Air raids and strafing all morning; the most savage attack was at 10:55 A.M. Everyone compelled to go to the hastily built refugio, *where we stand shoulder to shoulder. Sardine canneries could learn a lesson or two from our modern methods. One bomb at the entrance and we'd be packed for good.*

Before we even set up for work and while our belongings were still unpacked, we got orders to get ready for another move. Apparently, the army is not having much success in halting the fascist offensive. Though there is confusion and chaos among part of the civilian population and among some of the fleeing troops, our headquarters personnel and staff remain calm and organized. For us, when we cross the border, we go home. For the Spaniard, whether he stays or leaves, his troubles will have just begun.

26 January

We were prepared to move yesterday but the order did not come. This morning two camiones *loaded with our archives, equipment, and suitcases left for a rendezvous eight miles north, but we are ordered back because the commissariat is to stay in Figueras.*

Air raid at 9:00 A.M.; another at 10:30, but no bombs.

Tony De Maio from SIM (Servicio de Inteligencia Militar) is here. He told me of his work in the intelligence services and the various methods the fascists use to undermine the morale of the army and the population, including experimental methods of sabotage.

Among these methods he mentioned the use of the fifth column to cut water supply to hospitals, industrial enterprises, and residential areas; the interruption of electric power by sabotaging equipment and where possible destroying or blowing up equipment; and setting fire to fuel and ammunition dumps behind Republican lines, or anywhere else that would contribute to panic and demoralization of citizens and soldiers. He said that teams of trained saboteurs had been sent in by Franco and were already at work. Scores of them had been nabbed by military intelligence. The closer fascist troops get to Barcelona, the more openly the fifth column would operate.

27 January

Barcelona has been captured. It is reported that the enemy entered by way of Montjuich and landed troops, cutting off Barcelona at Mataro. Morale of the people is low; the will to fight is gone; fear of falling into enemy hands is rampant; how to get out fast seems to be the sole concern. Situation is grim.

Gallo convened a meeting of all HQ personnel at the temporary headquarters, but I wasn't there because I had already left for my rooming house to catch up on some sleep. In the morning he gave me hell and told me to stay put at HQ. I missed his report on the current military and political situation and the procedures for final evacuation.

28 January

After walking for the past three days from Barcelona, Juan Godoy arrived, tired, hungry, clothes torn and shredded. He had hardly slept for fear not only of enemy entrapment, but also of fifth columnists that were beginning to appear more boldly than ever. He proudly showed me two eggs he had bought from a peasant for 15 pesetas, so I gave him a chunk of bread with which to enjoy them.

A woman refugee from Barcelona got separated from her two children during a bombardment. One was a little girl of four, the other, shockingly, was only two months old. She is going crazy looking for them. We have joined in the search.

Angelita is also having her troubles. She is looking for her husband, José Palacio de Montesino, a member of the SIM, who has not been heard from for several days. She fears that if we're forced into France and she is separated from him she will end up in one camp and he in another. Then how would they be reunited?

29 January
Several more air raid alarms. Bombs drop, though not nearby. We hear the whistling of the descending bombs, then the violent, horrifying explosions. With each explosion, those in the refugio *drop to their knees, huddling next to their neighbors for safety and comfort—stranger hugging stranger. Women embrace their children closely and tightly; some scream and are comforted; those who cry have their tears wiped away by others who are just as frightened. A woman, mother of several children each clinging to one of her limbs, trembles in my arms, desperation in her eyes. We all know, but no one dares to say, that this* refugio *can, with one telling bomb, become our mass grave. Morale is at its lowest. The main topic of conversation is how to get to the frontier rapidly and into France. The roads are choked with vehicles, donkey carts, and thousands of refugees—all going in one direction, France.*

Frente Rojo, trying to rally resistance, features as its main slogan: "El camino a la frontera es el camino de la esclavitud" (The road to the frontier is the road to slavery).

During one of the bombardments, Canapino dropped to the ground and into a pile of shit. He smelled so bad that we stayed away from him while he cleaned his trousers and shoes with precious gasoline.

Bombings today were particularly bad. Only nine enemy planes did the job. The antiaircraft batteries here cannot be compared with those of Barcelona. They seem to be smaller; we see shells sail through the air and explode long before they reach their targets. Not one enemy plane was in danger from our firepower. The total number of bombardments today was not less than five, maybe six; two of them were serious.

How terror-stricken the population has become!
Today's line of resistance: Solsona, Vich, Calella.

* * * *

I am working on the Brunete period—I should say that I'm trying to do so under these impossible conditions.

That day I wrote my last letter from Spain to my family:

Figueras, 29 January 1939

. . . I know you must be much worried. By now you are aware, perhaps alarmed, at the unbelievable and disastrous turn of events in Catalonia, especially Barcelona—the capital city— the loss of which does not necessarily end the war. After all, Madrid

and the central part of Spain are still solidly Republican, and the people of Catalonia—the northern small area still loyal to the government—are fighting with their backs to the French frontier, resisting and clinging to every inch of ground, retreating only when forced to or when the odds are so desperately and overwhelmingly against them that there is no other choice. This resistance is necessary and in the interest of Catalonia as well as for all of Spain. It gives to other areas, still loyal to the Republic, time to prepare a counteroffensive.

The tragedy of the Spanish people unfolding before us affects me emotionally and deeply, as it does all Spaniards around me. I am well otherwise, although I would not be so healthy if our group had not gotten out of Barcelona at the time we did. It was less than two days after we slipped out of the city that Barcelona was overrun by the enemy. For weeks before we left and up to our last moments, the city was under severe and constant bombardment. The pressures on us were enormous. Aerial bombardments were so bad that at times everything seemed to have the shakes: the houses, the buildings, the church bells, the plates on the tables, and the tables themselves—even the ground we walked on. When it was impossible to get anything done during the day, we worked at night.

Presently, we are in Figueras, a town a few miles from the French border—the small ancient village with the big medieval fortress I wrote to you about in what now seems like ages ago. It is here where we were first quartered in those earlier, happier, and more promising days of January 1937. We go about our duties as energetically as ever, hoping the tide will turn for us, but even here we are dogged and menaced by frequent appearances of enemy aircraft.

A couple of days ago an American popped in to tell me that Si Podolin was at that very moment in a train at the town's railroad station and that he was on his way back to the States. Since an air raid alert was in progress, I counted on the train being hung up until after the all clear sounded. Despite the antiaircraft racket, I raced down to the station, only to find I had just missed the troop train. My hopes of seeing Si and of giving him a message for home were dashed. I was so shook up that I sat on the tracks with my head in my hands, disappointed and sad. How I wanted to see him! He then could have told you how much alive I am. Since Si and I served in different units—he in the artillery and I in the infantry—we did not see each other more than a couple of times in our two years here, though we kept contact through mutual friends and by infrequent correspondence.

I have not heard from Fred Lutz, who left Spain for home at least a month ago. If he has gotten home, remind him how he felt when he was here and did not get letters from home, or from his best friends.

Let me remind you of what I told you in my last letter: when I've finished this last assignment for the Political Commissariat of the International Brigades, I shall come home but, if possible, I'll first visit our relatives at La Grand'Combe.

The sole purpose of this short letter is to assure you that the fall of Barcelona did not trap us in the city.

My affections to everyone.

Salud!

P.S. A friend is carrying this letter with him to France, from where he'll dispatch it to you. I doubt if, at this stage, any mail is getting out of Spain. Sorry I have delayed so long in writing.

30 January

Cloudy with occasional rain, the kind of a day we've grown to welcome, for it means no enemy planes, no bombs.

There is no news of the battlefronts—a sign of bad news, usually. Our communiqués are quick to announce successes, slow in admitting defeats and retreats. A communiqué of two days ago reported fighting in the sectors of Mataro, east of Manressa, and east of Solsona.

No electricity—no heat—I'm snuggled under a heavy overcoat, with a blanket around my feet, while working on the period dealing with the Aragon battles, from materials that seem to be detailed, accurate, and plentiful. But my fingers are stiff and cold.

Figueras is now becoming better organized: services for the community and the military are increasing. There is less chaos, greater confidence, and a growing feeling that perhaps we can do today what the Madrileños did in November 1936: halt the retreat, resist, turn the tide from apparent defeat to one of hope and victory.

31 January

Usual 9:00 A.M. air raid alarm, but the customary appearance of enemy planes followed by bombs did not take place. Four air raid alerts, 12:30, 1:40, 3:05, but no bombs fell. During the 5:00 o'clock alert, the enemy bombers were frightened off by our antiaircraft fire.

Gallo returned from a mystery mission after two days' absence. He's tight-lipped. Godoy paid another visit; this time he wanted cigarettes.

Fighting is taking place at Santa Maria, Moya, Caldas de Montbuy.

1 February

Air raid at 9:00 A.M. sharp; another at 10:00. This one was serious. We did not hear the usual whistling of the falling bombs, just the many distant thuds followed by the explosions. From the sound I would say the enemy is bombing the still congested highway or the railroad station, or both. Because Barcelona is now enemy-occupied, the local trains have no place to go, the station is inoperative. The highways are filled with people evacuating toward France. Obviously, the sole purpose of the bombardments is to cause terror, panic, and demoralization, and to prevent evacuation of Catalonia's most active antifascists.

Yesterday, our commissariat was dealt a telling blow. While Ernst Blanc, political commissar of the 11th (German) Brigade, was riding with a Polish officer, chofered by Puns in Gallo's staff car, they were ambushed and riddled by machine-gun fire. The Polish comrade was able to escape to tell the tale, but Blanc and Puns were wounded and captured, or killed. To me this was a personal loss as well, for Puns and I had become great friends. He was the finest Catalan I had gotten to know; dedicated to the Republic and loyal to his job, he never hesitated to drive day or night anywhere along the fronts. He had successfully driven Gallo and others through similar entrapments and never boasted of his achievements. He loved everybody and in turn was truly loved by all. Like others, whenever I had to go to the front, it was Puns I turned to. When I wasn't successful in getting him, like others, I was disappointed. I was pleased when he told me once how much he liked being with me because, he said, he found me easy to communicate with. Always when driving with him, I insisted on sitting up front beside him. He liked that. He was about my age, short, stocky, and powerfully built. He would have made a good bodyguard, even to the president of his country. After all he had gone through in the past three years, he did not deserve to die, especially in what now looks like the last days of the war in Catalonia.

2 February

    Today's rain did not stop enemy air activity. Seven air raids took place starting at noon, but our chasers successfully fought them off.

    Because of the food shortage we had only two light meals.

    On the third floor of the house where I'm rooming there is no running water because of the lack of sufficient pressure. So to get water, I had to go down to the well and haul it up with a bucket, then carry it to the third floor. But I gave up after I attached the bucket improperly and lost it in the well.

3 February

    At noon Gallo summoned us to an emergency meeting, with orders to get our personal and commissariat property packed for another move. Where? He didn't say. He didn't have to. Everybody packed quickly and anxiously. The many air raid alerts and the explosions only served to speed up the process.

    When Angelita, another woman, and I dashed to our rooming house to collect the balance of our belongings, we were caught in a surprise bombardment, not preceded by the usual air alert. Bombs fell first, then air sirens sounded. The unexpected explosions drove us into a doorway, where we ran into a mother who was ignoring the bombardment and nursing her fifteen-day-old child. She said she had no other milk for her baby and that her breasts were nearly dry.

    At our commissariat headquarters, we dressed a Spanish woman's wounds. She had been badly hit by bomb fragments.

    Bombs hit the CRM (Republican Military headquarters), Calle Wilson.

4 February

    We left Figueras at 6:30 A.M. for La Junquera, four miles from the French border.

    There is so much going on that I don't know where to begin to write, or what to say. I don't have to. I shall never forget what we are experiencing these last days. People by the many thousands, the wounded as well as the healthy, are all moving in one direction—France. Gerona has fallen. Catalonia is lost.

All the peoples of the world are in the International Brigades at the side of the Spanish people

NINETEEN

Retreat to France

From Figueras, about twenty kilometers from the border, we joined hundreds of thousands of Spaniards seeking to leave Spain for the haven of France along the single highway choked with cars, trucks, mules, civilians—men, women, and children—with their personal belongings, and soldiers, some in partial uniform, with their weapons and parts of machine guns. We plodded endlessly, it seemed. Impatient motorists, as in every country, stupidly persisted in blowing their horns, as if that could speed up movement. They were properly cursed with an eloquence of which only an angry Spaniard is capable. Cars ran out of gas and had to be shoved off the road. Everyone in the vicinity helped because it meant speeding up the march. Children cried and trailed after their slowly moving parents. Lovers held hands firmly, unsmilingly, walking as if this were their last earthly mile. Donkeys brayed as they pulled their carts loaded with household treasures, playing their part in slowing down the exodus. The most heartrending sights were those of the wounded. At times it looked like a hospital evacuation: some had head bandages with blood still trickling from fresh wounds; others hobbled on crutches, a leg in a cast; amputees rested alongside the road, accompanied by comrades who themselves had been wounded. One had his face and head entirely bandaged except for the eyes. His right arm was in a dirty, blood-stained sling; his left arm was missing from the shoulder.

It seemed as though all Spain was in flight. Yet it was not all sadness, for some sang the "Internationale" and others waved their clenched fists in the air shouting that they'd be back. The peasants and their families watched from fields in apparent

213

disbelief. Some did not return the clenched fist salute as enthusiastically as they had in earlier and happier days when they blew kisses and smothered us with flowers and oranges.

For me these scenes brought to life the many colorful pictures we used to see in our school history books depicting George Washington's ragged, beleaguered, but courageous revolutionary army. It made vivid the pictorial scenes of our own war-torn country during the fratricidal War Between the States.

At times some of us rode atop our brigade truck, laden with headquarters supplies—riding shotgun, so to speak. Buried also in the truck was my straw-type suitcase with personal papers, diaries, and other mementos. I came to Spain with one suitcase and I was leaving with one, or so I thought.

5 February
    The women members of the Political Commissariat of the International Brigades separate from us and walk toward the French border. The men remain with the truck. For the first time I am in civilian clothes.

Because we would be climbing and hiking through the steep and dangerous Pyrenees at night to bypass French border guards, the women had been asked by Gallo and concerned husbands to take their chances by walking into France accompanied by a French citizen, who would keep track of the group and keep in touch with the individuals and the families involved.

Within sight of the border, Gallo ordered our caravan to fall out and abandon the truck and other vehicles and their contents.

Leaving the truck behind, we climbed to the top of a slope overlooking the road jam-packed with refugees fleeing toward the French border, with its internment camps and, for most of them, an uncertain future. This was the last lap; for many there was still the real danger of not making it across the border because of enemy aircraft returning with their bombs and wanton strafing. Rumors were rampant that the French government was closing the borders to further refugees, and with the enemy at our heels, anxiety grew. Every minute seemed an hour.

On the knoll where we were assembled, we were urged to surrender our weapons. Tucked in my right boot under my civilian trousers was a small pistol that I didn't want to part with; but when it was explained that these small arms were to be distributed for use by the remaining underground fighters, I could not in good conscience keep it. Apparently, I was not the only one hanging onto a weapon. Pistols, guns of all types (in Spain there were many varieties) suddenly cropped up from everywhere. Even a bayonet was thrown into the pile. There was an air of finality about this last act of ours on Spanish soil, a realization that the war for us was over, even though the central zone was continuing the resistance.

We huddled around our group leader for a briefing session. He surprised and delighted us by saying that we would be crossing the border at night to slip past the French border patrol and so avoid internment. He also introduced us to two Frenchmen who were to be our guides. When the second guide was introduced, he looked at me and I at him; suddenly and spontaneously we flung at each other in wild embrace! The Frenchman danced in my arms and kissed me on both sides of my face. In rapid French, with animation, he told the startled onlookers why the fuss. Even if one knew no French, one could have told what the Frenchman was saying by just watching the rhythmic movement of his wiry body and quick hands.

Alonzo Elliott, a linguist, translated for me what I already knew. It was February 1937, two years almost to the day, during the intensity of a battle at the Jarama front, that I first met this little Frenchman with a long nose, thin lips, and sunken cheeks. Our newly formed Lincoln Battalion, in its initiation under fire, was on the attack alongside the seasoned French battalion, called the 6th of February. As we moved toward the enemy through an olive grove, darting from tree to tree, this Frenchman and I dived simultaneously behind the same tree stump during a burst of enemy fire. There was hardly room for one. He knew no English, nor did I know French. "A fine kettle of fish," I thought. We remained huddled together for a few minutes only, though they seemed like hours, and exchanged comradely greetings while waiting for a lull. We shivered and shuddered at the rapid staccato of machine-gun fire that splattered in front and around us. We clung so close that if any bullet had struck one of us it could have easily killed us both. We vehemently cursed the enemy in our respective languages, and then separated. That was the last I saw of him till this moment—two years later. We were surprised at such quick mutual recognition and, I guess, overjoyed at seeing each other once again—alive.

Elliott and I, with others doing the same type of work and staff members of the International Brigades, some forty of us, crossed the treacherous Pyrenees during an all-night trek. One of the guides walked at the head of our long single-file column, and the second, my battlefield friend, brought up the rear. The night was without moonlight. It was so dark that one could not see the man in front of him. The guides had us form a long chain—each of us grasping the hand of the man in front and extending a hand to the man behind. The lead man followed the forward guide while the rear guide made sure no one was left behind.

At one point, while we were rounding the side of a mountain on a narrow path, wet with the night air, my foot slipped and the chain was broken. The rear guide nimbly sprinted past and reformed us, moving through the moonless night like a car with its headlights on high beam. Silence was essential; no one spoke; no one smoked; no one sneezed or coughed; and if anyone breathed, we couldn't hear it. Each time the chain was accidentaly broken—it happened too often because of our inexperience at night-walking on strange, wet mountain paths—the discipline of silence was maintained. While crossing a rocky stream into France, one or two of our guys slipped on the mossy rocks and fell headlong into the icy February waters. That scene, in normal circumstances, would have probably evoked hilarious laughter. To us it was tragic, for the least noise or carelessness might have attracted the frontier guards, whom by now we considered our enemies, and meant arrest, jail, or concentration camp. We helped the drenched and shivering out of the water and gave them sympathy, warmth, and comfort. The guides, on the other hand, familiar with every stone and rock, barely got the soles of their shoes wet.

In this group of refugees were men who were among the leading forces of the International Brigades. Their capture, as it later turned out, would have deprived Europe of some of its greatest underground antifascist organizers and fighters in World War II. Joseph Broz later became famous in Yugoslavia under the name of Tito. The Frenchman Tanquy, who accompanied us to make sure each step of the way was carried out according to plan, helped organize the resistance to the Nazis in the Paris area during World War II. He came to be known as the liberator of Paris since his forces opened the gates for de Gaulle's entry. Hans Maasen, a German coworker at International Brigade Headquarters, returned to his homeland as soon as World War II broke out and from Leipzig organized a secret radio transmissions team that beamed anti-Nazi programs for the duration of the war.

After crossing the border successfully, we were met by a bus that drove in and out of dark mountain passes with headlights turned off until we got to a drab farmhouse deep in the French countryside. Hot food was waiting for us, and a few of us had to be reclothed. I got a new pair of shoes that almost wrecked my feet. By nightfall, after a few hours of sleep on the hay in a big barn, we moved on again till we got to the town of Ales, north of Marseille.

The local police were friendly to the Spanish Republic and obviously part of the conspiracy to keep us out of the hands of the French government. They escorted us to a loft of an empty building, where again we ate, slept, and hid while waiting for our next move. As a matter of fact, the police were so friendly that when I made it known that I had relatives in the nearby coal-mining town of La Grand' Combe, the chief himself chauffeured me on a visit to the house of my aunt, uncle, and cousins. He knew exactly where they lived, in a two-story, soot-covered frame house, whose second floor opened out onto a mountain coal mine. When I knocked, the door opened and I saw a little woman with a broom in her hand, sweeping. I could not mistake her; she looked like my mother, though a bit younger. She stared at me and, though we had never met before, exclaimed in Italian, "My, aren't you my nephew John?"

Later I learned how she recognized me without my first identifying myself. When I was graduated from high school, my mother sent her a picture of me in cap and gown. And there it was sitting on her old-fashioned wooden icebox, the kind we used to have in our own home back in the States. This photo was to cause me consternation later in the evening. In the meantime, the accommodating police had sent for my uncle and cousins, who were at the mine. They arrived for the surprise reunion covered in coal dust and wearing lamp-lighted miners' caps.

During supper, my little cousin Yolanda, about five or six years of age, tugged at my shirt sleeve and, pointing to the picture on the icebox, asked if that was me. When I smiled, "Yes," she said, extending her arm and hand in fascist salute, "You are a fascist." "I," giving the clenched fist salute, "am a communist." I bristled! Her parents explained that all these years they thought that because I was in cap and gown, I was a priest, and priests to them at that time were fascists. After I told them that the cap and gown was an American custom upon graduation from school, I was forgiven amidst toast after toast of homemade wine. One of my coal-miner cousins, feeling by now that I could be trusted, boasted that he was the leader of the town's Communist band and proudly showed me pictures of his band posed with their musical instruments and wearing red kerchiefs around their necks. Most, he said, were Italians. My relatives, like Italian immigrants in the United States, lived in their own little ghetto, clinging to their native country's language and culture. It didn't take long for the word to get around that the son of one of their own was in town and the house was quickly besieged by *paesani* wanting to see the *Americano*. Some even claimed to know my parents and my oldest brother, Joseph, who had been born in Sicily.

I gorged myself on my first good full-course Italian meal in more than two years.

In the face of this splendidly cooked dinner, and I'm sure they went overboard for the occasion, I forgot, or chose to ignore the fact that my stomach had gradually shrunk in Spain from lack of food. I could not possibly have held all that good chow. That night I gave my cousin, with whom I was sleeping, a bad time by dashing in and out of bed, disgorging the spaghetti, meatballs, sausages, and desserts until there was nothing left, not even the pleasantries of the night before.

Several days later, Alonzo and I were told to go to the Ales railroad station with prearranged *friends*, who would see us off like visiting relatives. Then we were to report in Paris to an address that we had memorized. Our other companions were likewise dispersed to various parts of France. Most ended up in Paris, where we later saw some of them.

In retrospect, for the French, who organized our every move with cloak and dagger precision, it was just another dry run. This trip from Spain to Paris—by bus and by rail, walking, sleeping in a barn, in an abandoned loft, in the dressing room of a Paris theater, and in other strange places, and tiptoeing about noiselessly, often in the shadows, but always hiding—was carefully planned and flawlessly directed by the French. We didn't lose a man. No wonder the French, following Hitler's invasion, organized the underground and the Maquis resistance so quickly and efficiently that they were able to conduct a brilliant and resolute antifascist struggle.*

The destination for Alonzo and me took us to the end of the line by Metro, a private nook in a cafe in a remote suburb of Paris, where we were greeted by Luigi Gallo, who once again directed our work and the work of other language representatives on what were now the archives of the Spanish Civil War. Because these documents were prepared at the request of the Spanish and for the Spanish, everything of importance in English was translated into that language. This, of course, was also true of the French, the Italians, the Germans, and others.

We were assigned an apartment in the Montmartre section of Paris belonging to the Italian Palmiro Togliatti, whom we knew at the time as Ercoli. He had gone from Spain to Algeria and was not yet back in Paris. His wife and mother hosted us hospitably while we continued the documentation begun in Spain. We thought it quaint and wonderful when Mrs. Togliatti and her mother served us in bed each morning with a tray of coffee and croissants with butter and jelly, a typically French breakfast. Today, considering our more advanced consciousness of women's role in society, I would be embarrassed to accept being served in bed by our hostesses. The knock on our bedroom door came always while we were still asleep, and Alonzo and I never quite agreed if this morning breakfast ritual was their way of hinting to us that it was time to get up and get to work.

During one of those days I got a mysterious phone call advising me to go to a certain warehouse, where, to my surprise, I was ceremoniously presented with my suitcase that by then I had given up for lost. It had been gone through, but I could discover nothing missing. One look around the warehouse, and I could see where the contents of our truck abandoned in Spain had finally ended up.

Once a week we slipped out of that confining apartment to meet with Gallo in a

---

*The French Maquis resistance movement of 1939–45 consisted of irregular, underground forces committed to fighting the Nazis and internal fascists during World War II.

back room of a restaurant, usually in a Paris suburb after the last stop of a Metro line. We discussed the material we presented and talked about the next batch of work. After a good meal—unlike in Spain all meals were now good—we separated until the following week, same time, different place.

In Paris, I also kept in touch with Victor (Ajzner), who had been among the last group of volunteers that, in the retreat from Spain, had walked in an all-night trek over the Pyrenees to avoid hostile French border police. He, too, was working on the archives, though for the Polish section. We occasionally got together and, at his insistence, always met on a long, padded bench in the Louvre fronting a designated painting. This great center of world art was a safe and discreet rendezvous area for illegals in France, and that was where we parted in April 1939.

I wasn't to see Victor again until twenty-seven years later, purely by accident. Among hundreds of others from many countries, we were guests of the German Democratic Republic in East Berlin in July 1966, commemorating the thirtieth anniversary of the Spanish Civil War. My son Kenneth was with me. During one of several small conferences, I sat at one end of a twenty-foot-long table, signed the usual lined yellow pad, and passed it on. By the time the pad got to the other end of the table, I noticed someone push back his chair and quickly walk toward me. It was Victor. At a lengthy dinner afterward, we filled in the years.

He told me that at the outbreak of World War II, in September 1939, he was seized by the French gendarmes and detained as an illegal alien. From prison he made a determined application for enlistment in the French army. Accepted, he changed his identity documents to those of a Frenchman. Once again he was in the midst of battles. This time he was captured with his unit by the Germans and became a prisoner of war. Despite the firing squad, endless interrogations and tortures, and the fear instilled in the prisoners by the Germans to encourage informers and provoke betrayals, not one revealed Victor's true identity. And Victor was not only a veteran of the International Brigades—in itself a terminal crime in Nazi eyes—he was also a Polish Jew.

After his liberation from near death by the Soviet Red Army, he returned to his devastated homeland, and with the same selfless energy, devotion, and vigor he had displayed on the European battlefields, he took part in his country's reconstruction programs.

Today Victor, now Dr. Seweryn Ajzner, is a respected historian and scholar specializing in histories of wars against fascism, and particularly that of the Spanish Civil War. The archives section of Brandeis University Library in Waltham, Massachusetts, which he has assisted in developing its outstanding collection on the Spanish Civil War, has some of his works. A copy of his latest book (written in Polish, naturally), which he sent me, is in the historical archives of Rutgers University Library in Camden, New Jersey.

By April 1939, Lon Elliott and I had completed our work, and we turned over all material to Gallo. Lon went to England, and I went to the U.S. Embassy for a passport since mine had expired four months earlier, a condition under French law that made my presence illegal. Embassy personnel expedited my departure.

The five-day voyage on the trans-Atlantic liner to New York seemed long and was disturbing. I failed to unravel to my satisfaction the inconsistency, as it appeared to me, of a world basically antifascist and anti-Hitler refusing to help a people dedicated to the side of the democracies and eager to introduce land, industrial, political, educational, and social reforms that would bring Spain more quickly to the level of the more advanced countries of Europe and America. As we now know, in less than six months the world was joined in violent and catastrophic conflict.

TWENTY

Return Home to New Battles: An Epilogue

Before leaving for Le Havre to board the SS *Washington*, I was summoned by Gallo to the Paris headquarters of the French Communist party, where I was greeted by André Marty, organizer of the International Brigades, Palmiro Togliatti, leading Italian Communist now back from the Algerian route he took out of Spain, and Luigi Gallo, commissar general of the International Brigades. With wine, cheeses, and French pastries, they wished me well—an unexpected small surprise farewell party. This was the first time I had ever seen the three of them, together or individually, relaxed in this manner. Especially Marty, abrasive disciplinarian, who was always austere, now seemed to be a warm person. Before I left, they gave me in a small film can a microfilm of some of the documents I had worked on. It was incomplete, they said, but it was a start. I was asked to deliver the film to Earl Browder, then secretary-general of the U.S. Communist party. I was pleased that some of the records of the American participation in the Spanish Civil War would be available to us so soon. And the request did not surprise me because the original work on which we had spent all these months was done at the suggestion of the Central Committee of the Spanish Communist party. Though it was their property, the Spanish and French parties were simply sharing this information, at least in part, with the American party.

I carried that film can in my side pocket all the way to the United States. Not long after my arrival in New York City, I visited Earl Browder, and in the presence of John Gates, the last political commissar of the Lincoln Brigade, I explained the contents of the microfilm and gave it to him. I watched him put it in his center desk

221

drawer, and as far as I know, it was the last anyone had ever seen of it. Bob Minor, the cartoonist whom I had gotten to known in Spain, was also present but was not a participant. He was waiting for me to read the galley proofs of an article he had written for a magazine about the situation in Spain.

Life for me had to go on; I had no time to mourn. To challenge my depression over the events in Spain, I caught my breath and threw my efforts into the unfinished task of organizing workers of the Campbell Soup Company in Camden, New Jersey, just a few short blocks from my home on Benson Street. My mother, a worker on the chicken line, asked for and got the Number One union dues payment book of Local 80, United Cannery, Agricultural, Packing, and Allied Workers of America, CIO (UCAPAWA-CIO). She wanted it to be known that she was number one union supporter. She attended every union meeting; though she knew no English, whenever I got up to speak she applauded even before I opened my mouth. If she was a loyal union (or son) supporter, hundreds of others quickly responded with equal enthusiasm. Former fellow workers, friends, and neighbors helped me renew my self-confidence when they kept telling me, "We were waiting for you to get back."

The union rolled on. We won a National Labor Board election overwhelmingly and moved quickly for a negotiated union contract with improvements in wages, hours, and conditions of work in this giant of a cannery, with 5,000 year-round workers and 10,000 during the summer tomato season. The 1930s began for Campbell workers with depression, unemployment struggles that ended in defeat, and strikes that also ended in defeat. The first year of the 1940s, on the other hand, promised a decade of hope: the first union contract ever, the right to job protection, seniority rights, greater dignity for workers, and the right of representation without fear of employer reprisal.

The dizzying momentum of this victory took me next to Chicago, with others organizing Campbell workers in that city. The plant was not as large as that in Camden, 3,000 year-round workers, but it was a sister plant and Camden workers wanted it organized for reasons of solidarity. Here, too, we gained victory. When I rushed back to Camden, I found workers of other industries knocking on our union door. Twelve hundred cigar workers from the La Palina factory of the Consolidated Cigar Company came singing into our union hall. After a short strike, they too got their first union contract, a milestone for the cigar industry, which was largely open shop. Five hundred Siegel Cigar Company workers shortly followed suit. Their strike was longer and more bitter. We enlisted the support and mediation of Camden's mayor George E. Brunner, to get an agreeable settlement.

Two hundred Knox Gelatin workers of Camden had long wanted a union. We met weekly and secretly in the dank cellar of a neighborhood bar that we entered through a trapdoor. Over hot dogs, peanuts, and beer, we mapped organization strategy. In time the workers won the right to union representation and a union contract.

When we organized tobacco workers in the American Tobacco plants in Trenton, Philadephia, Charlestown, South Carolina, and in the Midwest, UCAPAWA changed its name to FTA—Food, Tobacco, Agricultural, and Allied Workers Union of America.

I spent the next three years in the U.S. Armed Forces. Treatment of veterans of the Abraham Lincoln Brigade in the U.S. Army generally depended on the attitude of superior officers toward the Spanish conflict. Like other veterans with whom I had spoken, I found decency and support among both officers and enlisted men. But I had a problem with the army intelligence and the FBI, and it started at least thirteen months before I was inducted, although I did not learn this until 1975, when I got ninety-two sanitized pages of my U.S. Army file under the Freedom of Information Act. The letter below, signed by the office of the adjutant general, is dated July 29, 1941; I did not get my greetings from Uncle Sam until September 12, 1942.

HEADQUARTERS THIRD CORPS AREA
UNITED STATES ARMY
BALTIMORE MARYLAND

B/AS

000.51-Sub.Act.   *July 29, 1941*
I2 (I) (7/29/41)(1026)

Subject: John Tisa,

To: Commanding Officer, 1301st Serv. Unit, New Cumberland, Pa. (Reception Center)
    In the event that the subject should be inducted and arrive at your Reception Center, a report of his arrival will be made to this headquarters by radio, care being taken to refer to the file number cited above. A separate report of his assignment when known will be made by indorsement hereon.
    By command of Major General GRANT:

JOHN B. RICHARDSON
Colonel, A. G. D.,
Adjutant General

In April 1943, at Pueblo, Colorado, where I was assigned to an overseas outfit, I was approached by an officer from the army personnel records department, who told me that he was familiar with my file and said that he had been a supporter of the Spanish Republic and had contributed money to that cause. His brother, a dentist, he said, had treated the teeth of returning volunteers at no charge as a tribute to them and in memory of those who died in a great cause. He added that what he was about to tell me was in strict confidence. He related how my incoming and outgoing mail was being opened, studied, and copied and that everything that I said or did, as well as where I went and people I met, was being recorded. Even the phone call from the Democratic mayor of my hometown, Camden, George E. Brunner, seeking my support in discouraging Carmen Parenti, a friend and fellow trade unionist, from running for the state legislature in competition with his choice, had been recorded. I was not surprised at what the officer told me, except for his next statements: "Your service record is marked 'not to be assigned to sensitive duties' " and "You are being shipped out of here and will never be sent overseas."
    I was handed my orders transferring me out of my overseas army air corps unit to Tinker Field, Oklahoma City. The file I obtained under the Freedom of Information Act confirmed that the information the lieutenant had given me was indeed accurate.

I learned, too, that the reason I was put to work in the orderly room was because I was to be under the "watchful eye" of the squadron commander. Since my outfit was headed for overseas, I gave a talk entitled "The Effects of Artillery and Avaiation Bombardment and Protection Against." Though the talk and discussion afterward were well received and highly commended by officers and enlisted men, intelligence gave the order I was not to give any more lectures.

At Tinker Field I requested transfer to overseas duty. At that time such requests were permissible and usually acted upon favorably. After several days the squadron commander told me, "You don't have a chance." He said it was out of his hands, so I was put to work as a clerk in an aircraft repair hangar. During the year I worked there, the officers and the enlisted men and women I worked with were called in by intelligence and interviewed about me. I never feared investigation, then or now, but I did resent the unfavorable reflection it cast on my character especially when those interrogated were questioned about my conversations, the literature I read, how I spent my spare time, and so forth.

In 1943 I applied for Officer Candidate School at the urging of my superior officers. Though I met all qualifications and passed the examining board, nothing came of it—this at a time when experienced officers were at a premium.

When the army orientation program was initiated at Tinker Field, I was asked by base officers to work on it. I did so for about nine months. The personnel records file I obtained in 1975 included a letter from my superior officer, dated 22 December 1944, expressing high regard for my conduct of that program.

During that period of orientation assignment, I was sent for four weeks to the School for Special and Morale Services in Lexington, Virginia, for advanced study of the army orientation program. From among the many enlisted men at the school, three were selected by the colonel in command to go to Officer Candidate School, to be commissioned as orientation officers. I was one of them. It was a high honor and I was delighted. The school teletyped a request for my release from Tinker Field. The response came back negative. Again it was army intelligence that stepped in to block my advancement.

Not long after my return to Tinker Field, I was by special order transferred to Normoyle, San Antonio, where I took up duties in the orientation section. A few days later I was summoned by intelligence and made to fill out once again long questionnaires about my life, work, background, and activities. Then followed face-to-face interviews with intelligence officers. Again I was being investigated.

In February 1945, less than a week after these interviews, after more than two years in the air corps and despite superior ratings and letters of commendation by every officer under whom I served, I was abruptly transferred into the infantry and shipped to Camp Howze, Texas. Again I was training, with a fifty-pound pack on my back, making forced marches during the day and night in rain and wind and doing the belly crawl through obstacle courses with live machine-gun bullets whistling overhead. It was not a happy time for me because I viewed this as punishment I did not deserve. During my third week of "training," I was surprisingly promoted to cadre. As cadre I occasionally gave orientation talks. I was determined not to let intelligence beat me down. Officers and enlisted personnel of the orientation program who sat in on my lectures and discussions asked their superiors to transfer me to their program for full-time activity. Again I was told that an unseen power said "No."

I myself requested the classification section to transfer me from field cadre work to administrative work. Orders were already cut for me to take over as sergeant major of one of the battalions. The next day the orders were revoked, and I was shipped to another company of the same battalion as field cadre. I was cheated out of a promotion and continued crawling through mud and negotiating obstacles courses.

When Camp Howze was about to close, I asked the classification section to ship me under my regular MOS (Military Occupational Specialties) number 274 (Information and Education). My lieutenant told me, however, that base intelligence phoned and prohibited this.

I wrote a three-page, single-spaced letter to the general in command and recited the above details, and more. I closed my letter as follows:

> Sir, this is only part of a long, and to me, ghastly story of how I tried to be a first class soldier but have not been treated as a first class American. Was it a mistake for me to have joined a group of far-sighted Americans in fighting Hitler and Mussolini's drive for power during years when the American government and people still couldn't believe a second world war was impending? Instead of my experiences and abilities being utilized for the benefit of the army, I was penalized for being a "premature antifascist."
>
> In spite of all this obvious discrimination, I gave my best to the Army at all times. My performance record shows high achievement in any task to which I was assigned.

I requested separation from the army as promptly as possible. I sent copies of this long letter to the intelligence services, to the War Department, to my senator and congressman, and to the national office of the Veterans of the Abraham Lincoln Brigade. Three months later, on 3 December 1945, I was at home with my family once again.

Within a few weeks, I returned to my union, and at the 1946 convention I was elected director of organization of FTA-CIO. We initiated organization wherever there was a demand for it. In North Carolina we succeeded in organizing the leaf tobacco warehouse workers in the cities of Rocky Mount and Wilson and in the areas around them. We organized the Camel cigarette workers in Winston-Salem, North Carolina, and conducted a long strike fiercely fought by R. J. Reynolds Company, which pitted half its 10,000 workers who were white against the other half who were black, to hold back improvements in wages and conditions of work for all employees.

On the West Coast, we organized the fresh fruit and vegetable packing-shed workers, who called themselves, "fruit tramps," because they traveled the circuit; packing melons in Phoenix and Yuma, Arizona, moving to Imperial Valley, California, for more melons, or Salinas and Watsonville to pack lettuce and other vegetables, or the San Joaquin Valley to pack tomatoes. Many went for apples in Oregon, others went by boat from Seattle to the fish canneries of Alaska. Thousands of these workers, most of whom had known the hardships of the Oklahoma dust bowl days, fought hard to build our union and defend it at every turn.

Other veterans of the Lincoln Brigade also continued the struggle in whatever way they could. Those who returned from Spain's battlefields in 1938 immediately launched a nationwide campaign demanding that the United States lift its embargo against the Spanish Republic. But the Republic fell before a change in U.S. policy could be effected, despite the heavy pressure from American public opinion, which was moved by the plight of Republican Spain.

In June 1939, Lincoln Brigaders joined in a formal organization, Veterans of the Abraham Lincoln Brigade (VALB). We raised funds to aid the many victims of Spanish fascism, particularly political prisoners and their families, sought the release of prisoners of war, and took part in every activity that might contribute to the rebirth of democracy in Spain. These efforts made us targets for harassment and persecution during the repressive McCarthy years. But we were not deterred. We strove even harder to give both moral and financial support to the forces of democracy struggling to free Spain of fascism. For Spain was our heritage, our great instructor.

INDEX

Index

Abraham Lincoln Battalion. *See* Lincoln Battalion

Aguirre, escape to France, 118

Air attacks: civilian targets, 139, 159, 175, 178–80, 186, 194–95, 197, 199, 201, 204–10; military targets, 36, 39, 61, 121

Airforce, Republican, x, 36–37, 39, 112, 118, 187, 199; newspaper layout signals, 72

Ajzner, Seweryn (Victor), 143, 196, 205, 218

Albacete bullring, 35–36

Álcala de Henares, 77–81

Ambulance service, 106–7. *See also* Medical service

American Federation of Labor rejection of plea from Spain, 14

American Revolution, perception of by Europeans, 151

American volunteers: black, 24, 27, 51, 144, 148; enlistment of, 15–16; new recruits, 69; outfitting, 16–17; transport to war, 17–20. *See also* Lincoln Brigade; Volunteers

An American Testament, 190, 194

Anarchists, 72, 176, 179, 201; militia, 113–14; women, 113–14, 176; youth movement, 177

Angelita, 203, 205, 207, 210

Anglo-Italian Pact, 195

Anti-fascist Italians, 121

Anti-fascist partisans, 120

Anti-Hitler German socialists, 48–49

Aragon front, capture of Italian pilots, 140

Archives, evacuation of, 206

Artillery attacks, 66, 73, 104, 156

Auxiliary support, lack of, 52

Badajoz massacre, xi

Banderos del Tercio, 162

Barbershop at the front lines, 63, 68–69, 71

Barcelona: bombardment of, 133–36, 139, 143, 151, 159, 197, 199, 201, 204–6; final weeks, 193–201, 205–6, 209–10, 213–18; Pioneer Children of, 188. *See also* Civilian living conditions

Barthel, Jean, 73, 79, 99

Basque defeat, 118

Basque provinces, Catholic church in, xiii

Bates, Ralph, 96–97, 99, 101–3, 112–13, 116, 118

Battles: *16 February 1937* (Suicide Hill), 39, 41; *22 February 1937*, 41–45; *27 February 1937*, 47; *14 March 1937*, 57–58; *5 April 1937*, 60–61; *15 December 1937* (Teruel), 125; *July 1938* (Ebro), 155–63

Beeching, William, 159, 177, 180, 188

Bilbao, fall of, 114

Blanc, Ernst, 128, 130, 149, 209

229

About the Author

The son of Sicilian immigrants, John Tisa was raised in Camden, New Jersey. Active at a young age in trade unionism and the young people's Socialist movement, Tisa joined the first group of American volunteers in Spain in January 1937. Because of his special role as Brigade historian, he was the last volunteer to exit Spain in 1939 during the general retreat from Catalonia. Resuming a prominent career in union organizing, then serving again in World War II, he was later to be scrutinized by the United States government during the McCarthy era. Continuously an active member of the Veterans of the Abraham Lincoln Brigade, Tisa was a committed leader of peace activities during the Vietnam War, and became an outspoken advocate for the rights of veterans. He now lives in Florida with his wife, May, where he continues his writing and political involvement in the cause of freedom.

John Tisa has been the prime source for many books written about the Spanish Civil War, including his own: *The Story of the Abraham Lincoln Brigade* (written between battles in Madrid during 1937), *The Palette and the Flame*, and contributor to *The Book of the XV Brigade*.

RELATED BOOKS

Nicaragua
The People Speak
Alvin Levie
224 pages   Photographs

Crisis in the Philippines
The Making of a Revolution
E. San Juan
256 pages   Photographs

Women and Change in Latin America
June Nash and Helen Safa
384 pages   Photographs

Longshoremen
Community & Resistance on the Brooklyn Waterfront
William Di Fazio; Introduction by Stanley Aronowitz
208 pages

Class and Culture in Cold War America
A Rainbow at Midnight
George Lipsitz
264 pages   Photographs

Victims & Neighbors
A Small Town in Nazi Germany Remembered
Frances Henry; Foreword by Willy Brandt
216 pages   Photographs

Steelworkers Rank-and-File
The Political Economy of the Union Reform Movement
Philip Nyden
176 pages

The Presidential Election Show
Nightly News Coverage of the 1984 Campaign
Keith Blume
256 pages   Photographs

Women's Work
Development and the Division of Labor by Sex
Eleanor Leacock and Helen Safa
256 pages   Photographs

The Politics of Education
Culture, Power & Liberation
Paulo Freire
240 pages   Photographs

Marxism: The Science of Society
Kenneth Neill Cameron
240 pages

Tribes on the Hill
The U.S. Congress—Rituals & Realities
J. McIver Weatherford
320 pages

Education Under Siege
The Conservative, Radical, and Liberal Debate Over Schooling
Stanley Aronowitz and Henry Giroux
256 pages

Community and Organization in the New Left, 1962–68
The Great Refusal
Wini Breines
208 pages

BERGIN & GARVEY PUBLISHERS, INC.
670 Amherst Road, South Hadley, Mass. 01075